SHINING THE LIGHT V

THE TRUTH ABOUT
- David Adair at Area 51 • SSG Downs Military Planes
- Zetas Re-create the Past • True Purpose of the Mayans

HUMANITY IS GOING TO MAKE IT!

LIGHT TECHNOLOGY RESEARCH

SHINING THE LIGHT
BOOK V

HUMANITY IS GOING TO MAKE IT!

THE TRUTH ABOUT

- The Corporate Model
- Zetas Re-create the Past
- The True Purpose of the Mayans
- SSG Downs Military Planes
- David Adair at Area 51
- Grid Lines Rising

Light Technology Research

Cover art: Balance
by Robert Lewis Arnold

ISBN 1-891824-00-7

Published by
Light Technology Publishing
P.O. Box 1526
Sedona, AZ 86339

Printed by

MISSION POSSIBLE
Commercial Printing
P.O. Box 1495
Sedona, AZ 86339

Robert Shapiro is a man who has grown up with the experience of extraterrestrial contact. From age twelve he has had a series of personal UFO contacts. Throughout his life there have been communication with beings from several star systems and dimensions. The development of his career and lifestyle has come as a direct result of this communication. Robert has been a professional channel for over eighteen years, and although he can channel almost anyone or anything with an exceptionally clear and profound connection, he most often channels Zoosh, who describes himself below. Robert's great contribution to an understanding of the history and purpose of humanity is his epochal work, *The Explorer Race*, and he is one of several channels featured in *Sedona Vortex Guidebook*. When he is not channeling, Robert is a shaman and spiritual teacher in his own right who lives in Sedona, Arizona. He is available for personal appointments and can be reached at (602) 282-5883; P.O. Box 2849, Sedona, AZ 86339.

Zoosh ensouled the first planet that humanity experienced as souls and he has been with us ever since, for "about a trillion years." He is witty, wise and compassionate. He says about himself, "It has been my job and my purpose in life to follow the birth of your souls on your journey to re-creating the universe. My job is to be your companion, your guide, occasionally your entertainer. I have to nurture that sense of mystery — it's not as if you're going to have it forever.

"It is my job to help you get there, to help you to understand your experience and to observe everything. And, in time, to remind you of the everything you are in one of my many guises."

Contents

Preface

Dear Friends,

Some of the information at the end of *Shining the Light IV* was not easy for the mind and heart to accept, but in our commitment to bring you the truth about what is really happening on this highly polarized Explorer Race training planet, on which we're completing graduate school in how to be creators, the truth has both positive and negative facets and energies—although recently they seem more outrageously positive and negative than usual! The secret to graduating is quite simple in theory: make all choices from the heart, based on love for all beings and all of creation including self, choices always based on the highest good for all concerned. But when you throw in the subconscious, one's false beliefs based on judgments from past and future experiences, habits and addictions, desires and hormones, our linear mind and all of the stuff we are resolving for ourselves and the rest of creation, the plot thickens.

There are new elements being added to this global soap opera, which is "Can these Earth humans attain atomic technology without blowing up the planet or parts of it; resolve the previously unresolvable issues left over from previous creations; find a use for negativity as itself (as curiosity and a lust for life and adventure); do what no sentient being has ever done before—live in the physical body as it transforms from third to fourth dimension while the human focus changes from the physical me/mind to the less dense physical we/heart/soul—and do all of this before the planet they have polluted becomes unlivable and the very school they need for graduation is trashed?"

In the midst of living in the above mellow drama, we were told that the tyrants who are attempting to control all of humanity are getting more vicious and powerful. Remember Don Juan saying that if you want to advance quickly, find a tyrant, because the challenge of overcoming the resistance will make you stronger. Well, we are allowing some highly creative tyrants here.

Zoosh through Robert Shapiro says, "It's all in the timing." We have been receiving and printing information about the sinister secret government (SSG) since the beginning of the *Journal*, but it was only after a picture of the Hale-Bopp comet with an "object" traveling with it was posted on the Internet that we asked certain questions and were given unsettling answers. Although the Hale-Bopp comet had been photographed since at least mid-'95, only after an unusual photo was posted on the Internet and some information came from the remote viewers did we ask questions about it. This process seems to indicate that *since we have a very positive, powerful source of help from the light,* we can now be told of the increase in potential aggravation by the dark side.

We must remember to put all of this in perspective—that these energies are reflections of us, that the SSG can exist only because of our energies of fear, anger, doubt, judgment and so on. Zoosh says that if we would eliminate our cynical attitude and regain our expectation of goodness and hope, we would cut their power by 40%! I am old enough to remember when America was a more positive, pleasant place—when we trusted our neighbors and the government, believed in truth in advertising and picked up hitchhikers without fear, when being a Good Samaritan was a way of life. Now two generations have been fed the big lies of fear, lack of hope and "expect the worst" since birth, as part of the SSG's master plan to totally control the population, leaving us in need of a severe attitude adjustment.

The good news is that the 32nd-dimensional lightbeings inhabiting the vehicle traveling with the Hale-Bopp comet, who are here to help us get through these times, are also our reflections. When we stop and remember that we are lightbeings, immortal and, in our natural state, totally loving aspects of the Creator, lightbeings who chose to participate in this training as part of Creator's master plan to train His replacement, then we can play our roles with zest and humor without getting caught up either in the e-band of humans who still think they are the parts they play in the drama, or in the emanations of the SSG, who want us to follow their script instead of letting us write our own.

So read this book with a light heart to get the whole picture, but don't give away your power to your fears. "We're given only what we can handle" is a basic training rule. The point here, as I understand it, is to be aware of all of the old control and manipulation energies that the SSG is mirroring to us (we have all played those roles in other times, other places and probably even more creatively) so that we can see the consequences of those thoughts and desires. We must release all such energies before we can move into 4D, let alone before we can be entrusted with the power of creation.

We are now at 3.47 on the dimensional scale to 4.0 and beyond. As YHWH through Arthur Fanning said, "Arise your vibrations" and intend to move to 3.55, where SSG-type energies are like an old, half-remembered bad movie.

We print the following summary of the essence of the information that ended *Shining the Light IV,* much of which is suggestions we can well use now.

ASSISTANCE TO HUMANITY*

- Our original heart energy, kept for eons inside the planet so we could stay in polarity, is now being released increasingly rapidly.
- This ship came to align you unto joy. These beings came with authority. As they moved through systems, the energy was so powerful that humanity automatically aligned to their thought. You will not have the ability to think the game of not [love] but the way they hold the thought.
- We're bringing forth more light, and it will activate the brain, perhaps causing pressure in the temples. You exist in here [soul], your greater force inside the body in safety. It aligns to the thoughts of your lightbody around you. Vibrate that lightbody, quicken it and feel it inside the soul area; the flesh will change its texture and become permeable for both energies to move freely through.
- In the next ten years humanity will begin to understand that the body and the planet are for the attainment of your spiritual wisdom, building power within the soul forces of the wisdom of spirit, not dogma or building a church or having the only truth.
- You're getting assistance from many beings, many energies. Even some ETs will start to show up to alter some of these thought patterns to get you thinking in another way.
- These are challenging times. Later you are going to learn that the only important thing is your spiritual wisdom; the wisdom of your soul accumulated in the darkest of times and the happiest of times and your accumulated spiritual power, which will take you into forever.
- A vehicle was headed this way that had your extraterrestrial brothers and sisters who are working with the Creator, radiating energy that is your natural knowledge, like an inoculation for you to remember who you are and drop the drama of your personality. The purpose was to make a giant leap forward to get past the 3.50 mark, but *you* had to do it. This energy was radiated toward you, but you had to catch it and use it.

* This summarized the channelings in November 1996 when Comet Hale-Bopp was rounding the Sun.

DIMENSION
4.0

3.55

3.47*

3.0

*YOU
ARE
HERE

Zoosh through Robert Shapiro — December 3, 1996

Last August you said we had reached 3.49, but recently you said we were at 3.47. Why the discrepancy?

This relates not only to the nefarious activities of the SSG, but also to a degree of *reluctance* to move forward.

Remember that you were hurtled forward, jumping quite a bit, then there was a little vibration and you started creeping forward. Some souls here are reluctant to express the responsibility for creations, even their own, so there is a slight move backward. Granted, the SSG has mostly to be "credited," but you cannot go back any further than 3.47. They can drag you that far back, but that's it. To go forward you must be pulled forward, *but you must also push.*

WHAT YOU CAN DO:

- Let go of cynicism (see boxes below), thereby eliminating 40% of the power the SSG is drawing from us.
- Release anxiety at moments in your everyday life by projecting gold light physically (blow it out) toward those who stimulate that anxiety.
- Constantly remind yourself how much you have in common with others, letting go of perceived differences.
- Practice feeling love as heat in the chest. When you can hold this heat, add the feeling of gold light. This is true transformative alchemy. In a group, it multiplies dramatically. As you physicalize the light, it enters the particles in your body, then the constantly moving mass of Earth, cycling through others.
- Send love/gold light to the beings on TV whenever you hear about violence.
- For your protection, project gold light at the SSG. If you do it *physically*, it's ten times more powerful than *imagining* gold light. In a meditation blow it toward them. It's much more powerful.
- In your meditations move around (in groups or alone), feeling and broadcasting the gold and white light. This will integrate the light into the physical world. When you are not physically active, the light will simply support and sustain you.
- The symbol of a pyramid on your clothing at your chest will allow you to think from within the safety of your soul. It was designed that way as a safe haven. The incoming energies we are directing and assisting have come to awaken.
- Focus on the energy. The light will give you the ability to successfully network with other beings of like feeling. Know that you are empowered to manipulate thought so that certain beings can't establish a thought for you to believe in. Once you are self-empowered, they can't manipulate you.
- Be gentle to one another, compassionate. Surrender into your loving self. Center within it and feel safe and secure. You'll draw in more light.

Keep it simple:
methods for transformation are simple.

Cynicism
The belief that human conduct is motivated wholly by self-interest; the expectation of nothing but the worst of human conduct and motives.

1

SSG Realizes That Humanity Must Be Customers, Not Slaves

Zoosh through Robert Shapiro
October 17, 21 and 24, 1996

[On October 15 due to interference the channeling had to be postponed and the following is an explanation of that interference.]

Temporary Warping Due to Arrival of Teachers
Helping Negative Sirians

There is a serious interference with a bending of light rays. In this area light rays are bending to accommodate the arrival of certain beings who will assist in the evolution of the beings [negative Sirians] now in occupation and assimilation at the 3.0 dimension. The point of entrance of these beings is about 25 miles due north of here. It is causing a warping, a curving bend of light rays, which is causing some unintentional interference tonight.

Apologies to those who have gathered, but this warpage of the light rays should be over within fourteen hours. Certain individuals might have a little difficulty maintaining connection with their physical self during this time, and this can cause a wide variety of symptoms—everything from exhaustion, headache—what are basically annoying discomforts, distraction.

When did it start?

It really started about three and one-half days ago, but has built to its most powerful level about an hour and a half ago. It will maintain that level of intensity for another three or four hours, then drop off rapidly.

Who are the beings?

These beings are teachers of light who have adapted themselves to work with beings who are essentially rather negative in character. This means that the teachers must arrive greatly expanded, then reduce themselves on their way through the temporary veil between where you are now and the 3.0 beings. As they reduce themselves, it creates an equal and opposite energy reaction, meaning that as they get smaller, the outward energy becomes more impactful, not unlike the reaction in an atomic detonation, where the energy implodes before expanding. This is basically a law of light physics, so it's still in operation in this part of the universe and something that cannot be helped. It is for a good cause, but it happens to coincide with this evening's channeling. It will affect different people in different ways. It might actually make some people feel better. But it creates a difficulty in channeling.

The negative Sirians who were here bothering the people on the planet—when that planet recently exploded, did they leave and go to 3.0? Or are they still milling around here?

They're still milling around here. They are being cajoled to move toward 3.0, but they won't do it on their own, so an interesting program has been developed. Authorization has been made to segregate these beings, move them to a place of their own underground and initiate them sufficiently so that they can function as what I would call teachers' aides. They have been told that they cannot go with you and that if they try to stay where they are as you move on dimensionally, they will simply be destroyed. Thus their choice was either destruction (which they wouldn't choose intentionally) or initiation—sort of conversion by the sword. They have naturally chosen conversion by the sword. To do this they have to give up a great deal of their discomforting energy and in the process a lot of their competition. As you know, competition, although you have found good uses for it, is basically associated with discomfort.

They are now assembled in a location not too far from the outer edges of the icecap of the North Pole, from where they are being very slowly and gently moved to a position in space about 182,000 miles from Earth (but not where the Moon is). From there they will be refracted using light to the 3.0 dimension and held there in stasis for about thirty days, during which they will be treated by the lightbeings to reduce and transform that extra discomforting energy. Then they will be linked to certain light-producing phenomena not unlike a star, through which their energy will gradually be transmuted in about another 45 days to something equivalent to perhaps 1½% to 1¾% discomforting energy. They need that much to relate to the other individuals from that now-deceased planet from Sirius. In this way they will then be able to assist their people and also assist the lightbeings who are coming to teach them. By experiencing this transformational process, they will understand how the process works.

How many beings are there?

I should think no more than 30,000, give or take a dozen or two.

So they're going to be totally gone, along with all the annoying little things they've been doing?

They will be totally gone from your planet in about a day and a half. They are now gathered up near the North Pole.

All right!

This is not to say that you won't still have some things going on here, but *they* will not be the cause—not directly, anyway.

Understand that these things happen from time to time. I might add that part of the reason you had the tape difficulty was because the energy was being warped somewhat nearby. There was a refraction that impacted a very narrow corridor along this house, and it affected various other magnetic happenings as well. For example, there were an unusual number of power surges around the Earth during this time. I don't think much equipment was ruined, but a few computers crashed, unfortunately. These things happen.

Recent SSG Rebel Decision to Loose Chupacabras

What would you like to say for the magazine regarding the secret government—what they're doing, what we're facing at their hands for the next couple of months?

You've got some rebels running around out there. Some people within the inner circle of the sinister secret government want to just wait and see what happens, which is prudent. But as is often the case in an organization, especially a highly organized criminal organization, there's always a few loose cannons. A couple of beings involved in your basic loose-cannon operation recently made a decision to release some hybrid beings, which is designed to cause a little panic in the population.

Now, for some time there have been a few (not many) beings similar to this running around on the surface, but mostly they have been unable to access the surface very well, so their comings and goings have been infrequent. But now a few of these beings have been released to the surface. Sometimes they're called the goatsuckers, sometimes chupacabras.

Yes. You've already talked about that.

We talked about this already?

You said they were from the second dimension and they were looking for sheep to find their history.

Yes, but I also have to tell you that there's a variation of those beings now that have been released within the past eight months, and these beings are truly lost. This means that their genetic substance has been altered and they have been placed within an environment that is incorrect for them. They amount to a combination of several beings, and this genetically altered being cannot survive for more than a couple of years. They are highly manipulated through dimensional portals. I just want people to know, if they hear stories like this, that this is a being made up of several parts (some of which are ET, *none* of which is human) and that other beings, perhaps a little wiser, will pull these beings out of this reality.

How soon?

I should think within a year and a half. It might take awhile because they're constantly being pulled into dimensional overlays where it's hard to find them.

Where specifically are they coming from? Where were they created?

They were created down in the southern tip of South America. They have been released in one case several miles north of Buenos Aires, one up near Venezuela and several in Mexico. And one or two are occasionally being released throughout the Southwest desert. But I don't think that heavily populated places will see these beings because the more people there are around, the more likely people will see them. This is really designed by the rebel force of the sinister secret government to create fear, which is their number-one marketing tool, as you know. This rebel sect's whole idea is, How can we grab power? If you looked at them as warlords, you wouldn't be too far from an application of their identity. But you also have to understand that the inner circle of the sinister secret government is inclined to take a liberal view, meaning that if it's successful and creates more money for them, then they'll say, fine.

If it turns out that people just become more lackadaisical about exposure to unusual beings (which will prepare you for contact with true ETs), then the secret government will consider it a disastrous failure and terminate the project on their own (they've given it maybe two and a half years to sink or swim). And they will also probably terminate the rebel members of the sinister secret government. If necessary, they are willing to terminate members of their own inner circle, and they have the capacity to do so. No member of the inner circle is entirely safe because they have built into their physical selves a means by which, if all the other members focus entirely on a certain thought (I won't say what) accompanied by a certain feeling (I also won't say what) and direct it toward these members, no amount of shielding can protect them.

Have they ever done that?

No, they haven't, but they have the capacity. This is actually a bastardization of ET technology.

But why are these beings so similar? Have they deliberately created them to be similar to the second-dimensional beings in Puerto Rico?

Yes. They've created that intentionally so that they can say, "Look, these beings are real. They have a history." You understand? They don't even have to say it; others will say it for them. They'll say, "Oh, they started here and here they are. They're spreading." The whole idea is to suggest that they're spreading.

But they definitely have no connection to those second-dimensional beings that we talked about?

That's right. They do not have a direct connection.

Are they dangerous to humans? I mean, what if a human sees them? What's the smartest thing to do?

If a human sees them it's best to give them distance and be reasonably confident. For what it's worth, you probably cannot bring one down with a bullet, so don't try. But they are susceptible to electric shock. Nevertheless, I don't think you'll be able to do it. The best thing to do is to just look at them. If you need to go somewhere, back up. Keep looking at them, don't turn your back.

Are they third-dimensional?

They're not really . . .

You said they're interdimensional.

Well, they're not interdimensional. They're being pulled in and out of interdimensional portals by the secret government, but that doesn't mean that they're interdimensional. Just be aware that they are being manipulated. They are in that sense victims, though I don't like to promote the use of that word. Nevertheless, that's the situation here. Any tastes they might have for animal blood is purely acculturated and not part of their true existence within the separate beings that they are.

It's like creating a Halloween character. They want people to be afraid of them.

That's exactly what it is.

SSG Manipulating U.S. Government to Equalize Prices with World Prices

We've been getting so much literature about boxcars with chains built into them and big warehouses in the middle of the country that say they're Sam's Club but are really full of arms. Are they preparing for some of this melodrama that we heard of years ago in terms of controlling the citizens?

Let's just say this: Most of the legitimate government people have no idea that they're being manipulated by these beings, but there are elements within the sinister secret government that have put out to legitimate governmental circles the idea that if certain changes are made (in the United States, not so much in other countries), the citizens of the United States won't stand for it and would pose a true threat by defending their rights and becoming militant organizations. This is because the citizens of the United States have been raised on the mother's milk of revolution (meaning the Revolutionary War); even the Civil War has been so glorified that the idea of fighting for some just cause is almost spoon-fed to students from grade school on up. By the time you get to college you get more of a world-view. So there are these individuals who are saying, "If we do this, then this will happen, so we must be prepared."

Now, the changes would be, for starters, an equalization of certain worldwide phenomena. For instance, gasoline per gallon in this country is unusually cheap (not counting other countries that might subsidize it, such as Mexico). In Europe, for example, gasoline costs significantly more, sometimes twice as much or more. You might have a cartel that wishes to say, "Okay, we're now on an international economic system!" For what it's worth, the international corporate powers do not represent one religion or nationalistic group; please get that thought out of your head. When you let yourself be manipulated by that idea, you're absolutely tools and toadies of the sinister secret government. International corporations are really in a position right now (as anyone can see, looking at the consolidation of banks) to create an international, unified economic society.

I've said for a long time that the initial world order will be based on the corporate system. Well, they're really very much in power to do that. The interesting thing is that at the top of corporations right now (aside from their desire to make money) there is some sense of responsibility to the citizenry at large, believe it or not. I'm not trying to glorify corporations and say they are God's gift to the world, but there is some sense in many corporations that they've got to look after the people. It's a bit of a mini-government in itself.

Getting back to their goals, there is a pretty fair chance (40%) that there will be a real move toward having things cost the same in all places where corporations are. They are in fact creating an international economic model. This might rule out places like Cuba and China somewhat, particularly Cuba, because they are genuinely independent. China is a little more involved in free trade with the world and Cuba with part of the world. We're looking at the intent to fix prices.

Expect Rising Gas Prices but More Jobs in Next Three Years

Now, the government of the United States will resist blatant price-fixing. But they're disinclined to do too much about price-fixing when it comes to products that are seen by the public as being essential, such as gasoline. I'm not saying to run out and buy a hundred gallons of gas and store it in your garage, but the chances of fuel prices going up significantly (over two dollars a gallon) within the next two or three years are quite strong in the U.S., because this represents a true cost, from the international corporate point of view. These corporations are going to pool their money in some places, not to save the poor, but to create a price based on what the item actually costs. In Europe you've got a significant profit built in that is designed to motivate corporations to find more oil, at least on the theoretical economic level. In this country, because of a certain degree of competition, prices are lower.

You might ask, "Is there any product where the price is going to go down?" I'd have to say that this is probably not the case. However, corporations are becoming increasingly sensitive to the idea that by creating a class of very poor people, you're creating people who can't afford to pay for their products. So corporations will begin to find means to get people off the welfare rolls and into jobs that pay better. Right now there's resistance to the minimum wage, especially from smaller businesses. Places of business will automate even more, and you'd be surprised how little resistance there will be to it. As a matter of fact, people might like it because it seems modern and exciting. There will be fewer people working at places, more people available in the work pool and more work found for them to do.

Basically, the international corporate model for the world order has been coming on for a while, and within the next two and a half years it will be locked in. So even if you have a government that is strongly connected to the church or a philosophy or even a government that is autocratic, you will still have to experience the corporate model of world society.

Understand that right now as I speak, the United Nations, which I perceive as a primarily benevolent organization, is a model for what can be done that is good through a corporate-modeled organization. The United Nations is basically a good thing, although it is involved in entirely too many so-called police actions. I don't think the United Nations really makes war very well, but they do make peace well.

SSG Will Eventually Stop Involvement in Drugs

The sinister secret government now is primarily involved in making sure that their slice of the pie is large and in acknowledging that even

though they control and manipulate legitimate businesses and corporations, at some point (and they're understanding this now) they're going
to have to step back and say, "We can't manipulate things any longer.
We can't create a class of drug addicts who are highly damaging to persons and property." The irony here is that the sinister secret government
has such a large stake in the affairs of human beings now that they are at
the point where they will withdraw all of their efforts toward making
quick cash through the sale of drugs either by manipulation or taking a
percentage. And they're going to come down hard on those who are involved in this.

Marijuana is going to be legalized. Just face it and understand that
heroin, crack cocaine and drugs such as that that lead to violence (either
because of what they release within an individual or because the individual has a habit that has to be fed) will be targeted for elimination. Certain things that are considered scientifically as being nondestructive will
be allowed, and marijuana isn't destructive (though it is psychologically
and emotional addictive) if you don't have other drugs to move on to.
You will have marijuana that you can smoke or consume in some way
that will be mildly impacting—not hashish, though. They're going to
outlaw that. And they're not going to be mister nice guy, like law and order. If you're caught growing or distributing drugs, you just disappear!
It will be a crime like that. It's going to be something the sinister secret
government or highly organized crime will simply eliminate.

This is going to happen probably in your lifetimes, probably within
the next 20 to 25 years. There are a lot of would-be chemists out there
who will try to reproduce stuff. But once the sinister secret government
and organized crime withdraw their energy from it and say, "We've got
to put a stop to this, because we're so involved in legitimate business and
legitimate corporations that this is hurting us. We're shooting ourselves
in the foot every time we deal drugs, and we can't tolerate it from *anybody!*" And that's going to be the end of it, with the exception of marijuana. You might say that is a benefit.

The sinister secret government is still going to be in power in 25 years?

SSG to Fade Away and Join the Legitimate
System to Make More Money

No, no, no. The sinister secret government is going to gradually fade
out of existence because what you've known as the sinister secret government will not so much be uncreated as gradually come into the system.
Understand that the best way to involve people in something more benevolent than they're currently involved in is to bring them into the system. And the sinister secret government somewhat unintentionally has

brought itself into the system by becoming highly involved in legitimate corporations.

And banks.

I don't want to single out banks—legitimate corporations, and I'm not going to say which ones. I'm just going to say that organized crime has been doing this for some time, and highly organized crime (in the form of the sinister secret government), even loosely organized crime and up-and-coming gangs, are getting involved in legitimate corporations because they find they can make more money. The curious thing is that the minute they get involved in legitimate businesses, they eventually become disinclined to be involved in illegitimate businesses because they can see that this is actually harming profits. This isn't because of morals; it's a monetary decision. The sinister secret government is at that point now. Even organized crime is very much at that point now. I'm not saying highly organized crime and organized crime are your friends; they're not. But highly organized crime (the sinister secret government) and organized crime (that you know and understand) are past the 50% mark in recognizing it. The gangs will be the last, but they will follow. If they don't, they will cease to exist. So they will follow for their own best interests. Thus ends our lecture on the criminal conspiracy for the evening.

Personal Weapons Will Fade; Other Changes

So all of these contingencies about rebels probably won't make it into this reality where they'll come door to door and take your weapons and herd you into railroad cars?

I don't think it will come to that. I think that people are gradually being conditioned that personal weapons are unsafe. And in all honesty guns have only one purpose. I understand that this society is based on a revolution, aside from being based on colonizing. And in a revolutionary colonial system the tendency is to want to be armed for various justified reasons. But within 20 to 25 years at most, personal ownership in this country (though borders will be more blurred in the future) of any weapon shorter than thirty inches is unlikely. You'll still be able to fight with swords (those people who are interested in that). And you'll still be able to do target shooting with rifles at some point, but the chances that there will be an allowance for private ownership of handguns or concealable knives is highly unlikely. If you look around the rest of the world, you'll see that that's the tendency if not already the fact.

Some people have said, "The people will revolt if these changes come," but I don't think that's the case. And I'll also say, for what it's worth, that a lot of fear about "what if" is only fear. Some of it is based on misperceptions, some on gossip and some on scare stories. Probably the bulk of it is based on misinformation—things that were not understood clearly.

So yes, you're going to go through some changes, especially in this country, some of which you won't like, but you will adapt to them. For starters, look at your debt! It's going to have to be paid off at some point, you know. A major gasoline tax—twenty cents per gallon—would go a long way to pay off that debt. I'm not expecting large groups of people in the United States or its protectorates to be rounded up and herded into camps. I'm not expecting this for political or nationalistic or racial purposes. I know there are some people who fear that the United States wants to build machine gun towers at its borders. I think that's a temporary backlash that looks like it will happen. I do think that borders will be beefed up, but it's not so much to keep people from leaving the country, so don't worry about that. I do think that you will see a little bit more policing, but I'm not expecting concentration camps in this country or even DP (displaced persons) camps. I don't think it's going to happen. There are some people making contingency plans just in case, but anybody who's been in the military or the police or even politics knows that large organizations are always making contingency plans. I don't want to give it much energy and I hope you won't, either.

Weather

Okay. On a different topic, will there be more snowstorms and blizzards in the next six months?

Are you asking, "Is it going to be a long, hard winter?

Yes.

I don't think it will be any worse than any winter you've experienced in the past ten years. There will be places that will have some major snowstorms, so if you can buy heating oil now, buy it because it's a little cheaper now. I'm expecting an unusually mild winter in some places and a fairly severe winter in other places, but I'm not going to go on record too much. You'll probably have some pretty good storms in the Northeast, so be prepared. Lay in a good supply of heating oil and go ahead and buy that down jacket. But I am not expecting a bone-crushing, hundred-year winter.

War, New Religions and an African Land Grab

All right. What about the war situation? Is it going to go on as it is, or are we going to have a lot more little incidents—or what?

You'd be surprised at the pressure to stop the war in the Middle East. As a matter of fact, it's so strong that the United States was secretly (not publicly) highly criticized for its recent missile attack on Iraq, even though one might easily justify it. That's how strong the worldwide pressure is for peace in the Middle East—or at least the absence of a shooting war. I think you'll find that the full power of the United Nations (including the United States, perhaps reluctantly) will force Israel back to the peace table and to the original agreements. And if Israel does not comply, U.N. troops will come in to defend the Palestinians and everybody else. No one, certainly not the world corporate model, is going to stand for going backward, not in a place that produces such vast amounts of the world oil and has vast oil reserves.

It is also a place that will be the staging ground for certain new religions. I can't say too much about that now, but I want you to make a note of that: *staging ground for new religions—Middle East*. I'm not saying that any of the religions in that area will be eliminated, but that there will be zero tolerance for going backward in the peace accords there. So Israeli government, be aware, and if you haven't already noticed, if you think your citizens are marching in the streets right now to protest decisions to return to the warring days of yore with the Palestinians and others in the area, you haven't seen anything yet! Get ready for countrywide strikes and student demonstrations the likes of which you've never seen, because the people are not going to tolerate backward motion.

You mean war?

That's right. Backward motion would be war. You see, those who are in power now are basically fundamentalist. Believe it or not, you don't have to be involved in Islam or Christianity to be fundamentalist—there are fundamentalist Jewish, too. They are in power, and there is not going to be any tolerance for that. Nor will there be any tolerance for wars in the Middle East in general. The U.N.'s going to come down hard on that. In five years people will no longer be shooting at each other. That power exists.

What else? Skirmishes in Africa? This is probably going to go on for a time. (This is a sad situation we've talked about in *Origins and the Next 50 Years of the Explorer Race* that will be released at some point in the near future.) People on a semicorporate level who wish to make a land grab in Africa are encouraging warfare there. I think the U.N. is also going to step in and the corporate model is going to put a stop to that within the next two and a half years. The reason is largely because of vast (even today) mineral, oil and coal deposits. They can't be having wars when they're attempting to mine and improve the quality of life for the local people. Of course, they won't honor the tribal customs except scholastically, by studying them, but they will attempt to improve the lives of the people by twentieth-century standards.

I don't want to sound as if I'm waving the flag for the international corporate model, but understand that this first world order that works on the practical economic business level is a lead-in to the more benevolent world government to follow. It has to start there because that's what people can understand.

So the old practice of the secret government arming both sides of a battle to create sales of weapons and go back and build it up afterward, that's over?

No, no. I'm not saying that's over; I'm saying it's drawing to a close. Just like the sale of drugs to make quick money is also drawing to a close.

That's wonderful.

The Corporate Profit Motive Will Raise Quality of Life

Ultimately any corporation knows that if it wants people to buy its products, they have to be alive; and they have to be happy if you want to have ultimate sales. The products have to improve people's lives. Eventually you're going to see more benevolence from technology because the more the corporations continue to merge (which is natural) and get involved on governmental levels, it has to know what it's doing. And it will eventually become more efficient. Efficiency is not always humanistic, as anyone who has studied history knows. But in this case efficiency will lead to something more humanistic. This is largely because some beings at the upper levels of the major corporations—and certainly the individuals in the sinister secret government—know that eventually trade and sales are going to take place between this world and other planets. And the business world wants to be positioned correctly for the time when they will sell Earth products to extraterrestrials and the people of this planet begin buying products created on other planets. They also know that the benevolent extraterrestrials you're soon going to be in contact with will not encourage or even allow such sales unless your governments agree to a certain standard of humanistic practices.

You will begin to realize that if you want to make money or even have influence, you must bring up your standards as well as the quality of life of people around you to get the ET contracts, because the people in the extraterrestrial trade organizations you'll be dealing with have certain philosophical standards, and they won't sell you things you want to sell to the public unless you act in a certain way. So you are arriving at the time when you will realize that many practices that might have seemed benevolent on the surface were not in the end. Those practices on other planets have been basically eliminated through interaction with other races from other planets. You're easing into that right now, and there's no stopping it. Once that's settled, things are gradually going to get better, but you won't notice this initially in this country for probably another fifteen years or so. People who are paying attention will notice it now, but others won't begin to acknowledge it until they have to.

ET Escapees from Underground

Supposedly there were three beings in Brazil (humanoid ETs). Three young girls saw one of them. And it was reported that one or two of them were in the hospital. We think they were dead. Can you tell us anything about that?

Remember what I said before about a lot of beings who are being shocked to the surface? To some extent what's also going on is that some ETs are escaping from underground. There's a lot of breakdown in the sinister secret government's authority underground because they're going through a radical shift; they're gradually legitimizing. And there's a breakdown in power underground. A lot of beings are really ETs, and people who have been keeping control of them are . . . well, it's just sort of a breakdown of power, and a lot of ETs are now able to escape to the surface. When they get to the surface, if they remember how (if they haven't been down there too long), are calling to be rescued. But they don't have the sophistication to know who's a friend and who's a foe. So not all of these beings are getting off of ships. This is why sometimes when people come across these beings there is no evidence of a ship having been there, because they have come up to the surface out of dimensional doorways—or in some rare cases, actual physical doorways. This was a case in which beings came up from underground.

Were they all killed?

Two of them are in what I'd call a dormant stage, meaning that they're not actually dead. Let's put it this way: One of them is now unable to get back into its body and will move on, on the soul level. One is in a dormant stage and might not (75% probability) get back into its body. One, I believe, has a pretty fair chance of being rescued.

Why were they held underground? What was the purpose? Where are they from?

SSG Kidnapped ETs for Biological Experiments, Now Releasing Them

About twelve years ago the sinister secret government developed means by which they could tap into underground bases of benevolent ETs; they couldn't drill holes there. By using dimensional doorways (they have that technology), they could reach through a doorway, grab somebody and use them for their nasty purposes.

As a basis for cloning?

Yes, and for biological experimentation and everything else nasty. This is what they have been doing. Within the past ten years (especially the past six) it's become obvious to a lot of people that there have been mass evacuations of extraterrestrials living underground. Underground civilizations have moved off temporarily to return later. That's why; they weren't safe because the sinister secret government (SSG) has that ability. But the SSG is no longer grabbing beings because now they realize that these extraterrestrials are going to be our future customers. Now that the SSG is legitimizing, they are confused about what to do with the people they've grabbed, whose extraterrestrial governments (for lack of a better term) have demanded, requested or required their return. So in some underground areas of the SSG they are releasing the beings, hoping to curry favor from the ETs. The people who were assigned to guard these beings feel like, "Why should we bother? This isn't working out. Every man for himself" and so on. They're just letting people go. But the word has gone out by the SSG not to harm any ETs or otherworldly visitors and to try their best to help them get repatriated, as it were.

What star system or civilizations are they from?

Several civilizations. I'll tick off a few: Andromeda Pleiades, Orion, in three cases Zeta Reticuli and in one case Antares, several from Sirius. The list goes on.

Where were the ETs who showed up in Brazil from, one of whom was taken to a hospital? There was a drawing of one in a UFO magazine.

I think these beings are from Sirius.

Negative Sirians or . . ?

No, no. They were not negative beings.

That's great. This relates to where our civilization's going in the next fifty years.

Remote Viewers' View of the Future

Material seems to be circulating about the government doing a lot of remote viewing. The scientists who have projected into the year 2000 have seen that then only 20% of the population is left on this planet, and it looks totally different. I am curious—is this 3.0 dimension? Does this not concern us?

Thank you. That's a good question. This basically has to do with a potential future. This bleak outlook (20% of the people left and worldwide disasters decimating the population) is still a possibility, as I've said before—but not much. I don't think that's *your* version of your planet. Most likely this is something that happens at 3.0 or possibly 3.1. Now, for those who are seeing a benevolent future yet only 20% of the current population (which is still quite a few folks), this might be something at the 4.0 dimension or beyond. So it depends largely on what scientists and remote viewers are seeing. If they're seeing something chaotic and miserable, and perhaps beings who do not actually look human, they're *definitely* seeing 3.0, where the formerly negative Sirians are living. On the other hand, if it's benevolent, it's at a higher dimension. Allowing for where you're going in the next fifty years or so, it could be you, but only if it's reasonably benevolent.

Inevitability of Birth Control

Now, there's something I haven't said, and I have to bring this up. I've sort of hinted around about it before, but this question stimulates it. Is it likely, people have asked, that there will be restrictions on the birth rate in the future? It is not only likely, but you can count on it. I'm not saying, have kids now before it's too late.

This falls into alignment with people being unable to give birth because the planet has too many people on it (we've discussed that before). It also falls into the realm of necessity from a corporate viewpoint, because the corporate-model government will begin to realize that there are too many people. They're not going to put you in boxcars and send you off to camps, but if people stopped having children for 25 or 30 years, there would be a radical but natural decrease in population. Chances are, there will be a control on future population, but not as rigid or as harshly enforced as in the People's Republic of China. It would be a similar model, only not as harshly enforced, where a couple, if they are potent, will be allowed to have no more than one child. That's likely—count on that. And it might also be that for 10, 15, 20 years even, couples will not be allowed to have *any* children. I don't want to say how, but it will be possible to do that without coming into your bedroom and saying, "You sleep in separate beds."

The potential of a drastically lower population is there because there are too many people here, and Mother Earth will eventually summon her reserves when it comes to her immune system, which is simply microbes. If she summons 5000 microbes, you're going to have 5000 new diseases. Science isn't ready for that, so you need to be okay with the idea that births will become rare and that children are a valuable treat.

The remote viewers saw that there were probably all kinds of diseases that would wipe people out, so I suppose that's 3.0.

I think so. I believe it can be that. We talked about this before, did we not, when you were pushing 3.47? If enough people come to believe that those diseases will be virulent, it could still happen, but it doesn't have to. The option is available for the population to be reduced in benevolent ways.

In the long run, but not by the year 2000.

I know. I'd say it's the lower dimension. I'm going to stand on that; I'm not going to budge off of that.

Frog Mutations and Toxic Wastes

Also, there's these mutated frogs that have been discovered in Minnesota that physicists and scientists are very upset about, thinking that this is a result of ultraviolet rays. Is this a microcosm of what might happen at 3.0 dimension?

I can't talk about that at length, but that isn't at 3.0; that's happening right here in your reality. It has to with exposure to toxic wastes. A lot of frogs spend time underground. If you search around enough, you'll find serious toxic wastes there. On the spiritual level, it's a warning. Some things just cannot continue now (in terms of technology) because you don't have the capacity to deal with the wastes—obviously, certain chemical and biological weapons and certain technologies. So the whole experience of needing to have a more sacred relationship with the garden and the animals there or with farms and the animals there (insects, as you call them) is essential.

I think other work has been done here; I don't need to add to it. You can find out what to do. If you're going to produce poisons and they're going to run off into places, they're going to affect human life and human birth and other life, too. And frogs, who are very spiritual beings, are going to be inclined to *show you* what's coming if you don't do something. Frogs, I might add, are one of the few beings who are willing to commit mass public suicide, and they have done it before. You see them hop out on the highways and you can't avoid them—that's mass suicide. That's always them saying, "You've got to stop what you're doing. You've got to start living in a more sacred way." That's the basic spiritual message. Obviously, it's possible for science inadvertently or even intentionally to create highly poisonous substances. But you don't *have to* try and create them. They're out there in the natural state of being.

So there are many beings around that also have mutations, but we're not aware of them yet?

Beings?

I mean animals that live underground or are there often. Frogs aren't the only animals that this is happening to?

That's true. It could happen to human beings. What I'm really saying is that Mother Earth has the ability to produce toxic substances. Please don't feel like you have to emulate that level of creationism. But yes, if you're asking, "Are potential birth defects in a large sense possible in the animal kingdom as well as the human world?" Certainly. But why have it?—just change. I know it sounds ridiculously simple to say and highly complex to do, but as your world becomes more connected, more interconnected, it's not going to be bureaucratic. You will make a decision at the top and it will go all the way from the top to the bottom in a couple of weeks. It can be applied. It's true, dioxin has been buried; they tried to hide it. "Oh, shove it in the ground. We won't see it. It won't be on the surface; it won't harm us." But everyone knows, Earth is a living organism, where things are always moving around. At some point you're going to have to go find it, dig it up, transform it. You might need to find really spiritual people to transform it or you might have to go park it on the Moon for a while until you *can* transform it.

So this must mean that there's a lot of toxic stuff up there in Minnesota.

Well you know, any state with some wide open spaces in the past forty years (of course, there are fewer wide open spaces in Minnesota now) or even twenty years ago would be highly susceptible to the burial or, more likely, the dumping of toxic waste. And I'm certainly not ruling out radioactive toxic waste. This has more to do with conventional things, as well as a spiritual message from the frogs.

Computer Chips in Prisoners

I think you covered everything very well. We're really saying not to look at all these fear-based things that are coming across. I got several memos that apparently were lifted from the files of a major computer company that mention research regarding a chip that they're putting in prisoners that enable them to control them completely.

That's real.

The implication is, once they're tested on the prisoners, God knows who else they're going to implant.

That is real. This was envisioned by others and it's true; it's coming. It is a very small group of prisoners they're putting them into, not everybody. It's an experiment that you have to expect. They've got these for animals already. "Oh, put that in your animal. Mark it with everything and then go someplace." We've discussed this. Yes, that's real, that's coming. I don't think you can stop it.

But they're not going to put it in all the people?

I think eventually they will. It will probably be installed at birth. In a lot of ET civilizations you have this.

But this isn't just to mark people to find them. This is for total control. They can put you to sleep for 22 hours.

Yeah, but that is not going to happen.

They can turn you off completely.

That might happen. You want this technology to be applied as lightly as possible. Let it happen (eventually, not now). It's very likely that in the long run all prisoners will have this implanted. However, it is possible that once they complete their sentences, including parole, it will be removed. That's real possible; it's being researched for that. But will this particular kind of chip go into the general public? I don't think so.

Good.

I do think that there will eventually be a chip of some sort that will be used for the general public. Not just for tracking, but for other purposes—basically the ultimate mini-Social Security card that will have lots of information about you. I don't think you're going to be able to avoid that one. Now, it's possible you might if it doesn't happen for 25 years, but I think it's coming sooner than that.

It will be an opportunity to employ magic (true magic) because some of you might have to get past it. But in terms of going into prisoners—oh, yes. They'll have to get some of the bugs out of it. But yes, I think it's really going to happen. Ultimately it will be used for benevolent purposes for prisoners—to keep them from fighting with each other. It will make them more docile, true. It's frightening, but it will be sufficiently frightening and controversial in intellectual circles, to say nothing of religious circles, that I don't think there will be any chance of that particular chip in that form being used in the body of the average citizen. It will get a lot of publicity by simply getting put into prisoners. It is possible that even after they finish parole they might not have the technology to get the darned thing out. That's what's going to create a lot of the controversy.

Well, this one they can. They can take it out under cover of just sending somebody over for a medical exam or something. This was three or four pages of what alleges to be a secret, confidential, eyes-only memo that somebody mailed in a plain white envelope.

I think that it is a project on a very small scale now that is in application because the technology exists. I think that ultimately the device will, in the case of prisoners, be put someplace where it would be difficult to remove. Ultimately it will probably be implanted at the base of the skull or someplace like that, where you can't get rid of it without killing yourself. They don't have the technology that involves simply putting a collar around your neck. But for what it's worth, the actual intentions are benevolent. It will get enough publicity, believe me—worldwide—to prevent its widespread application as a control mechanism for the civilization.

Good.

Nonlethal Weapons Testing on the Public

I want to talk about something briefly. Ever since the 1700s and the 1800s, in the early days of law enforcement those who have acted as police have wanted a weapon that would be practical but not lethal.

Especially in modern-day policing you'll find that fully 40% of the most dangerous calls are domestic disturbances. And if husbands and wives are fighting, the last thing in the world the police want to do is go in and shoot somebody. But it's surprising how often somebody gets shot or is terribly injured.

So for years the police have been saying, "When are we going to have something we can actually use?" For a time they thought they had it with a little electric gun, but it wasn't practical for many reasons.

It is interesting that in circles where one would least expect it there is great interest in nonlethal weaponry—in the military. So there is a market in the police community and potentially in the military community. The idea is basically to apply electronic warfare to more mundane situations or smaller skirmishes.

I bring this up briefly because it is beginning to be overwhelming. You all know that electronic and electromagnetic pollution are out of hand. Not only are there microwave generators in every house, but you've got satellites blasting you with microwaves! I might add that fully 40% of the aggravated cancers are largely stimulated by electropollution and/or microwave radiation. I'm not talking about skin cancers or cancers that show up at the end of a natural life cycle, but cancers that are aggravated and become inflamed.

As if that were not enough, weapons tests are being done on unsuspecting individuals, meaning the testing is done largely on the mass public. Granted, it isn't done in New York City or Washington, D.C. (although there have been a few experiments in Washington). It is generally done in the areas of small towns accessible by underground or clandestine bases.

This has been going on in Sedona for a while and certainly in many other spots. This testing has been done mainly in the West—in Texas, Oklahoma, Wyoming, Montana, Oregon, Washington, California, Nevada, Arizona, New Mexico, Utah, Colorado and Idaho. There have been exceptions, such as the tests in southern Florida and an outrageous amount of testing on the nonvolunteers of Cuba. You'd be surprised what your government—or more often the case, government contractors—does under the guise of nondestructive testing.

I bring this up because it is time to decide how much defense is too much. The idea of a nonlethal weapon is terrific, but it ought to be tested on volunteer subjects. I see no reason why prison inmates shouldn't be paid or compensated in some way for this hazardous work. It's outrageous that they are often paid with a brief furlough from prison. There ought to be something more for them because prisons are terrible enough already. And they are outrageous in their concept; if you want to separate people from society, that's fine, but you don't have to send them to concentration camps.

Electonic Warfare and Mind Manipulation Must Be Stopped

I support nonlethal weapons, but I am not keen on the way they're being developed. There is no question that the sinister secret government applies electronic warfare to the manipulation of people's thoughts and feelings.

You all watch these shows like *Star Trek*. It's one thing to have a hand-held self-protection device that immobilizes someone without injury. They basically go to sleep and then wake up. I'm all for that. But it's another thing to ask: "How can we manipulate the public so they will follow no matter what we say or do?"

While I fully support the development of nonlethal weapons to be substituted in situations where lethal weapons would have been used, I do not support the methodology for the testing. And I would like to see you as citizens do something about it. Those of you who want to work on the spiritual level, excellent. But even if you don't work on the spiritual level, write your Congressmen. They might feel powerless as individuals, but if you get enough of them to petition the Defense Department or the Attorney General's Office, something will be done. The main thing is, *let's stop testing mind-manipulation devices on the unsuspecting, involuntary public.* And for those who do volunteer, let's see that they are properly and justly rewarded.

Can you be specific about what devices we're talking about?

Basically, electromagnetic devices and even extra-low-frequency (ELF) devices. As a result of extensive research in neurochemistry, these devices are known to affect the body's hormonal system and secretions or electrical stimulations within the brain. Much of this research has been not only to discover the feel-good pill (which I've mentioned before), but to lead to a way to control people in a nonviolent way so that the people will be nonviolent. And while that seems very benevolent on the surface and the goals were initially justifiable, there has been an outrageous amount of manipulation and testing on the general public. The problem is, when private industry develops such things, there is a tendency for a lot of mischief to take place.

Your Group Conflicts Are Meant to Solve Unsolvable Conflicts

So I am all for nonlethal weaponry, but I'm not for mind manipulation—and I am certainly not for microwave and electropollution. It is necessary, I understand, as you're going through this stage to clear up the unresolved issues of your creation. Let's look at things in the larger picture, as I like to do—for instance, the wars and struggles between certain nationalistic groups and religious groups over the years. Instead of Catholics and Protestants (as in Ireland), let's change it to Martians and Venusians. The minute we change that perspective, we understand that one of the reasons you have so many fragmented social or religious structures is because the ultimate intention is *to create methods of peace for unsolvable conflicts* that have occurred on other planets and other cultures. When something is unsolvable in a place where conflict is not allowed but basic conflict has been demonstrated, outsiders will step in and resolve the issue with a benign police force, saying, "We will seek to have this resolved elsewhere and we'll apprise you of the solution so you can apply the solution with your people." You might ask, "How is peace kept in the universe?" This is ultimately the answer when there are individuals who might be inclined toward arguments or violence.

Ultimately that's the direction you're going here—moving toward a policing force that will use nonlethal weapons and say to people (even warring groups), "You clearly can't resolve this. We're going to work on this resolution somehow, but for now we're going to have peace here. That's how it's going to be." It might be hard to imagine that people will say okay. But they learn that they're not being ignored, that someone's just cause is not being cast aside and that resolution will be accomplished someplace.

Now, Earth is a place where resolution is being striven for. In another context, that's the future of law enforcement, even between two individuals who have perfectly just causes from their points of view. Someone's going to come along and say, "I'm sorry, but you're not allowed to fight. Not only are you hurting each other, but your anger and your battle is affecting others. We're going to put a stop to it. A resolution will be created and given to you to work out." Thus law enforcement is gradually going to evolve into becoming what it was always intended to be: peace officers. That's it.

2

Facing the Antichrist within Self Is Humanity's Challenge

Zoosh through Robert Shapiro
January 1997

What started this was the letter on the Internet from someone who said he was a covert black agent from the Vatican. He had gotten into a secret computer connection that was tracking the Hale-Bopp comet. His letter says that his parents and his brother and sister were later murdered because he knew about those secret files.

And this was put out over the Internet?

Yes.

This is a hoax. I'm not saying that the writer did not believe what he wrote. But he is not a covert agent for the Vatican. The Vatican does have a police force, but they don't go all over the world to do things. A lot of this has been blown all out of proportion on the basis of recent fictional works by popular authors.

Putting something out over the Internet is basically like sending an anonymous letter. I'm going to say that the person was expressing his point of view, but he is not officially, unofficially or in any way associated with the Vatican. And the Vatican is the Catholic Church.

So they're not tracking the Hale-Bopp comet? The next day on the radio show it said that Gore and members of NASA went to the Vatican, like they have some kind of supersecret situation room or war room.

The Vatican is interested in developments. They don't have a war room. I wouldn't call it a situation room because they're not that centralized; they're not organized that way. But they are interested, they do keep track of things. Through various generous bequests to them over the years and because they have money, the Vatican has a lot of fingers in a lot of different pies.

Understand that the Vatican has the long view—which, I might add, a lot of religions don't. And that is: "What will happen to us if everything takes place that's been predicted for years by beings all over [including myself], if the Second Coming happens within people? Will we be needed by the people? How can we best serve?" Believe it or not, they have asked those last questions. I know that everyone wants to think of the Vatican as the enemy, but they are not the enemy. They are occasionally weak individuals, meaning not dedicated to the cause to which they have sworn, but they are interested in what will develop. There is a thought in their minds that this represents something along the line of signs and wonders. That's part of the reason that they readily recognize signs and wonders all over the world.

If you've been paying attention to the news, you'll notice that the Vatican is much quicker to say, "Yes, this is a miracle, this is true." It isn't cynicism; they're just more alert to signs and wonders at this time. They believe that there is a very good chance that this approaching comet and its companion have to do with signs and wonders. That is why they are willing to use science to study it. But they do not make their decisions based on science. The Church is not a science-ordered community and it is more than a dogma-oriented community. At the very highest levels there's a lot of knowledge, a lot of awareness, and there isn't much restriction of that knowledge within the higher circles of the Pope and his advisors. (We need to include the Pope's advisors here.)

They want to know what this is about. They think they *might* know, and they want to be kept abreast of it, not so they can control anything (these are *not* the bad guys), but so they can see how they could best serve.

I thought they'd been taken over by the bad guys.

No. What has gone on in the past, not only within Vatican City but also within the Catholic religion itself, were a lot of things for which they are either ashamed or wish they had not done. Certainly some of it has to do with what they did during World War II. But if you had to pin them down, they would say, "We did what we had to to preserve our people and their immortal souls."

I'm not saying that this excuses what they did, because they could have changed things. They didn't know then how powerful they were. They didn't know that if they had spoken out strongly to German citizens against the Nazis and that if all religions had said, "Don't do this—it's threatening your immortal soul" and so on, they would have undermined the power of the Nazi political enterprise so much that it might have never gone beyond the borders of Germany.

Think about it: Suppose the Church had come out and said to Poland, for example (where there are a lot of Catholics), "The Nazis represent the antichrist. Fight to the last man!" Blitzkrieg or not, Poland would have fought to the last man, woman and child and the Nazis would never have gotten into and past Poland. They probably wouldn't even have annexed land there. The Church now knows that, but they didn't know it then.

This falls under the heading of regret. So yes, there have been terrible things done in the name of the Church by its representatives, and yes, they need to clean house. I believe this housecleaning is going to take place within the next ten years. As I say, younger ones are coming up. Don't be too surprised . . . the next pope is going to be quite a character, and the one after that also.

What about the antichrist?

The antichrist has always been in existence within the human being—that is simply the choice to do evil instead of good. *That* is the antichrist and has always been. From the action of a person who mugs somebody on the street and expresses in that moment something that could be loosely categorized as evil, all the way to somebody in the sinister secret government who will stop at nothing to hold and secure power (and lots of stops in between)—*that action and thought* (in the form of the fantasy of an evil act) *is the antichrist in application.*

This is important to put out there, because people are not going to evolve in their spiritual application in some mysterious way. They have to be shown step by step. My job as the end-time historian is to tell you that if you have even a fantasy about destroying somebody, that is a representation of the antichrist. Just be aware of it. Awareness gives people their power. It also gives them the responsibility for their actions, and ultimately that is what the Explorer Race school is about on Earth: giving you the responsibility for your actions, which you don't get in many spiritual planets.

If you take an action that is different from the prescribed norms and even accepted latitudes of life on the Pleiades, for example, and that action harms you or someone else, you as an individual within that society are not held responsible. Your mentor is held responsible. Any reprimand goes to the mentor. That's how it works there.

They do this because they believe absolutely in the idea that once you're a mentor, you're capable of hearing something critical (you don't get to be a mentor until you're an adult in that ability) without it harming or affecting you as a soul. But if you are young and you do something outside the bounds of their philosophy that is harmful to yourself or someone else, they believe that if they directly criticize you, it can create a potential for a self-fulfilling prophecy. That is, if you tell somebody he's bad, then he becomes bad or he overreacts, leaving behind the essential elements of his personality, and he goes on for the next 150 years or so trying to get back to his home personality.

In my example here, if you did something evil even to a minor degree on the Pleiades (and it would be very minor there, I can assure you), you would not have to pay the piper. Here it's different. You've got to pay the piper. Here you learn about responsibility; you learn about consequences. I am talking with such feeling about this subject because it bears directly on the Explorer Race. If we're blaming somebody, what does blame say?

You're bad.

What else?

You did it wrong.

What else?

I'm judging you.

Yes, and *I'm not taking any responsibility* for what has affected me *because it's your fault.* You can clearly see how that does not fit into the Explorer Race lessons you are here to learn on Earth. So anytime we even *say* that the Vatican (an incorporated body that represents millions of people) is evil, we are essentially setting something up. It's the same thing as saying that the blacks are evil, the Jews are evil, the Arabs are evil. We create an enemy, and as a result that enemy must be, in the minds of many people, punished by any means necessary. After years and years and years and years of saying that the Jews are evil . . . that is why during World War II millions of people—little children, babies, women, adults—were taken away and murdered in the most heinous way, to say nothing of gypsies and any "enemy of the state" or military prisoners. And everyone who was in a position to do anything about it—which included the Allies and the heads of governments, even organized bands of powerful individuals, organized crime—turned their heads away and said, "Well, they killed Christ, so what?" If you keep repeating the lie long enough, people will say, "They're the enemy and they deserve anything they get."

That is exactly what happened. Even in the highest circles of power in your government—as good and as beloved a man as President Franklin Delano Roosevelt was and as many good things as he did—Roosevelt still turned a blind eye when people said to him, "Bomb the concentration camp crematoriums. Bomb the railroads that go to the concentration camps. What will it hurt? Bomb the trains so they can't take people there and use them for their evil purposes."

With all their bombs, couldn't they have sent a few bombers to do that? They couldn't do it, not because of any good reasons (I'm picking out FDR only as an example; there were plenty of others), but because they had been raised in a society that had nurtured the lie that the Jews killed Christ.

Can you not see how this is a test? It is crystal clear that it is a test. Here we have the opportunity or choice to say, "The Christians are evil" or "It's the Vatican." We are hearing, "It's the Christians; the Vatican is evil." If we say the Vatican is evil, then we just take the shoe off of one foot and put it on the other. We will have created an enemy. I'm going on about this, my friend, because it is vital for everybody to understand that *as long as we create an enemy, we express the antichrist.* Never forget that. It needs to be published, because people are going to hear this sort of judgment. In the publishing business, information constantly pours in to you whether you want it or not. But the Internet is now becoming pervasive. In the coming years it will be a force of such great power that people will be stunned. That is why lies must be answered.

Why did this person put this out?

Because he as an individual belongs to a religion, and he also has personal feelings, that believe the Vatican is evil and must be destroyed at all costs. He doesn't *think* like that, but that's the *feeling.*

Understand very clearly that this could happen to all Catholic people, millions and millions of them. The highest levels of the Catholic Church have known this for years. As early as the 1700s they understood that someday there would be a severe threat to the Catholic Church and all Catholics, and that pogroms (the word for killing or hurting the Jews because they killed Christ) might someday happen to Catholics all over the world. The shocking part of it is that the people who would commit the atrocities against Catholic people would themselves be Christians. They were told that this would happen.

So when World War II came around and Hitler was rising to power, the Catholic Church was desperately afraid that this was going to be the moment when they as the Church—the Vatican and Catholics all over the world—were going to be brutally murdered. If the Third Reich had won World War II, that is *exactly* what would have happened. This is why they made this crazy compromise with Hitler; they thought that was the time that had been prophesied. That is also why they proselytize people to join their church with so much passion. It is also why they encourage Catholics to have many children. The idea is, "if we populate the Earth with millions and billions of Catholics, there's less chance (with Catholics all over the world and everybody getting used to them) that we will be persecuted."

I can assure you that they have been told this in visions, dreams, by spiritual means and by documents they trust, because the documents have other predictions that came true. They said that someday what happened to the Jews in World War II would happen to them, only worse—meaning that every single Catholic everywhere would be tortured and murdered, and the Church would be eradicated. Further, it would be done by Christians (not Moslems) of other religions who believed they were on a holy crusade. (Understand that the Catholic Church is a sacred organization.) As a result, the people of the world—everyone—would be condemned by God and God would destroy the Earth!

They have supported the inclusion of the book of Revelation in the modern version of the Bible so that people will think about that as a possibility: that someday God could destroy the Earth. This is very important stuff.

Now is the time for the secrets to be revealed. That's why I can reveal these things, sometimes in an innocuous remark or by answering an innocuous question that you might ask. You've seen old movies where they have a spring-loaded trap door you can stand on and it supports you. It can support thousands and millions. But someday the trap door springs open, and you didn't even know it was there.

That's the trap: *blaming someone,* especially a vast group of people. It starts out innocently, by saying, "It's the Vatican." Everybody with a political mind and intelligence would understand that this means Vatican City, Rome. But the vast population of the world hearing that thinks it is Catholics, because who is the Vatican? Who is the Vatican in Tijuana, Mexico? Who is the Vatican in St. Louis, Missouri? Who is the Vatican in Paris, France? Who is the Vatican anywhere around the world? Catholic people. I urge you to publish this. I urge you to publish what I'm saying, because the final test, the challenge in your face, is the antichrist—and the antichrist is *in the person, every individual.* The antichrist represents blame: "Look—*they're* the enemy." It starts out so innocently. Think about it.

I had no idea it was so powerful.

The Jews were pervasive in the time of Jesus' life. Jesus was a Jew. We know the story. The Jews were later blamed even though the people who committed the murder of Jesus were the Romans—in other words, the Italians. Where is Vatican City? Is it anywhere near Rome, do you think?

What would you do if you understand that story, and it looks like *you're* the ones who bumped off the Messiah? Are you going to say,

"Well, all these other people were here and *they* didn't do anything about it"? Let's say that a man walks down a street with a machine gun, shooting people at random. There you are with no weapons. The police capture the man and afterward everybody says, "It was *your* fault!"

"What do you mean, *my* fault? I was just walking down the street. How could it be my fault? It was the man who had the gun."

"No, no—you didn't do anything to stop the gunman. It's your fault."

What's the difference? When you're busy placing blame you know there isn't any.

Remember who the Explorer Race is. Where did you come from? You came from places where you blamed each other, and those resentments were brought here. *You must get past those now!*

Is it not interesting these days how an innocent remark can bring forth such a wealth of material?

We'll use this, because a lot of people will have read that letter on the Internet. It circulates everywhere.

Let's not use anybody's name. Let's just say it was from an anonymous source on the Internet and the story was repeated from person to person. After a while people tend to say, "Well, this must be true." They don't remember where they read it or heard about it, but it becomes true because it has become, intentionally or otherwise, the Big Lie.

3

From Your Light's Point of View, Resistance Is Futile

A Sirian through O'Ryin Swanson
February 5, 1997

You call this energy that is coming into the Earth new, but if you visualize yourself going down steps when you came into the third dimension, leaving energy that was too refined for the density you were lowering yourself into at each step, and at the bottom turning to come [back] up these same steps, what you're facing now is your energy that you left there when you were at that step coming down. Unfortunately, your memories have been wiped; there is nothing in the conscious or subconscious that has a glimmer of understanding of these energies. That is a downside of wiping out the failures to keep your enthusiasm up.

So you and humanity are now dealing with energies that the human body—the living organs, the cells, every conscious particle of you—thinks is new energy, that it is dangerous, that it is invading you, that you have to put up resistances to it, that you have to form a barrier to it, that you must protect yourself at all costs. But, beloved beings, it is only because you have not just forgotten, but you have had your memories removed. Coming down into this dimension was so traumatic; fear was used as a prod and as a method of descension. In that sense, the fact that you don't remember the fear is positive. But if there could only be an awakening to the realization that this is *your energy;* these are particles of the electricity that is yours, that has been stored as if on "this shelf" or "this step." As you come up each step now, the energy that you left as you went down, [at] each parallel step you are only recovering more of who you are, specifically, individually. It seems like a great, swirling amorphous energy mass, but it is only your own energy that you are contacting, connecting to—the part you left because you couldn't take it any lower.

We urgently wish to express to all humanity that the best way to handle this is to relax, to open your arms, your body, your energy field, to allow the energy lovingly to caress you, to join with you. It is not an invasion; truly it is a merging, it is a reconnection. And these steps go on and on and on, so the harder you make it for yourselves now, the more resistance you're going to build up to the future steps. Our heart aches to show humanity that it is not something to fear. These are very loving, very powerful, very specific parts of yourself that you had to leave as you went down the steps so you could be confined and encapsulated in the density where your greatest lessons would be learned.

But now it's over. You're coming back out of that compressed, intense focus. You are expanding to become what you truly are—not that you will become what you truly are in the next few years, but every acceptance of this part of you that you honor and accept and allow to join with you is part of expanding into the being that you truly are. You had great courage [in] allowing yourself to leave parts of yourself *at every step*—great, great courage. It is as if a warrior went out to meet the dragon and left his warrior tools behind, and went with nothing but his bare hands and his wits. That is all you were able to take into that encapsulation. But now, coming out, all the blessed gifts that you have heard about, that are part of your natural heritage, part of who you truly are, are coming again to join you. Allow it, love it, open to it! If we could talk to all of humanity on this planet, [this] is what we would say: "Open to these energies." When the body sees these energies as an invasion, it puts up barriers, it forms antibodies, it constricts chakras and organs, it affects the breathing, it affects the way the actual body works, and it's not meant to do that. It is meant to joyously join you now—joyously and lovingly and with a sense of, "Ah! You've been gone so long! It is so good to be back together with you!"

We have always been watching you and loving you—always—and we are so proud of you! Because you've done it; you've done it! Not just for yourselves, but you have done it for all of creation everywhere. It might seem to you that nothing has changed, that you're still constricted within this dimension, that you have difficulty, that your physical life is hard and has many challenges and there are so many difficulties and so many hurdles, so many obstacles. But this is just the last few seconds of the melodrama. The more of this energy that you can contain, the better you can deal with what you perceive to be these challenges. The more energy you can embody and the more you can bring into your auric field, your energy field, into your very organs, into your very physical body, the better equipped you will be to handle what you perceive to be these hurdles and difficulties. *Resistance is the only hurdle you have left; give it up, let it go!* Do not resist what is the next step for you—the expansion back into who you are.

You have been here in this limited place of very heavy lessons and experience for so long that you have forgotten anything except what is here in front of your face, as they say. But know that as long as it has seemed, it is but an instant in the totality of who you are, and it is finalizing itself now. It is ending. The experiment is over. You, the experiment, have changed the way creation will exist from now on; you have done it! So please allow, bless, ask to receive the energies that are you, let them flow. Accept them in a way that will give you strength. These energies will give you strength and they will give you love and they will give you courage. They will give you insight; they will give you all that you need to meet all the challenges that lie before you. Just allow them into you, accept them, love them. They are *you.*

We ask that everyone may know of this so that they do not see this as an invasion. We will continue to attempt to inspire and to contact all of those who are open so that they can know this, so that they can understand this.

4

SSG, Terrorists and ID Implant: Use Benign Magic to Change That Reality

Zoosh through Robert Shapiro
February 6, 1997

Zoosh speaking. I said some time ago (as have others) that the eventual intention of those people who influence the people in your government is to have placed in the bodies of the citizens of the United States (and eventually the citizens of the world if they can figure out how to do that) identity chips that can hold a vast amount of readable information as well as what I would call impacted, or deeper information about you. I would say that within the next three months probably the first part of this plan might go into effect. I want to put the word out now so that those of you who consciously create your own reality can create a different reality for everyone.

There is a second operation going on in the deep-projects area of a rebel intelligence outfit. They are in no way under the authority or command of any American intelligence operatives or directors. They plan to encourage the sealing of the borders of the U.S. and to create a permanent identity, a MARK, probably within the palm of all American citizens. This will not be something secret. People wouldn't have to carry IDs or driver's licenses around anymore. It will have conventional uses by the regular government, so it will be easy to sell the idea. The idea is to stage an event or series of events whereby it will appear that a small group of foreign individuals has infiltrated into the U.S., most likely from Mexico, to commit terrorist acts against U.S. government buildings and public buildings of various larger to midsize U.S. cities. The ultimate intention is to create an urgency that United States citizens, even at birth, have implants within their bodies that could instantly reveal significant amounts of information, using something like the scanner you have in department stores and supermarkets, and be able to immediately identify a U.S. citizen.

Here are the targets I feel ought to be the most vigilant: offices of elected officials—first, federal office buildings. I encourage passive security devices, because their monitoring capabilities are pretty good. Next, facilities such as hospitals—Veterans Administration hospitals such as Walter Reed and the like. Those in the intelligence community who are concerned about potential terrorist actions, look for people who appear to be foreign nationals, but mainly look for connection to deep-cover operations within the U.S.

This operation is well past the planning stages. (There is an outside chance that a unit might try to cross the Canadian border, most likely in North Dakota, Montana, Idaho, possibly Minnesota.) There are three teams, mostly likely crossing the southern border in a land operation; the policing community knows thatground penetration is easiest.

This information is directed to those in the intelligence and policing communities, people in the security business and general citizens, especially those in the metaphysical community and the enlightened community, to see what you can do to change this reality.

Remember that to change this reality, you can't cancel it. You can, however, attract a different reality. For individuals and those working in groups especially, try to plan a fairly benign future for the continental U.S. for *the next eight or nine months to a year.* The window of opportunity for this operation is considered to be within the next six to nine months, but I think there is a potential for it to happen sooner. Let's try and change this reality. That's my flash.

Who do these teams work for, the secret government?

Not directly. They are involved in a deep-cover operation in a rebel outfit of a known intelligence service associated with the United States. Should it come to light, don't blame this intelligence service. There is no officer or agent that I'm aware of who knows of this group. Although they do not work directly for the sinister secret government, they are financially supported indirectly by it.

They want to create a dramatic incident to encourage a permanent installation within the bodies of all U.S. citizens that will on the surface be a built-in ID card. Impacted beneath that level of basic information (born to, social security number, parents and so on) will be a capacity that can be activated within ten to fifteen years that will function effectively to profoundly influence your behaviors. It will be externally sourced by a form of broadcast electricity. Think about the ramifications. It would be possible, with this deep programming, to set up installations all over the country or even by satellite and broadcast certain "suggested" behaviors for whoever is wearing these devices. Think of the ability to manipulate people.

The influence would not be a dominant force. If it were, the individual would have a very uncharacteristic quality; it would superimpose itself over your personality. It is latent, but it would work with other influences, both subtle and direct, to manipulate and control your general attitudes and behaviors. I feel it could be used up to a 30% influence; they would never use it beyond 30% because it would alter your personality, and then everyone would catch on very quickly that something was going on.

How big is this group?

As a rebel outfit, not counting those they contract with who might think they are an honorable U.S. agency, they number no more than 1200 individuals.

Evidently the rebels don't know who really is funding them.

That's not true. They mainly generate their own funding, but they are supported *indirectly* (the key word). They get about 90% of their funding from smuggling. They smuggle whatever cash crop is available. They've been known to smuggle diamonds, but the primary cash crop these days is drugs; so they are involved in moving things from point A to point B. And since the sinister secret government is highly involved in organized crime, they essentially support this outfit by throwing business in their direction, though no one is aware of that. That's why I say their support is indirect.

But how do the 1200 rebels plan to use this ability to control the American people?

There is a small group of individuals (eight inner-circle members) who started this outfit, recruiting people they wanted. The 1200 would like for those eight to be in charge. This inner circle of eight is indirectly connected to the sinister secret government. They were encouraged or started up by somebody who is directly connected to the sinister secret government, but this circle of eight does not know that. They think *they're* going to have the power.

They don't realize they're puppets?

Exactly. And of course, if the operation were a success (and we want it to *not* be a success) and were completely installed, there would be a period of perhaps twelve to sixteen months when this inner circle of eight would feel victorious, feeling that everything was looking good, and then . . .

They would disappear.

They would not be heard of again.

Is it going to be universal, or just American? You called it a universal . . .

The intention is to start with the United States and then to try to make it worldwide. But I don't think they could succeed in doing it worldwide. They're going to try it in the U.S because it is now the most propagandized large nation, primarily because mass media is so good here. This is not blaming the media in any way, but suggesting that the instruments of mass media, primarily television but secondarily print, are easy to manipulate.

I can't imagine an American wanting or accepting this.

Of course you can't imagine it, but think about this: What if it came out in the press and was demonstrated that a terrible bombing took place at a hospital, especially one where the people are appreciated and admired, such as veterans or children. I'm not trying to encourage that, I'm just asking what if. If that happened once, twice, three, four, five times, people would be in a complete uproar to do something about it, and justifiably so. Ultimately, the elected governments would have to ask, "What can we do?"

Obviously, cards, badges and pictures are not foolproof. Forging documents these days is very sophisticated; the amount of counterfeit money floating around is appalling. In response to such a crisis they'll ultimately have to say there has to be some form of ID that is absolutely foolproof, because it's true from their perspective.

Wouldn't they have to prove that these terrorists were foreigners?

Oh, yes, but it's very easy to program people to do this. The best way to do it, of course, is to program somebody who thinks he's doing something else. In the past this has been done very effectively, and if it works, why change it? You have agents willing to sacrifice themselves for a cause, whatever it might be. More likely you involve people who don't know what they're doing, think they're doing something else or that they're working for a legitimate policing agency of the U.S. government or international police agency. Because it is so easy, we need to get lots of people together as individuals and groups to form individual and group visions to draw to you a different, benevolent reality of the future. That is, as I've said before, true benign magic. Change your reality. You can't cancel a reality—that takes a lot of energy and it's hardly worth the effort. But you *can* draw to you a more benevolent one by using very little energy, and the more people that are doing it, the better.

We were told that we would get into 61% negativity and that the highest we'd ever been before was 60.5. Is this negative time coming in the next two or three years?

Remember that the 61% negativity is only a potential, not an absolute. That's part of the reason I want to tell you beforehand about these dramatic things that might happen, so that you can change. I see no reason why you should be forced to go through 61% negativity, and I don't know any other consultant who feels differently. So yes, this is part of that. I'd like to see you change it, and I think you have the capacity.

5

How Spirit Works in the Universe

Lee Carroll

Kryon has told us that it is virtually impossible to visit an interdimensional place and interpret it correctly with our single-digit dimensional human minds. Even with great discernment and enlightenment there is a vast amount of information that simply isn't recognizable by any human living in lesson on the planet today. And yet this is how most predictions are obtained.

It's like sending an anteater to review a meeting of humans attending a lecture on the workings of the incandescent light bulb. The anteater covers the event and comes back with the news. He tells the other anteaters about the strange beings there: how they smelled, what color their fur was, if there was food, and how he was almost stepped on—and that's it! The anteater doesn't have the concepts of spoken language, of why the meeting was held or of the science being discussed. What he got was only a fraction of what was there, and most of it didn't even pertain to what was happening. When any human is given an interdimensional vision, he is fortunate to get a fraction of the real essence of what is taking place.

Internet Information

As usual, there is information flying around that is not tempered with understanding, wisdom of enlightenment or common sense. The most dramatic statements are being grabbed up and passed along. Sometimes those reporting the sensational end up writing their own news! This phenomenon is possible because the Internet is a free venue of information that does not have to be validated or verified in any way to be electronically published. The freedom of the Internet is awesome (Kryon is very fond of it), and it will serve this planet well. Kryon has told us that "when everyone can talk to everyone, there can be no more secrets!"

But you have to temper what you see online with the reality that anyone can say anything, and it looks just as important as anything else. Stated credentials are often bogus, and sometimes the information from one source (usually stated as "anonymous for security reasons") becomes the proof for another source, which is then unknowingly (or purposefully) requoted and rephrased by the original source to validate it!

This is not a criticism of the Net, but rather a statement of fact for those who tend to believe everything they read, even on a computer screen. I am an Internet surfer, and so is over one-fifth the male population of the United States (according to PBS radio in a reported survey taken in December 1996).

Comet Hale-Bopp

I asked Kryon, "What is physically out there that astronomers are calling Hale-Bopp?" He winked at me and said, "Frozen methane gas." This wasn't good enough. I asked Kryon, "There is sensational news about this astronomical unit. Is it important to us?" The answer, "Yes." I continued: "Kryon, is it sensational?" The answer was yes. This got my heart going, and in a moment I will give you what Kryon said about Hale-Bopp. First, however, let's start with what we can see, and what science has to say about it.

There is no covert blackout regarding Hale-Bopp, at least not on my computer. There are better times to see the comet than others due to known astronomical anomalies, so the viewing dates have some gaps, but that's a common denominator for all telescopes, amateurs and pros alike. Some have suggested that there hasn't been a good large-telescope photo since August.

In general you should know that almost daily reports are available from current viewing by at least four United States sources (the Hubble telescope, Hawaii's famous telescope facilities, the University of Maryland and JPL) as well as from other places on the planet (the Canary Islands, Japan, Slovenia, Belfast and Australia). There are actually far more than these, but you can find these specific sources all at one address on the Internet: www.eso.org/comet-hale-bopp. These are all institutional Internet pages from around the world.

The Hubble space telescope isn't always focused on Hale-Bopp because it has a viewing schedule that is intensely competitive with other agendas and agencies. This can't be any surprise to anyone, since it is the only large orbiting telescope in existence. It is actually giving Hale-Bopp more time than had been scheduled due to the increased interest.

Others will tell you that the so-called blackout is government-based. This could be so—but the whole world? An interesting thing about the Net is that a conspiracy of this kind would have to include every telescope facility on the Earth, and all the countries involved would have to cooperate in the lie—no leaks, no kidding. (Having been to the United Nations I can report to you that it takes years for countries to agree just on where to sit. Take a look for yourself.) There is a great deal of international daily updated information regarding the comet—some scientific and some not—that is very available and very current.

Let's look at some of the physical facts. Hale-Bopp is not a new visitor. It has a large elliptical orbit around the Sun and is part of our solar system. It was discovered in July 1995 by Alan Hale. Its nucleus (the hard part) is about 40 km wide (about 25 miles), which is medium large for a comet. Its coma (the expanded gas around it) might get to be as large as 70,000 miles wide as it gets closer to the Earth and is excited by the solar wind. It will not hit the Earth or the Sun, but instead will come within 93 million miles (.914 astronomical units) of the Earth at its closest range on March 23, 1997. Take a look at this date; Kryon speaks of it later.

Photos of the comet from amateur astronomers and professional facilities alike show that it has spiral vents, is breaking up to some degree as it sheds ice and gas due to the increasing solar wind, and its luminosity varies from week to week, again due to the dynamics of the debris being burned from its surface. The comet has been extremely cold for almost 3000 years, and now gets to put on a show for us this spring as it gets closer to the Sun and is excited by the solar wind. Those familiar with comets understand these dynamics. The solar wind will greatly affect the object, giving it its comet tail, and causing it to have what is called outbursts, a known phenomenon of all comets due to dust illumination and the clumps that break off of it and continue with it. This makes it luminous one day and less brilliant a week later.

Okay, so much for the science. The sensationalists are telling us that following this comet is a spaceship, and in this spaceship are thousands of entities that are going to do—what? Well, that depends on which message you believe. Some say it will be like the movie Independence Day—an invasion, and the end. Others say that the ship will disgorge its inhabitants close to Earth to rescue us (I'm not certain from what). Others tell us that the ship is here simply to transmit messages from the Federation (a name shared by certain channels and the Star Trek series) that will assure us that we are okay. These messages will tell us that we are not to be afraid and that all is well—nothing hostile.

There is some similarity to all these messages, but some sound like the Borg (again from Star Trek) and others are benign and definitely spiritual. Unsubstantiated and anonymous sources on the Internet are also claiming that there are encrypted messages coming from this ship. What is the truth?

In a moment I will tell you what Kryon has to say, but you might say, "Kryon is just one more message from one more channel. How can I know what is the truth?" Kryon again asks you to discern for yourself and use spiritual common sense, but he also says this: "After the comet comes and goes, and you see there was no expected drama, revisit this message and glean the truth from it." But didn't Kryon say it was also sensational? Yes, let's keep going.

Remote Viewing

Remote viewing has been practiced since the 1950s and both the United States and the former Soviet Union had covert programs that used it to some degree. It has validated successes and some dramatic failures too, so it can be hit and miss, depending on many circumstances. If you find an experienced remote viewer, the chances are high that he/she used to work for the government. Make no mistake, remote viewing is not a spiritual talent nor is psychic ability. Both of these gifts are metaphysical but do not necessarily carry love-based enlightenment with them. They also do not automatically mean that the person with the gift has integrity. It is important to unlink these abilities in your thinking from that of spirituality. There are remote viewers and psychics who are very enlightened and also those who are working for governments with agendas that would make you unhappy, to say the least.

Trained, experienced remote viewers have been used to view Hale-Bopp (according to Art Bell radio-show interviews), although little is known of their spiritual posture. They have astounding, sensational information. The entities are really there (they say), and, in addition, the accompanying object is more than four times the size of Earth! Realize please that no photo has shown Hale-Bopp with an object that big tagging along. A 25-mile diameter object next to a 32,000-mile diameter object traveling in tandem wouldn't just raise eyebrows—it would be headline news around the world, and not easily hidden. The comet would appear to be like a baseball traveling with something 1200 times its size, like a blimp, for instance. This particular scenario is not visible (at least not in the photos from the larger Earth telescopes). Also of honorable mention would be the gravitational effect on the orbits of all the planets in our system (not to mention astrological aspects) from an object four times the size and mass of Earth casually sailing into our solar system. Gravity, anyone? It would not be subtle.

Photos from amateurs and the larger professional telescopes, however, seem to confirm that there is indeed an object with the comet (but visibly not 1200 times larger). Astronomers tell us that it is simply a clump that fell off, and that it probably will be joined by other clumps—such is the way comets work. Sometimes the accompanying object disappears, however (timed photos confirm this). This is really odd, but again, astronomers have explanations.

Realize, please, that science is biased against the metaphysical; this is not new information to any of us. Established science will always try to explain odd things in terms it understands or pretends to understand, and I can't blame them, for this is their truth. You won't ever find a report in a scientific journal that tells us that the "unexplained gamma-ray bursts for the past four years are either (a) energy from a black hole or (b) angels." Here is the beginning of a very real unexplainable scientific attribute of Hale-Bopp, which Kryon says will pass without visible incident except that which is astronomical in nature.

"Kryon," I say, "is there something four times the size of the Earth accompanying the comet called Hale-Bopp?"

"Depends on what you mean by size," says Kryon.

"Okay, Kryon. Tell us what we should know. Please explain what is happening in the best way possible."

6

How to Release Discomfort by Transforming It

Zoosh through Robert Shapiro
February 17, 1997

Well, all right. I'd like to make additional comments on the so-called antichrist energies that I talked about recently [see chapter 2].

Now, I'd like to suggest that there is an unconscious action going on that is affecting certain individuals more than others. I talked last month about the antichrist in terms of what it meant to the individual. It is essentially hate, prejudice, violence against another person or against oneself. For those of you who have not found a constructive means to release pent-up angers, resentments, even depression, I encourage you to do so. I told you a while back that Mother Earth could not take your excess energies of discomfort. But what's happening now . . .

And the Master of Discomfort didn't have to take them anymore. [See "The Master of Discomfort" in The Explorer Race: The Creator and His Friends.*]*

No. Now, there is something going on that is a bit of a problem. I think that you as beings can work it out, but while it's happening it's creating what I would call a backflow, not unlike what occurs in pipes or occasionally at the mouth of rivers, which creates problems. As I said before, you need to release your discomfort by transforming it. You can't just hurl it out in the space around you, because you already do that when you feel that discomfort. You need to transform it by some vigorous *physical* process—whether through some form of sacred dancing or some form of martial art or shadowboxing. It has to be something where you're moving your legs and arms and your whole body's moving. If you're incapacitated, then you can move your arms around, perhaps, and while you're sitting you can hop your legs up and down. If you're totally incapacitated, just move around the best you can.

The idea is this: Because there is so much discomforting energy being released by Mother Earth and by you as individuals (which is a good thing), it's creating a backflow that's affecting very specific peoples—those who are most closely connected to the Earth, for sacred or even cultural reasons. This is most often native peoples: Native Americans, native Africans, even native British people (whom you might find in the north and a few other places in the U.K.). It is certainly affecting older peoples in Asia and Australia and people in parts of Europe. Those who are directly connected to the land through culture or through sacred manners have this backflow energy entering them.

Even farmers?

It could be farmers, but only if they have a sacred connection to the land—meaning that they love what they are doing, have their hands in the soil regularly and understand that the Earth is a sacred thing—farmers who have a strong sense of godliness, whether it be [through organized religion] or through what I call *natural religion.* Specifically, people such as these are being affected and are acting in ways that are not natural to them as individuals. They might have more of a tendency to be on edge or have a greater tendency to be violent with little or no provocation. (Please do not read this as that all farmers are violent, which certainly is not the case.) It is particularly affecting some native peoples who have special connections with the Earth. I'm going to mention a few tribes that are being impacted in a way that is disrupting their lifestyle.

The Australian aborigines in or near cities are being affected this way. It started happening about three months ago from today's date [February 17], and has built to the point now where I need to say something. It's affecting the Dineh (Diné) tribe, also known as the Navajo nation. It's affecting the northern tribes, but to a lesser degree; this includes the Cree and the Sioux. It is also affecting the Cherokee nation and a few other tribes. The ancient peoples in Africa are being affected, as well as the Bedouins, who have a sense of being one with the Earth in their tribal customs.

Other groups that are suffering from this backflow energy are the Inuit, also known as Eskimos, and some older traditional peoples in Iceland. Now, I've singled out a lot, but I don't want you to feel that I've mentioned them all.

I mention this because you as individuals now have a responsibility that is greater than that to yourself. I have always said that your first responsibility is to your own personal creation, but now you have a responsibility that goes beyond that, which is typical in creator school. First, your responsibility starts at home, and then your responsibility is expanded to other peoples—very often peoples you've never met and might never meet.

This is what I'd like those of you who are more conscious to do. When you have the time (don't disrupt your entire life) or can devote the time, I'd like you to find some means of spontaneous (this is necessary) sacred dance you can do—meaning you don't *think* about how to dance. If you want to dance to a drumbeat, that's fine; ideally this drum is being played by a person rather than recorded on a tape, but if a tape is all you've got, okay. It doesn't have to be a traditional dance. I'd like you to dance from your emotional place of being, which essentially resides in the solar-plexus area. So connect with your solar plexus and dance as best you can.

Those of you who can't manage to do this or think about it, then shadowbox or jump up and down. I'm sure you can think of other ways. We need to dispel that antichrist energy by being physical in some way not associated with work—meaning that when you're working (sawing wood, splitting logs or anything) you have to be mentally alert. You have to pay attention and you're following reason as well as making careful physical movements. The release of these energies doesn't work very well this way. It has to be spontaneous physical action, and it needs to be constructive. If you can do this, it will begin to change some of the chemical backflow energy that is affecting a lot of people who are close to the Earth.

Does one need to focus on the intent of doing this as part of the process?

Yes, one needs to be alert to the fact that as you're jumping about in one way or another (don't be concerned with being too precise; let it be spontaneous motion), you might be processing more than your own feelings. Once you feel clear (I'll let *you* discover how you feel clear because I don't want to program your experience), you will actually have more energy. Continue as long as is comfortable for you, or do it more than once. In this way you will be *able* to process energy that is not your own.

The idea is to begin by processing your own energy, because your body needs you to do that. Once you've processed your own discomforting energy, you will know it; you will feel more vital, amongst other things. Then continue moving as long as you have the stamina to do so (don't injure yourself, but keep going as long as the stamina is there) because you will process others' energy. You don't have to think about processing it; it will just happen. In that way you will not draw to you discomforting energy that is not associated with you. The action of the physical, spontaneous energy—jumping around, moving, being physical—tends to radiate your auric field outward in a way that processes energy all around. And it will carve a big hole in the discomforting energy waves that are around you.

Is there any value in asking that the violet flame be used?

You can use whatever spiritual means you like, but I feel it is most important that you as individuals make some effort. This isn't a spiritual exercise exclusively. It's a physical/emotional exercise that allows you to experience material mastery within a spiritual circumstance. Remember, you are all here to learn material mastery, which is why you're in a physical body, and the physical consistently has some form of consequence to deal with. It's not a requirement. I'm just asking you to do so because many tribal peoples are suffering needlessly. You might ask, "Why are they so affected?" When you have a sacred relationship with the Earth, there is no separation between you and the Earth. You *are one* physically. This means that if the Earth is sick, you also have a tendency to get sick. There is no artificial boundary between you and the Earth, so when the Earth is overwhelmed with discomfort, you might be overwhelmed as well. I'm not saying to you spiritual people, "Don't create a spiritual bond between you and the Earth"; I'm saying, get more physical and transform the discomforts within you. And if you can transform some that is 'round and about you, so much the better.

7

Grid Lines Rising above Planet

The Master of Plasma through Robert Shapiro
February 18, 1997

H*ow does it work with the grid lines and ley lines? They're part of Mother Earth's energy body, yet they feed us too, right?*

Yes, but there is an interesting point now with what is ofttimes referred to as grid or ley lines. These lines are no longer where they were; they are rising above the surface. In time there will be an expanded grid all around the atmospheric area of Mother Earth. This will protect her as she moves through dimensions. Grid lines and ley lines are able to do this by expanding, becoming larger by moving outward and maintaining a roughly spherical shape around the planet. As a result, some of you are having bizarre experiences when a grid or ley line goes right through your home or business or wherever you are located. They are moving outward away from the planet.

Right now most grid and ley lines, with a few exceptions, have cleared the surface of the Earth where it is little higher than 4300 feet above sea level. Certainly those lines have not yet cleared places that are five, six or seven thousand or more feet above sea level, but they will. It is not a formula, but as an average, the lines are moving outward from Earth to form this grid at the rate of about one-quarter of an inch per hour, which is quite rapid. Because of the discomfort energy that Mother Earth is releasing, these lines are often clogged with this energy, which needs to be purified.

So those of you who work on such things might ask that as the lines come to the surface, any energy of discomfort be transformed and purified and cycled to where it will do the most good. In this way we can get the grid above the surface of the planet looking pristine. If you were to see it from a distance, its color would be not quite white; it would be white tinged with gold. There would be this hint of gold light about it.

How deep were they before they started moving?

Any given ley line or grid line can be several hundred feet to perhaps only a few feet below the surface, depending largely on surface activities. If there is mining or heavy construction, it is deeper. If the land has lain relatively untouched, it is closer to the surface. This tells you, of course, that in the natural state of being these lines would be closer to the surface to nurture the planet and the population on the surface and also to support and sustain the weather. Part of the reason the weather has been so erratic in recent years is that many of these lines had to go deeper inside the planet to escape the disruptive effects of mining and heavy construction. Heavy construction in this case would mean a large building with subbasements and foundations down four or five stories or some such thing. This disrupts a lot of earth.

How far above sea level will the lines go?

They will go out into space and eventually look not unlike the cover

Regaining Cosmic Antegrity by Joseph Boike

of your magazine here [March 1997 issue, see inset].

I was going to mention that!

That is why I brought it up, because that illustration is quite prophetic. This grid will act to protect the Earth and also hold to the Earth any discomforting energy should it become an extreme situation—extreme being more than 55%, which is a possibility. It will keep it from radiating out beyond the outer layers of Earth's atmosphere. It is most probable that this structure around Earth will be roughly 500 miles above the surface, so this is perhaps beyond the atmosphere.

And beyond the satellites, right? I don't know how far out the satellites go.

Beyond most of them, but it will not harm any space traveler. One could easily fly right through a line and be unaffected.

8

A 45-Day Zeta
Restructuring of the Past

Joopah through Robert Shapiro
February 20, 1997

Good evening. This is Joopah. I'm here tonight [for the *Explorer Race and Beyond* book] because there is a pervasive energy in this sector of your galaxy now that is coordinating your times and space with our past times and space. The feeling is odd sometimes because there's a sensation of something foreign. There's also a sensation of something not quite right. This intersection of our two worlds has in large part to do with the uncreation of some of our more troubled past on Zeta Reticuli. This extreme of discomfort is a temporary anomaly, but because my people are so intimately involved with your people and your time, this restructuring of our past is moving energetically right through your present moment.

The purpose of my visit tonight is to remind you that your future is now less likely to evolve into our society—on the soul line, you understand—than it once was. This is advantageous. Our society is moving up in dimension rapidly, really to get out of the way of your evolution and growth toward your new future. Your new future is much more geared to exploration and physical activity. Most important, it is being structured by you to avoid the pitfall of expanded intelligence being perceived as a panacea for all that ails your society.

Speaking as one who has experienced, in my seventh-dimensional body, expanded intelligence, I can assure you now (in my ninth-dimensional body) that it is not a cure-all. It just tends to override the other bodies of existence, the mind being only one of those bodies. The physical, the emotional and the spiritual are also very important. Time changes; time lines are shifting even as we speak. So for the next few days, really starting today and for the next 45 days, it would be useful if people could pay more attention physically. I will tell you why.

Our Past and Yours Are Changing

Because of this phasing that is going on and because your souls at one time were going to evolve into being our souls in our society (which is deemed unnecessary now), the phasing is creating a minor shift in time structure. Because your souls are no longer going to evolve into our souls, this frees up our soul chain to evolve differently, and as a result our past is changing. This is strongly suggestive, is it not?

If our past is changing, then, as you might guess, your past is also changing. This will affect all of you in the Explorer Race, because coordination with your new future necessitates a change in your past. This means that the impact of our society on your society will become significantly less. Many of the contacts that your people have had with my people over the past several thousand years will be gradually uncreated, since it is considered much more ideal that your people—Earth people and the Explorer Race—not meet my people from Zeta Reticuli on a social basis for another 450 years or so. Although it will not eliminate all past contacts between my people and yours, fully 87% of these past contacts will be eliminated. This will allow a significant and powerful change to develop for your people.

As you know, it was in the late forties and early fifties that my people originally contacted many different governments on Earth. These contacts led to some good things for both of our peoples, and some not-so-good things as well. Some of our people became unintentionally enmeshed in your political upheavals. Your own people evolved much more quickly because the technology we shared was corrupted and kept secret instead of providing your culture with an inexhaustible source of electrical energy, as we had intended.

The Corruption of the Crystal Technology We Shared

This technology had to do with crystals and atomic energy. By that time your culture had already turned atomic energy into weapons systems and a certain amount of electrical generating capacity. What our people shared with some of your people in the late forties and early fifties was a power-generating unit that could produce about one megawatt of electricity per cubic inch. There were no moving parts, and energy was generated largely through using the energy of the Sun's rays to bounce off the internal corridors of the crystal's internal reflections, thereby multiplying. As many of you know, crystals have that curious quality of multiple levels of internal reflection. (I might add that many of the ships from my society and other extraterrestrial ships can be small on the outside and large on the inside by using orders of magnitude and crystal reflection to create a larger inner capacity compared to outer dimension.)

This energy-producing device, when inactive, could literally be held in the palm of an individual's hand. It could be duplicated by a means that we did not share with your people, since we perceived that it would be useful to wait. We waited perhaps 20 to 25 years to see how you used the power. As it turned out, your people were pressing for the knowledge to duplicate the device, but since it had been used largely for experimental warlike purposes, our society decided not to share that technology with your society. That is when a breakdown in communications and general social interaction between our people and yours occurred. Some of your Earth people—most of them associated directly with that sinister secret government—began to manipulate other governments into shooting down our vehicles.

This started taking place in the late fifties into the sixties, and by the time the seventies came, most of our peoples' ships were no longer coming close enough to your planet or its moon to be affected by any weapons system that might be aimed at us. I give you a little of the background of your recent history so that you would understand that it has been perceived necessary by our teachers and yours as well to alter the original exchange of technology that took place during the late forties and early fifties so that it will have never taken place. In this way much of the power, manipulation and influence of your sinister secret government will be uncreated.

The Beginning of Uncreation and How It Will Affect You

This is why this time is so important. This work has been ongoing to uncreate those events for some time, but right now in this moment—at about 2:15 p.m. local time here in this area [February 20, 1997, in Sedona] began this 45-day crucial time period in which those earlier contacts will begin to shred. By "shred" I mean that there will be a rending or tearing of the time line through that connection of our society to your society in the late forties to early fifties. The past and future of our people and yours have had enough separation that we are now at the point where those contacts in the time mentioned are beginning to change.

This will have an extremely minor impact on your current technology, because most of the technology developed out of that exchange between our people and yours was developed and utilized in secret. The only trickle-down effect that I can directly trace to these exchanges of information and devices is in the field of antibiotics. Those of you in pharmacology and medicine might note that some of the more highly synthesized antibiotics will become less useful for your people; but perhaps more important, some of the more natural antibiotics will become more effective. Penicillin and natural antibiotics, including homeopathic remedies and even some electromedicine applications, will become much more effective. Originally your culture would have evolved these things without this contact between your and my people. I bring this up tonight because it is timely and would be useful to disseminate in some way.

How does this time shift affect beings in the alternate negative future?

Yes, a good question. After the 45 days (plus five more) are completed, it should make that alternative negative future about 55% less of a possibility, which means that travel between the two points will become impossible. Still, that alternative negative future will exist for a few years, certainly no more than 5 to 7 if things proceed benevolently. There will be a 15% degree of risk associated with this diminishing future possibility. Those who traveled from that alternative negative future to your present or your past will also be diminished in their energy capacity by 55%, which ought to greatly negate their impact upon your world.

How did this decision come about; what led up to this?

This decision was really made by our teachers and the elders in our society right around the time sequence of 1952 in your time, because we saw then that our intended purpose to provide all Earth peoples with an inexhaustible source of electrical energy was interfered with. When it was not put into the hands of the public in the form of open scientific forums, then our teachers and people discussed what went wrong and our guides and teachers advised us that we must begin an elaborate means to uncreate this contact. We have been working on that ever since.

Will these devices eventually reach the hands of humanity?

Either that will occur, or more likely the device will simply disappear. If we can intricately uncreate those contacts without harming the souls involved, both my people's and your own (this has been ongoing for some time), then the exchange of technology will never have taken place. You might ask, what technology would your society have given us? From our perspective, technology is not necessarily an evolved machine, but could also be the components that might become technology. Our society was gifted with pure quartz, some in the form of sand, some in the form of crystal. This is not a very common substance that we can obtain easily in our world these days. That is what you provided.

Since you're from the future, couldn't you have seen what would happen? Didn't you know about the secret government?

You have to understand that it was a calculated risk, not unlike the calculated risk that was taken by Jesus and his mentors and teachers and other sacred people of the time when they hoped to deflect you from some of the more catastrophic developments that you would experience and some of the suffering your people would go through. But as you know, the best intentions do not always bring about the desired results. I do not wish to compare our contact to something as sacred as Jesus' contact with you, but the intention was the same—to deflect you from a self-destructive course of action onto a more constructive one.

Uncreation of 87% of the Contacted Implants

Will this uncreation relate only to the contacts with the secret government and the governmental figures? The Zetas have affected every human on the planet by helping to change our lightbodies, and vast amounts of good have been done.

Yes, it will affect everyone. As I say, about 87% of the contacts will cease to be. This will mean a couple of things to the average person: It will mean that the devices implanted in people's sinus cavities or in the basilar area of the skull, which occasionally caused some discomfort, will eventually, if things go right, never have taken place. It will not, however, affect the invited implants that are closer to the midbrain and the upper terminus of the spinal column in the skull region, which most of you have, wherein the higher-dimensional implant organically interacts with your physical selves.

The higher dimension is intentional, so that there will be no displacement of tissues in those regions, since those tissues are so extremely vital and delicate. The points of contact of the device to that neural area of your bodies will occasionally stimulate certain brain chemistry that will help you and support you over these difficult times of the past 25 years and into the future by about 75 years—in other words, about a 100-year measure of experiential time. The brain now needs to produce more hormones or fluids that will more easily allow individuals to experience in the sleep state what I would call euphoric states, not as an addictive state, and to be enabled to readily access their higher-dimensional selves on the physiological level. This will greatly accelerate the evolution or the gradual upward motion from one dimension to the next. At least that is the intention.

Who are your guides and teachers? Who counsels you?

We are counseled by beings from the ninth to eleventh dimension of this universe, beings who have seen and ordained many of the great mystical people, some known by you but most unknown because of your lack of travel. These beings seem to have the capacity to resolve differences through their advice, to suggest best courses of action and thought, and to encourage best means of emotional expression and physical action. They have proved themselves to our society over the millennia by our having followed their advice, which has led us to good experiences. They originally came into contact with our society toward the end of the tumultuous times I referred to before [in chapter 10 of The Explorer Race] when in our distant past we had more inner and outer conflict with each other, when our desires superimposed themselves over obvious philosophical benefits—in other words, a struggle with our egos. These teachers do not claim any location, but seem to represent themselves more as motions or meridians of energy and personality, rather than a being from a location. They do not claim to be from a place, but from an experience.

But obviously the Creator and his friends must have concurred in this?

We believe so, since when we follow the advice of these beings, the impact on our society is benevolent. Surely if their advice was in conflict with Creator's, the impact would not be so benevolent. This is simply logical. Your people are still in the latter stages of belief in the power of the mind. But I am happy to see, from my long-distance observations, that the sacred heart and the demonstrated physical motions, dances and sacred ceremonies are beginning to receive more widespread exposure as being beneficial. This will ultimately allow people to see the mind as an important component but in no way superior to the body, spirit or emotions. This way your society will proceed along lines that do not inflict too much intelligence upon you, and thereby an addiction to thought.

Unbraiding Our Past Connection with You, Substituting Sirians

Since our souls are connected, are the Zetas part of the Explorer Race?

They once were, because of your distant past connection on the emotional-body level to our society and your potential future evolution on the soul line to become us. But since this has been gradually and intricately taken apart or unbraided, then there is less of an impact. So one might say that if things continue along this line, our involvement as a society as members of the Explorer Race will be uncreated.

You see, the connection to the past with the Explorer Race and our people had to do with the unresolved emotion or ego experiences of that past conflicting time of our people. Your people, the Explorer Race, took over those unresolved emotions and resolved them as you moved from one group to another in terms of expression or incarnation. It created extra work for you—well, not so much extra, because it was very similar to what you would be resolving on your own. It created slightly more, about 1.737% of resolution needed along the lines of sexual experience for your peoples.

This might have been one of the contributing factors to your society's general discomfort with the idea of what you call homosexuality (which is not at all unusual in other societies). This kind of interaction between individuals who have loving feelings for each other is normal. I think that the reason why most societies on your Earth at this time do not find this type of interaction between consenting adults to be comfortable and acceptable is because of that extra job of resolution you took from us that we as a society did not resolve. I think this because I have gone through many potential scenarios of your evolutionary resolution cycle.

So this small moment of discomfort with that type of behavior will gradually decline. It is really more about a 6000-year cycle that your society has dealt with, and there is only about another 120 to 125 years more for this attitudinal problem to exist if this unbraiding between our societies continues to be successful. It is hoped that such violence and prejudice and confusion around this topic will dissolve in time. We regret that we did not resolve this in our time, but I must also say that your souls were not in any way coerced to take on the resolution of our unresolved sexual dilemmas. You seemed to be interested in the challenge at the time. Hopefully, this past will disconnect itself from your souls, and in your future this type of interaction between the same-sex adults will be what ultimately allows your civilization to reach a better balance in terms of numbers on your planet. If this kind of behavior had not been scorned, many more same-sex couples would have come together and the birth rate would not have become quite so catastrophic in terms of overpopulation in the past 40 or 50 years.

What about the hybrid race? Is that going to be uncreated?

It will be disconnected from you. Instead of our people and your genetic structure, it will be our people's genetic structure and a split between the Pleiadeans and the Orions. The race will not be uncreated—that would be like uncreating soul expressions, and we have no desire to do that. But the component parts will be different. It will have some impact on that group of beings in that they are likely to be more artistic and less competitive.

I have a personal stake in that. Some of those beings are a part of me. Are they uncreated, too? Will they not be connected to me anymore?

Let's put it the other way. You will not be connected to them. They will not be uncreated.

My eye was healed when I was three years old; you Zetas kept me alive. I've had many, many interactions with you. Will these be uncreated, too?

Part of it will be taken care of by the fact that the events that led to the discomforts we assisted you with will not have happened or at least not have led to such levels of discomfort, or else your interactions will have taken place with the Andromedans or the Sirians. Instead of our people coming into such frequent contact with your people, it would be much better if the benevolent beings from Sirius would have been in greater contact with your people, not only because Sirius is so closely related to this planet, but also because your cultures, many of whom are still in existence today, have a significant amount of direct expression from their deep Sirian roots.

You know about the Dogons, but also there are other beings. The Pueblo peoples were influenced by Sirian beings (it might have been better to have been more influenced in terms of their own survival), as well as an ancient and honorable group of beings now referred to as the Hopi. These people would have been more benevolently experiencing their past and present had they been able to have the contacts with Sirius beings that are intended. For example, had those contacts been ongoing from A.D. 800, then most likely the Hopi people would have returned to the stars, which is their true home, in the 1700s. There are other Native American peoples who would have done the same thing. There are also some peoples from Africa, Asia, Iceland and a few other isolated places who would also have returned to the stars. Many of the native peoples would have returned to the stars, including a group of individuals whose descendants now live in Scotland. There are others, but I do not wish to mention them all.

So our whole history will be changed, especially those who have had tremendous interaction with the Zeta. We won't remember it, the memories will change, everything will change?

But think about the advantages for a moment. Right now you are focused on the sense of loss, but think about the advantages in having been connected to the people from Sirius, who have infinitely more in common with you even today than we have. For one thing, many of the people from Sirius look very much like Earth human beings, and if you were to interact with them today, if you were to put many examples of Earth human beings next to Sirian beings, you would say there seems to be a very striking family resemblance.

What about from the other side? My understanding that the whole point of the Zeta interaction with the humans was so that the Zetas would learn to understand the importance of feelings. Will you have not learned that?

Remember, I said that 87% of the contacts would be uncreated, but

13% of the contacts will have happened.

And that is enough for you to have learned the lessons?

Yes. You have to remember that a lot of those contacts between our people and yours occurred because the Sirians who needed to contact you were unable to do so. Their physical bodies are similar to yours, so their ability to tolerate certain radiations would have been similar to your own. Sirius has highly evolved high-dimensional beings, but the beings who would have contacted you would mainly have been (or most likely now will be) beings more closely related to you. Think about the experience of meeting beings from outer space who look like you—the fun, the fascination, the interest!

What about all the Zeta likenesses that are scattered everywhere—on the Internet, T-shirts, books, you name it? What will happen there? What will happen with the information you've given us in The Explorer Race?

Most of what I have said in *The Explorer Race* (and I think I can speak for Zoosh here) will still happen, because 13% of the contacts will be sufficient. Our faces will continue to impact the T-shirts. Instead of being considered frequently seen beings or horrific beings by those who have had unpleasant dreams about us, the dreams will be more beautiful and compassionate and, yes, tender. And there'll be nothing horrific about the contacts. They'll be celebrations, pleasures, not unlike what has occurred in the not-too-distant past between the Pleiadeans and those who lived high up in the Andes. (Those contacts are not happening so much today, but when they were, it was very pleasurable for all concerned.) Of course, we won't have been as involved doing scientific work with you. We will still do the work, but not be as involved.

Uncreation of SSG's Cloned Slaves Using Our Device

Perhaps most important for our people, your sinister secret government will not have been able to duplicate our genetic patterns in a corrupted way by utilizing the little cube that could have produced energy. You see, the device had a secondary application as a communications device. One could look at it under a magnifying glass and see things from our world. By using the device in a way that was never intended and utilizing it with their rudimentary time machines and genetic experiments, they were eventually able to capture and synthesize some of our basic building components (DNA) and create a race of slave beings who still exist, though in decreasing numbers, underneath the surface of the planet. These beings do the bidding, mostly underground, of the sinister secret government.

Eventually that will be uncreated, but it will take about another 75 years. I do not wish to speak uncomfortably, but it is more likely then that the sinister secret government will utilize human beings for that slave race; I am sorry. But that will also be eventually uncreated by your own spiritual abilities to uncreate your past discomforts. You can see that the sinister secret government has not only corrupted variations of our life form, but also has way too much power for its own good and yours. The Explorer Race books are still relevant, but some of what has happened will be uncreated or changed to allow a more rapid spiritual evolution by both our peoples.

That will include the Montauk work?

Now, most of the things discussed in both series of the books you refer to [the Montauk series, available from Light Technology] will still happen, but the events will change cosmetically. The events themselves will still have happened. They will be changed, you see, by your evolution spiritually, but they won't be sufficiently changed to say they didn't happen.

Now, if I might get personal again for a moment, your contacts will have increased. You will have had more contacts with Andromedans and several contacts with Arcturians, two of which would have taken place on their world. And you would have had many, many contacts with Sirian beings. So you would have had this education, and things would have been easier, including business things and publications and so on. You have really been fulfilling your destiny a little bit more the hard way than it would have been otherwise.

But that's going to change?

It is intended eventually. You have to understand that this is happening, but sequentially speaking, your own life will be over when this past is changed. Eventually, your soul-line experience will be impacted more by the Sirians than by the Zetas. Although you would have had contact with us, it would not have been as frequent and would have been more social.

Let me put in a request. The Zetas didn't quite get my eye fixed completely, although they saved my life. Can whoever replaces the Zetas in that experience fix it all the way?

Oh yes, because the people who will do the fixing will be people who have much greater understanding, since they are not limited by technology—meaning they won't be using technology at all, as you understand it. Technology is such a very slow way to do things, as my people are realizing. That is why our evolution will be much more along the spiritual path, and technology as we have known it will become much more organic and less mechanistic. So do not fret.

The Impact on Your Current Lives

I want to ask a question. After this 45-day period will there be any change in our personal lives that we can notice?

Only about three-quarters of a percent of people now alive will notice some minor changes, generally classified as slightly improved health, memory, intelligence and significantly improved psyche, if I can use that term to describe the personality and the dream states that sometimes drive you through your subconscious. Some of you will find life to be simpler, less complicated. There are a few people in their twenties who will live to be very old and who might actually be alive when the changes are completed, and thence their life will change while they are alive. This is only a few people who are now in their twenties, and this will be a really extraordinary experience for them. Imagine a person who in 75 years is 140 years old. This will not be at all unusual then. Imagine being perhaps 100 or 110 years old, but not decrepit. You are still vital, with only an occasional nagging, discomforting dream or an inability to hit that overhand tennis ball. You will be able to read as much as you want without glasses; you'll put them in a drawer and forget about them and that will be that. Granted, there are very few of those people now, and their experiences are considered unusual or anomalies, not the norm. If it were the norm, you would become distracted by it.

This is absolutely, incredibly fascinating information. So how will we experience these changes? They won't really affect our life that much while we're alive?

They won't affect your life that much. I think that the impact is negligible in the short run, but in the long run it ought to be profound. Anyone over 40 will not really notice much. It is possible that certain symbols will become less important and certain other symbols more important. This can be tested by either looking at a book of symbols, crop circles, ancient hieroglyphics or pictographs, you call them. You could try looking at them and see which ones appeal to you. Look at them again in about 50 days (to be on the safe side) and see which ones appeal to you then and which ones no longer hold your interest. Generally the symbols that attract you are intended to be reproduced by you in some way, perhaps by drawing it and then touching it. It is intended that they influence you, usually on the cellular level, sometimes on the energy-body level or the auric-field level, to evolve in some way that your soul has chosen, ofttimes in some more benevolent way, sometimes strictly affecting your interests or even occasionally your intelligence. After that you might find that other symbols are more attractive and seem more interesting. I don't want to say too much.

I understand that when the Zetas come back through time, it was easy to find the

Earth because the Zeta planet was once in this place or else the Earth was on the way to where the Zeta planet was—what is the connection? I've never understood it.

The reason was because of our intertwinement. It is easy to simply follow the Explorer Race time line; we essentially program the place and the time and simply follow your path. It was very simple navigation. In the future, the navigational system will have to be altered. It will perhaps take a little longer to get here.

What about you personally? You are a leader of the Zetas, the first one in the ninth dimension. Will this have any repercussions?

I don't think of myself as a leader, but more of a wayshower. I do not foresee my life being changed in any notable way.

Can you just say briefly how the Master of Discomfort [in Explorer Race: Creators and Friends] was connected to the really bad times on Zeta?

One of his component parts was involved as a manifested being of the time who attempted to prevent this exploration of our more dramatic sides, and because he was perceived as a threat by those who wished to promote this aspect of our behavior, he became the object of vengeance.

Did he have a name?

I will let him speak for himself. He had many unpleasant things done to him, and it was done in such a way as to affect him into his past and his future.

Is there anything else that you want to communicate?

I just want you to know how fond of your people my people are. Don't think for a moment that because there have been some discomforts on this old time line, our people in any way perceive Earth people as an enemy. We have always perceived you as wonderful beings. We have enjoyed our many contacts, and we have understood more about you from these contacts. We have even made self-discoveries because of these contacts. So do not be concerned that there is any residual animosity on our part. I think you will ultimately find that you do not feel this toward us either, because we have been mistaken for beings who have caused you some harm, through no fault of their own, by being manipulated by others. I would say that our future—in terms of Earth people and your souls as the Explorer Race—is assured and will undoubtedly be much more benevolent and even fun. Our people will eventually teach your people how to master time travel without the use of any technical device.

Wonderful. Thank you, Joopah.

Good night.

9

It's Time to Change Your Past

Zoosh through Robert Shapiro
February 24, 1997

Zoosh speaking. Well, surprise, surprise!

Do you have any comment for publication on what Joopah said? Do you want to have a postscript on what he said about the discreation of the contacts?

Yes, I can validate this. It is true, and that's part of the reason that sensitives amongst you will be feeling a little bit odd for the next few weeks. While it's important to pay attention when you're driving or eating so you don't shove that spoonful of ice cream into your cheek instead of your mouth and redecorate yourself cosmetically, I would say you have to make more of an effort to be grounded. It's true that there will be some slight anomalous energies or activities with your time and also with your density. As a result, you need to pay attention when you're doing things. Anybody doing anything dangerous, pay attention, stay in your body. Extraneous thoughts could cause more hazards. I think it's important to mention that.

You have to pay more attention for the next 45 or 50 days [to April 10, 1997] or so. The last five days will be sort of a fade-out. I've been watching and waiting on this for a long time. It was not clear to me or Joopah or others whether the time it would impact you physically would be now or next year. It seems to be now, and it will have some minor impacts. The unbraiding effect should create the potential for greater friendliness amongst your peoples, or at least a better chance for trust and less reaction, suspicion and such.

Well, the fact that the alternate negative future can't come here anymore is pretty awesome.

I think so. It doesn't eliminate the possibility of their impact, but it certainly greatly degrades it.

What were the criteria used to decide which 13% of the Zeta contacts would remain?

The 87% were essentially duplications of other efforts, and the 13% were essential contacts because they would bring about something benevolent for your people or theirs or even for other people. So 13% of the contacts were deemed to be necessary. Many of the contacts were essentially duplications of other efforts to make certain that everything was true, like scientific studies with an experimental group and a control group.

So even if the Sirians fix my eye, I won't experience any good effect for 75 years?

Well, by the time they fix your eye (though it might easily be the Andromedans), it will impact your next life on the linear scale of evolution in the sense that you might be very slightly less compassionate.

Really?

Think about it. Very often things that are perceived as handicaps, even if minor, will ultimately cause you to be more compassionate toward other people. When you have some challenge, you are disinclined to judge others who have a challenge, and you are also more often inclined to feel a sense of union.

I'd like your opinion or comments on what Joopah said—because we didn't really get into it—about the 87% of Zeta/human contacts to be uncreated. It feels to me like those of us who have experienced it remember the suffering and hardship involved with it, but don't really gain anything when it's uncreated. Would you discuss that?

Well, Joopah didn't elaborate much on that point, even though it might have seemed so. What he didn't say or wax on about too much is that those contacts—let me change the word "uncreating" to "recreating" . . .

Joopah said our old Zeta contacts would instead be with other, more benevolent and humanlike beings.

Let's consider the ramifications of what Joopah is saying, because you must always consider that. If the beings are more benevolent, yes, you might have beings from Sirius and even Pleiades and all that. The Zeta society is beginning to evolve now. Remember that years ago Joopah said that he had gone to the ninth dimension so that he could demonstrate the new style of being for their people. They're not all going to suddenly click into the ninth dimension, but they are going to adopt ninth-dimensional philosophies. When you are in the ninth dimension, the gold lightbody, you look at life differently. When Joopah speaks, all his people (the Zetas) can hear him. (I am tuning off that channel at the moment.)

What he didn't say is that the Zetas will still be contacting people, but they will be different, meaning that they will have adapted. They're doing something now. We're talking about something that takes place in time, so there's an 85% chance that those contacts will still take place, and, yes, there might be other beings on board such as Sirians and so on. The Zetas *will be there*, but they won't be the Zetas that you've met. They will be beings who are much more understanding and appreciative of the subtleties of emotional, vibrational (vibrational is something they didn't have in their old philosophy) and physical-nuance communication.

Even human beings have a little difficulty with the last, understanding what this gesture and that gesture means. The Zetas will be much better at that. What this means is that they will no longer need the device they used in the past to protect their physical selves at such a depth of power. They will be able to tone that down quite a bit. They will newly be able to interact emotionally, so people taken onboard the ships will not be so frightened. Humans will see beings onboard who look like them, and *they* will introduce you to the Zetas. Or the Zetas will be socially more adaptable, meaning that they will communicate immediately, not just calmly, but they will exude loving energy or humorous energy. They will simply evolve, and as a result the meetings that took place in the past will be different because it is changing in the present (to them, which is the future to you).

I think a sketch is required here. [Draws.] This is your present, the Earth. This is the Zeta future and this is your past. The Zeta future is changing (which is the Zeta now, but they're in the future). When they travel back into their past to contact you, they will be traveling back as their new, ninth-dimensional philosophical beings. And the contacts, no longer with seventh-dimensional beings who are not sophisticated enough to act outside of their own culture, will not take place the way

ZETA PAST | YOU PAST | YOU NOW | ZETA FUTURE (NOW)

they did. Now, Joopah couldn't say this, because if he had, he would have essentially propelled his own people down a path. But I can say it, especially if I shut off that frequency. That's really what's going on. I think that Joopah's statements are worthy of being published, but I'm attempting to clarify them here.

What about all the people who had these contacts over the years? You said they would be re-created over the next 75 years, but not within our lifetime. I felt this sense of loss. What's it all about? I mean, why did it have to be so difficult?

Now, just a minute. Let's not forget what you're doing here. You're learning to be creators. Do you want to stop your creator training? One of the things that creators must do—at least toward their advanced training, and their advanced training is what you're doing now—is learn how to re-create the past and the future *while* you are re-creating the present. These days you are re-creating all the time. Everybody is full blast into re-creation right now!

Everybody on Earth, you mean, or everybody everywhere?

Everybody on Earth. People in other places are leaning toward it, but Earth is where the action is. The issue here is that this is an example of *allowed re-creation,* meaning, that you yourself are feeling a sense of disturbance at the idea of having lost certain experiences you've only recently come to comfort with, or at least some sense of understanding.

Yes, but I can see how they colored my whole life.

On the other hand, you are concerned that this change in the past might affect the present and future.

I'm not saying that; but why do we have to go through this when we're really not going to gain anything from it and it won't affect us in this lifetime?

Are you *only* this lifetime?

Okay, how will it affect humans? All humans have been contacted . . .

Everyone who has been contacted by the *Zetas*—Joopah is speaking only for the Zetas.

Humans who went through that fear?

Who went through that fear. Now, not everybody went through the fear. Some of the people didn't go through fear and had no downside to the experience, so their context will remain as it is. And the people who had a little bit of downside that was important to their outcome of life and their pursuits (what their soul wanted to do and so on) might stay the same. But for people who had emotional scars from the experience, that must be resolved. How can you even consider being a creator if you could turn a blind eye to someone's suffering? How can you turn a blind eye *to your own suffering,* even though it happened in the past?

Remember, all the exercises I give people always start with themselves. Creatorship starts at home. If you can turn a blind eye to your own pain, you don't qualify as a creator because you would easily be able to turn a blind eye to other people's pain.

But that's what was so traumatic. So many people did, and it was not even in their consciousness. Their pain was buried, hidden from themselves.

The Need to Change the Past to Change Your Lives

Think about it. Think about the current situation in the world, how much trauma and misery and suffering is happening out there, even as informed as people are these days who live in modern technological countries. Think about how you can allow your brothers and sisters in Africa, or even in another state or town in this country, to suffer or be hungry or unhappy. You can do that because you have learned what your society has taught you and because of *what you became as a result* of your society's manners and mores. You have learned how to tough it out, and by so doing you expect others to do so, too. You don't think that way intellectually and you don't feel that way emotionally, but you have basically learned, by being raised in a society that was raised by previous societies and so on ad infinitum, that one must learn to tolerate the pain and misery so you can enjoy the happiness and all the other stuff.

The main thing is this: You cannot change the pain and suffering in the world of the present simply by angelic interference. *You must change yourselves, and you do not change yourselves by changing your mind.* You know that intellectually evolved, even moral people, can commit reprehensible acts or at least allow them to take place in their name. Your country, using the justification of drug wars and getting back at drug lords, went south of the border looking for Manuel Noriega (picking a name out of the headlines), bombed the heck out of the place where Noriega might be with the idea of killing him or capturing him, but in the process killed and maimed hundreds of innocent civilians. This was not publicized in this country even though all the news services knew about it.

Is it just that you are being controlled? It is that this level of suffering is embarrassing. People gradually found out about it, but what happened? Nothing. We could pick out something much more mundane that is on a daily basis, but the fact is, you cannot simply change your mind and everything gets better. It helps to change your mind to change your life, but it's not enough. You need to change your *life* to change your life.

We said quite a while back that you might eventually evolve into being the Zetas. The Zetas are now basically understanding that one. They know they need to change their past, and they want to change the way those contacts took place with you. With more exposure to ninth-dimensional philosophy, they realize that their ignorance about what you needed is not a sufficient excuse to say, "Well, we didn't know any better then." *It's not a good enough excuse!*

How many times have you heard human beings in the best of circumstances, say "I didn't know"? They *didn't* know, but that didn't change the fact that others suffered. Plenty of people in Germany said they didn't know about the concentration camps, and they *didn't,* most of them. But it didn't change the fact that people were suffering. Other much more mundane examples are readily available. But you have to change things.

So here's Joopah talking for his people because they want to change things, they want to be responsible, and they're not saying that because it happened in the past they can't do anything about it. They're not throwing up their hands and saying, "Okay, we didn't know then, but we know now." They are in fact saying, "We know *now,* and we can change *then.*" *That* is something you are going to have to do also. As you evolve up the line, reevolving, as it were, you have to be perfectly open to changing the past. If somebody has an emotional scar from his childhood, it changes his whole life. Maybe she was going to be a doctor or a college professor; maybe he was going to be a farmer, a really good one, but he turned out to be something else because of emotional scars from his childhood experiences. Why not change that?

When Joopah said that it wouldn't affect your lives now, he was talking from *his* level of consciousness. Joopah is very smart, but as those contacts are changed over the next seventy-five years (when you will no longer be alive in this life) and the planet and everyone on it is going up in dimension, it might be possible that those changes will be sufficiently complete that you *will* feel it in this life. Remember, *things that are changed in the past will also affect your future lives, even though they haven't been born yet in linear time.* They will even affect your past lives, even though, in time, they are over. We have to get past the fixed aspects of time. Creator training requires challenges, and this is a requirement, dead-bang, that put you right up against the impossible. "It's happened; I can't do anything about it," says you. Perfectly justified. But, says I, "Oh, yes you can!"

Understand that ultimately the purpose of changing the past is to change the present. Think about it. All the people all over the world that can justify, chapter and verse, why they feel *this* way about *them* (whoever "them" is), and after hearing their justifications, whether it's on a personal, societal, or even nationalistic level, one might say, "Well, I understand why you feel that way." But one could say to a more evolved spiritual being, which you are becoming, "Well, why don't you *do* something about it? Why don't you change the past?"

Homework

Here's homework for you and anyone else who wishes to do it. I would like you to pick one incident in your personal past. It can be something related to ETs or any personal experience. It must have happened at least five years ago; I don't want it to be the recent past. Then work on changing it. I'm going to give you instructions on how to do it. This isn't strictly a visualization. You know how to do it on the visualization level, so I'm not even going to describe that part.

While you're in the visualization to change the past situation, I want you to use your hands as if you were moving around clay figures in a claymation cartoon or dolls or toys when you were a child. Gently reach into your visualization, but don't just change it to what you want it to be. *Uncreate what happened.* If it was an injury, then put your hand up to deflect that injury and turn it into something more benevolent. Basically, *put your hands into the soup!*

You need to remember the experience. If the experience is too traumatic, don't relive it. Pick something you'd like to change that wasn't a gut-busting experience, at least for the first time and maybe for the first three or four times. And change it by putting your hands into it. As you visualize it, move your hands forward to move things around. You might even see your hands in your visualization. They'll be very big compared to the rest of the scene. If you can see your hands moving, that's fine. Your hands will be coming from the present into your visualization; that will cover more ground. Reach in and gently move things around, just as you might picture an invisible hand coming in and changing something more benevolently for all beings in that circumstance. Do it a few times, then forget about it and go on, but just make a note in your journal (if you have one) that you did it.

Don't think about it too much. After a few weeks, go ahead and think about how you feel. (If you have a journal, go three or four weeks down the line and put a little note saying, "How am I feeling?") This is an experiment—all creatorship training is. We're going to see if your reaching back into your past to change something could just maybe change the way you feel now. (It could happen immediately, but it could also happen in four weeks or so.) This is good for all of you; this kind of thing is good creatorship training.

You have to be very careful. You can't revenge yourself on anybody. It can only be used to create a more benevolent situation. For instance, if for some people it is a car crash, instead of the two cars hitting each other, they just miss each other completely and go on. Understand?

Yes, that sounds great.

10

Cloning: The New Ethics Forum

Zoosh through Robert Shapiro
February 24, 1997

All the news media now has this story about the cloned sheep. Are we very near cloned humans? Do you want to say anything about that for "Shining the Light"?

Good. This cloning gives you an idea now, does it not, that the idea of duplicating complex organisms is not quite as far off as you thought. I want you to understand that because technology precedes your capacity to absorb its impact, you will have the opportunity for many soul-searching conversations with each other. Don't automatically ban the idea of cloning human beings. This technology has its uses, not the least of which is to bring ethics as a topic out of the dusty closet and into the forefront of human discussion. After all, ethics has gone under many guises in recent years, not the least of which is human rights, and it has become somewhat unintentionally politicized.

Now there is a reason to bring up ethics on moral grounds, on the grounds of values and principles that reach across borders. If nothing else, it will help you to become a world citizen as you communicate about such things. And now that you have a world network on the Internet to do so, it is something I would be slow to ban, in terms of its research. I'll tell you why: Now, the chances of mass human disaster happening are not very great, certainly not in your lifetimes, but there is always that outside chance. So it would be useful to have this tool. On the other hand, this genetic ability will make it infinitely easier for any political group of "ins" to clone more of themselves, thus suggesting that the current "ins" might outlast the "outs." I say this because a cloned being would undoubtedly be very healthy, durable, and, well, not much different from cloned corn or even hybridized vegetables and fruits, which are hybridized for their sturdiness. The same techniques will go into cloning human beings, I can assure you. However, one cannot overlook the overwhelming potential for abuse.

But I want you to discuss it. I don't want to give my moral stamp of approval or disapproval; I'd rather say, discuss it and understand that even if you all decide that it would be better to wait it will roll forward no matter what, research being what it is. But if you can get into a world-wide rhythm, you might just be able to establish some ironclad ethical principles to apply to cloning as well as other sciences that have to do with the creation, perpetuation and nurturing of any group of beings. I think this new ability to clone is a lesson in creatorship that deserves attention.

11

HAARP Update

Lee Carroll
February 1997

I t was the April 1996 issue of the *Sedona Journal of Emergence!* [see also *Shining the Light IV,* chapters 12, 13 and 15] in which I and others first exposed the project in Alaska named HAARP (High-Frequency Active Auroral Research Program). Unmasked at that time with supporting excerpts from Popular Science, HAARP was shown to be a very dangerous project supported mainly by the U.S. military, with highly unpredictable implications toward our environment, wildlife—even humanity itself. It uses newly developed scalar-wave technology in a way that science is only beginning to understand but is forging ahead with at breakneck speed.

In the Kryon seminars throughout the country we have continued to mention this project, and have asked those who felt motivated to actively meditate in groups for the resolution of this problem. In both United Nations sessions (1995 and 1996) Kryon has mentioned it, and we believe that this not a political item, but a planetary environmental issue. Many have asked what progress has been made.

Both the TV programs *20/20* and *60 Minutes* have been contacted repeatedly to investigate HAARP. They can't help but know about it by now, since hundreds have written. Through the help of Paula Randol Smith (former producer/director and theatre owner), the HAARP information was also hand-carried in February to the director of *20/20.* Believe me—they know. Will they be fearful to go up against Washington? Time will tell, but the higher the profile of the average citizen's concern, the better chance we will have to get the entire story aired nationally.

The ERI

The best news of all is the formation by four individuals of the Environmental Research Institute (ERI). This group's endeavor is to allow environmentally conscious scientists and laymen alike to participate in the monitoring of projects worldwide. ERI will work with other environmental groups such as the Sierra Club and Greenpeace. It will be totally independent of the influence of any business, government or individual. The stated goal? To identify undertakings that are dangerous to the planet and expose them until such time that laws can be adopted that restrict projects from commencing without oversight. The full-time president will be Patty Meyers.

What can four individuals do? Here is a sample of what already is in progress: (1) Development of a documentary: two-time Emmy Award winner/director & producer Wendy Robbins and Paula Randol Smith are already working on private funding and planning. (2) Meeting with politicians at high levels: appointments have already been granted and are scheduled. (3) Celebrities contacted for help. (4) Public-relations efforts to bring HAARP articles like the one in *Popular Science* to many other periodicals during 1997. (5) Keep after *20/20* and *60 Minutes* regardless of rejection letters. (6) Coordination with the EPA office and the Right-to-Know Act. (7) Developing fundraising efforts and building a membership of other like-minded people who wish to participate.

We again mention that a well-written scientific and objective book, *Angels Don't Play This HAARP* by Nick Begich is available in many New Age stores. You can also send for it c/o Earthpulse Press, P.O. Box 201393, Anchorage, Alaska 99520. If you wish to know what this is really all about, get the book—and get ready to be alarmed.

We thank Paula Randol Smith, Steve Rother, Patty Meyers and Ron McCray for their vision to begin this process. Others of some influence will be joining the team representing many needed talents in public relations, the political scene, broadcasting and film work. We have even been told that Sidney Sherman, holder of film rights for the book mentioned above, might be starting initial funding for a film! The momentum is building.

So what's happening on the HAARP site in Alaska? A year ago no one knew how to get to it or even that it was there. Today not only is it no longer secret, but the government has set up a public relations office to greet visitors and show them all about HAARP and defend the experiment. Something happened in the past twelve months to create the change—perhaps it was the many who voiced concern and wrote letters. We are making headway! HAARP will be totally operational very shortly and will commence to blast 30-mile-wide holes in the ionosphere, as a starter.

If you are interested in being a genesis member of ERI or just wish more information about this endeavor, you can call (800) 965-2674; or fax (619) 748-7640. You can also e-mail RotherEnt@aol.com. For ERI to work, it's going to take members, feedback, ideas, funds, support and volunteers. I would not be reporting it here if I did not feel that it has all the potential that Kryon said it had. We are powerful beings, and we can change this planet!

February 28 Addendum

HAARP makes it to the mainstream scientific community! *Science* Magazine is acknowledged as one of the most respected journals in the world (www.sciencemag.org). The February issue of *Science* is a milestone for those of us concerned about HAARP, in that it is the first time the subject has been presented in this serious venue. The presentation was fair, and brought up many of the issues that appeared in the *Sedona Journal* last year. The story also revealed the impact that our write-in campaigns and Nick Begich's book *Angels Don't Play this HAARP* have made on the project. The good news is that HAARP has been delayed in its implementation!

Ionosphere Research Lab Sparks Fears in Alaska

"*. . . all this [detractors] is putting the project's backers on the defensive. While HAARP project director John Heckscher of the Phillips Laboratory in Boston vows that anti-HAARP activists won't stop the project, he allows that they may succeed in delaying its launch, which is scheduled for 2002.*

"While Congress has budgeted $15 million in the fiscal year '97 for HAARP, Heckscher says that all the legislative hearings, requests for information and piles of letters have slowed the project down."

—*Science* Magazine, February 21, 1997

I feel that your concern, meditation efforts, supportive energy and letters have helped with exposing and slowing this dangerous planetary experiment. This article quoted above proves that we are right! Many thanks to all!

12

A Zeta Hybrid Says Thanks

A Zeta through O'Ryin Swanson
March 5, 1997

W
e have heard the pronouncement of the changing of the past by the Zetas from the future [see chapter 7]. Because of the current uncreation, some of you have a sense of loss, because the experience, even if traumatic and fearful, was an important part of your awakening. You have a sense of loss because you feel that the beings you helped bring into life, your contribution to the hybrid race, gave you a feeling that you contributed something important even though there were memories of being controlled, being fearful and being invaded. With the news now that these contributions you made are going to be uncreated, there is a sense that you suffered and gave, had nightmares and felt invaded and abducted for no reason, because there will no longer be a part of you in those beings. Those beings will be part Zeta and part other races in your galaxy.

What you need to know is that even though this is so, you were a bridge. Without your cooperation and agreement, that hybrid race would not have been created. So even though this time track will be moved, know that without your contribution and willingness to be there when you were needed, this race would not be alive and flourishing now. The Zetas feel that the trauma and the pain, heartache, fear and all of the residual emotions in humanity resulting from their lack of understanding of humanity's emotional body and from their scientific approach to beings they did not understand *was not in vain*. It brought into the consciousness of the group soul of those who experienced interactions with the Zeta a realization that you are not alone; that there are other beings out there; that what you were taught by the controlling Earth rulers is a lie; that you are not the only ones who exist in all of creation; that they cannot control advanced technological races. Those of you who interacted consciously or unconsciously with the Zetas since the mid-forties were pioneers, courageous adventurers who, on a soul level, were willing to subject yourselves to unpleasant experiences because *you cared enough to want humanity to advance.* At the time this experiment in creating the hybrid races began, the Zetas feared that their race could no longer continue and knew they needed stronger, more physical and more emotional bodies. There was a fear also that humanity would extinguish itself. So there was, in a galactic sense, a valid reason for the abduction of men and women of Earth so that a new hybrid race could be born, live and become a bridge between two such dissimilar civilizations.

But everything changes, and the Zetas did not realize their destiny at the time that these abductions began. Things have moved so quickly now among humanity that it is clear they will not only *not* extinguish themselves, but they will highly distinguish themselves as they move into their destiny into the next dimension and beyond. Since all negative actions have to be uncreated at some point, the Zetas, from their new, more comprehensive state of understanding, decided to begin that process now so there would be less discreating of the negative experiences later on.

Those beings you helped create will continue. They will not be connected to you, but without you they would not be, they would never have been. As a joyously happy, uninhibited member of that hybrid race, I say thank you from my heart to all of you who helped us come into fruition. Even though the experiences will be uncreated, a part of your soul will always know that when brave beings were needed to do something beyond the understanding of the human expression, you allowed yourself from a soul level to subject your human expression to these experiences because you knew the value of what the souls of both races were trying to do.

Know that these experiences were not in vain. It is as if you built a bridge, and at a certain point one connecting piece is going to be exchanged for another. Without your contribution there would be no bridge between these races, that creation of this magnificent race of which I am a part. All of you, whether you remember the experiences or not, are owed a great debt—a *great,* great debt by our race. You had the courage to do this at a time when even the thought of something beyond Earth humanity was to some a nightmare and to some a great dream. To those who have remembered and brought their experiences to the attention of the public, and to those who still repress these experiences, I and my fellow beings say thank you from an area of great gratitude within our hearts, for making the agreements before you were born and for being strong enough to live up to them. Without you we would not be. It was not in vain, dear friends. We thank you and we will always thank you. And we bless you.

13

Archangel Michael

Zoosh through Robert Shapiro
March 11, 1997

P*lease tell me about this photograph [appearing later on the June 1997 cover of* Sedona Journal].

Here we have an unusual picture. You know, it's like they say, everybody talks about him, but not many people have seen him. When it comes to angels, they do not leave impressions like human beings do as a result of the interruption of the Sun's rays, but they will often leave such marks, though rarely are they captured on film. This is an impression of Archangel Michael.

It would be nice to put that [photograph] on the cover because so many people channel, talk about and love this being, and yet one does not often see his footprints.

Say a little more about what was he doing there that day, and what the story was.

The human being who took the picture [Jeanne Chapman] had had a dream on the deep-level consciousness within the previous week. I don't think she remembered it, but it's possible she might have by now. In her dream (understand dreaming is just another state of being) she was discussing the value of angels showing themselves on Earth— whether it was a good thing or whether it was more promise than delivery.

During that dream conversation, the teacher who was speaking to the dreamer said, "I will, if I can, make arrangements for you to be presented with some physical evidence of an angel's presence in the coming week, and we will see whether it affects you in a benevolent way and whether it might even affect others in some benevolent way." This was not what I would call an argument, but rather more of a discussion.

Understand, the teacher and the dreamer's higher self were having the discussion, and the dreamer's higher self were advocating the position that if angels were going to come to Earth, they ought to come to Earth in greater numbers and be seen by more people. Whereas the teacher said that if that were to happen, these sightings would undoubtedly be misinterpreted, and people would rush to the current religions rather than understanding that angels have always been communicators between Creator and the individual—not Creator and the church or any religion. Religion, after all, is a series of laws and rules by which a society is either governed or at least organized, hopefully in some way to make it peaceful and benevolent. I'm not speaking antireligion here; I'm saying that the purpose of angelics has always been to create a personal relationship between Creator and the individual. Because of the veil of ignorance that is dropped when one has a physical life on Earth, one does not often feel that personal relationship with Creator that one would like to feel. That is really a large part of the job of the angelics.

14

Notice to All Pilots, and Recent Activity in the Skies: Exotic or Domestic?

Zoosh through Robert Shapiro
March 20, 1997

I especially want to address these comments to pilots of commercial and military planes and also pilots of private aircraft. You might have noticed for the past couple of months, or will before too long, a slight change in the lift characteristics of your craft. It's not the wing design. Because of physical changes that are now phasing in—and in this case for about two and a half or three months, but more noticeably now—the density of the air and the air pressure is somewhat less than before.

I do not foresee great problems here, but I would like to recommend that pilots—to the extent they can influence this decision; for private pilots it should be significant, but not, perhaps, for commercial pilots—avoid overloading if at all possible. A commercial airliner could be loaded to its normal full capacity, but please do not exceed the maximum recommended capacity by more than 0.1% (one tenth of one percent). I'll tell you why. Because of the change in the density of the air, there will be less lift, less resistance available to move the plane, whether up, down or in making turns.

Some of you might have noticed some anomalies along these lines in the past few months, but for those of you who haven't, pay attention to this in the next few months especially, because it might become noticeable. Now, I do not think it will lead to any danger. It is a short-lived phenomenon, largely a result of resuming the forward motion in the change of density to the fourth dimension. It is happening in a small corridor or flap of time. It is less of a consideration for light and ultra-light aircraft pilots unless you are at the maximum carrying capacity of your vehicle.

I'm putting this information out at this time because I feel it might have to be factored in. Now, I do not expect you to take my word alone, but navigators and flight engineers, please note that you might need a little more fuel than usual to get to where you're going—and I'm not talking about headwinds and tailwinds here. If the air is only slightly less dense, it will make a difference. You could say, "Well, if the air is less dense, there should be less resistance to moving forward," but because there will be sufficiently less resistance, you won't have the usual buoyancy. Since commercial pilots usually have extra fuel, this is aimed more at private pilots: don't try and stretch your fuel to the next landing strip. Stop somewhere if you're running low on fuel; don't press it. Don't use the old calculations, just be careful. I feel that this is something that is passing, but at its zenith it would be most noticeable, which is about two and a half months from this date. After that, if all goes well, it should fall off sharply and you can go back to your normal calculations of flight time. The individuals most likely to be affected by this are those who are using standard calculations for lift in aircraft for transportation safety. I do not feel that this anomaly will have a strong enough impact to make much difference in other fields. That's why this message is aimed primarily at pilots.

Influx of UFO Sightings

Here is a newspaper article about a UFO seen over Paulden. Last Friday's newscasts indicated that many people in Phoenix, also some from Flagstaff and Kingman, have reported lights in the sky in specific different formations. Can you comment on it? Is there a good story there?

This recent spate of UFO sightings has to do, for the most part, with terrestrial vehicles, but there are extraterrestrial factors in some. The sighting over Wickenburg, Arizona, was extraterrestrial. The sighting over Salem, Massachusetts, by a few individuals was also extraterrestrial in origin. But many (not all) of the recent sightings in Arizona, are associated with technology of a very highly evolved sort that owes its origin to Earth, though the technology that powers the vehicles was originally developed from technology shared by extraterrestrials. These are genuine UFOs from space. But with the exception of the sighting over Wickenburg and the one at Deming in extreme southern New Mexico, most of these vehicles have home ports on this planet. Some of them have to do

Object seen over state a puzzle—was it UFO?

By Susie Steckner
The Arizona Republic

The first call reportedly came from a former police officer who spotted the strange cluster of lights moving very quickly across the night sky near Paulden, north of Prescott in Yavapai County.

The bright red-orange lights formed the shape of a boomerang, he said, with a larger grouping in the lead followed by a single light.

Reports poured in Thursday to Luke Air Force Base, the National Weather Service and the National UFO Reporting Center in Seattle, which logged the call from the unidentified former officer.

Four days later, there is no clear explanation for the object, described as both a triangle and a straight line, and varying from bright red to white to bluish white.

"We are confused about the exact details, but make no mistake about it," said Peter Davenport, director of the Seattle UFO center, "there was a dramatic event that took place in Arizona that night."

The National Weather Service can't offer any answers. Same goes for the officials at Luke.

"We just know it was not one of our planes." Lt. Col. Mike Hauser said.

"Everybody is telling me that we have UFOs stashed all over the Air Force," he said. "I'm not taking issue with what people saw, (but) lots of things can make lights."

Davenports best guess is an "ultrasophisticated craft" that did not come from this planet.

The first call to the center came shortly after 8 p.m. from the former police officer. Minutes later, reports were com-

ing in from Prescott and Prescott Valley, Dewey and Chino Valley.

Davenport said callers checked in from the east valley, Glendale and Phoenix. Some reported that, as the object moved south toward Tucson, it appeared to send out a red beam of light.

The last call that night came from a young man from Kingman, who was en route to Los Angeles.

He called from a phone booth, saying he had seen a large and bizarre cluster of lights in the northern sky.

Tim MacDonald, 11, was leaving his Cub Scout meeting in Phoenix when he saw the bizarre object.

"It looked like a stealth bomber," he said. It was in a triangle shape and it had three lights. It was moving very slowly. It was there for two or three minutes."

The lights went out one

with highly evolved, long-range technical advances of a fairly secret nature (obviously it's not too secret or they wouldn't be flying over cities) associated with your legitimate military. You know, when people have reasonably complex extraterrestrial vehicles available for study, one of the first things you look at is the drive system, then everything else.

Some aspects of laser technology can be traced directly to extraterrestrial weapons systems that were analyzed and duplicated to the best of the engineers' ability here in recent years. Most people know about lasers as weapons systems. They are not as powerful as the ET weapons largely because the gases, trace elements and the atmosphere of Earth are not as volatile as the stored gases that generate some of the defensive weapons systems on extraterrestrial ships. I might add that the ETs could have returned fire when they were shot down, but they didn't. If they *had*, it would have damaged not only the weapons fired at them but the planet would have suffered grievous damage as well. An ET has to be of a reasonably high calling or advancement to not shoot back when they know they can devastate the other party.

I feel that I'm not really giving anything away, because most of this has been discussed openly in commercial outlets elsewhere. We're talking about the U.S. government's highly secret developmental military aircraft. They've done it for quite a while. Certain elements of the U.S. experimental testing facilities have had the ability to produce vehicles that make *no sound whatsoever*. This technology has existed for quite a while—forty or fifty years. In the early days of experimentation it was not deemed particularly useful for obvious reasons, meaning that if you're in a shooting war and things are exploding, you don't need silent engines. But when intelligence services and other undercover services took a second look, they realized it had potential.

In the early days of this sound-eliminating system, there was a lot of hit and miss. Fuel consumption was exorbitant compared to that of a normal engine—that's another reason it wasn't too popular then. There have been other advances such as masking devices, whereby a helicopter or small plane could be made to seem invisible. I say "seem invisible" because if you stuck a pole in the air and one of these vehicles flew by, there would be a thud even though you couldn't see it. Even though invisible, it is in physical space. Most ET ships have this clever system. It is not totally integrated into the U.S. military yet for obvious reasons, but it is certainly present in some remote test sites.

To summarize, most of these sightings had to do with advanced experimental U.S. vehicles, so don't worry. You will hear other stories, and I'm not going to say they're wrong, because there is certainly a plot. Anytime any plots of the sinister secret government are foiled, they don't sit back and say "Oh, shucks." They are already planning, if not applying, some other plan. As any good general or admiral knows, you don't do just one thing. You try many things and hope that at least one of them succeeds.

Independence Day Scenario

So it is true that the sinister secret government has a plan, but I do not think it will work. It has about a 3 to 4% chance of succeeding. That is a small percentage, but it's there. The idea of the alternative negative future beings is to send vehicles here (which would be one way because they wouldn't be able to get them back) that appear to be extraterrestrial because of their technology, and stage a fake attack on Earth by ETs. The attack would be real, but the association with extraterrestrials would be faked, meaning that they pretend to be extraterrestrials. They would go out of their way to be obvious—flying over highly populated areas and committing nefarious deeds. They would hope to create a high degree of mistrust in your citizens toward extraterrestrials—although there are no negative-oriented extraterrestrials that have access to this space. (For that matter, there's practically no negative-oriented extraterrestrials at all.)

The ones who might be in alternative variable futures do not have access to this space; I'm talking about the potential of being invaded by some kind of monster ETs who want to come here and eat you. That's not real, although it makes an interesting movie plot. On the off chance (3 to 4%) that the alternative negative future, with its connection to the sinister secret government, has any semblance of success (meaning that they throw in everything but the kitchen sink and a little bit gets through), I want you to know that a certain mechanism is in place.

I'm not trying to suggest a massive conspiracy, because you don't need to have one if you can just sell the big lie. If you can convince people that something is true, then people tend to spread the story around. This is a journalistic mechanism, meaning that even if some small portion of a potential attack from the alternative negative future [ANF] gets through, it will receive a disproportionate amount of publicity.

ANF Desire to Create False ET-Attack Alerts

The governments of the world, especially that of the United States, having gone out of their way for the past forty or fifty years to deny the very existence of extraterrestrial beings, would never come out and say, "Extraterrestrials are here and they've come to destroy you." But reports will be released *as if they were real*—and I'm not borrowing from Orson Welles' *War of the Worlds* 1938 broadcast. As any computer hacker knows, it is easy to break into various journalistic systems, at least in the short run, and release information that makes it sound as if extraterrestrials have landed and are attacking.

Since the mechanism is in place to influence the media, the alternative negative future and the sinister secret government intend to influence it with false reports—even five minutes would be sufficient. They *know* it's sufficient, because when reports have been put out even briefly about something closely allied to what people believe, such as conspiracy theories, that information whizzes around the world and is talked up by many people. As everybody in journalism knows (to say nothing of people in show business and so on), if you're trying to get your point across and you don't care how, it's less important that what you say is true than that it is *believed*.

So this is fair warning. If you start hearing that extraterrestrials are here and attacking people or places or the military, look askance at it. The chances of this really being extraterrestrials from other planets and solar systems is about equal to the chance that you could, on a single small piece of paper, using a #2 pencil on a 3" x 5" piece of paper, write out *pi* to its stopping point. You all know that *pi* just goes on; its end is only theoretical, and you would have to go a *looong* way to get there. I'm saying it is virtually impossible for it to be extraterrestrial in nature—one chance in 565,000,000,000,000 (565 trillion). Even if it were, in spite of the odds, the ship would have to be a rebel ship, and I don't know of a rebel ship anywhere near striking distance to where you are (in 3.0 dimension, yes, but not where you are). So I don't think you have to worry about it.

They had been able to transport only people from the alternate negative future. How did they suddenly get spaceships?

They didn't. I said that if beings from the alternative negative future send their vehicles back from their future, it is remotely possible that a few of them will get through. It is very unlikely, but there is that 3 to 4% chance that some of them *might* get through, and if they do, they will try to pass themselves off as warlike ETs. The reason for this, obviously (many of you are really alert to this now), is that the genuine ETs have agreed that their next effort will be to contact the *people* of Earth and bypass the governments entirely. They're going to go for the average person, and they will make an effort to contact journalists, especially those they feel have the integrity to say, "This is *real*."

The extraterrestrials are phasing in that plan as we speak. When you see real extraterrestrial ships, you'll probably feel excited and good about it. There won't be any kind of uncomfortable feeling. If you spot a ship from the alternative negative future (or even some sinister secret government ships, of which there are few), they'll give you a creepy feeling. That is not just because of their underlying intentions, but because the mechanics of the vehicles have been developed along electrical lines, compared to the generally established magnetic lines of most extraterrestrial vehicles (certainly all that approach this planet). If you're around a magnetic vehicle, it will feel benevolent; you'll feel good. That's another benchmark.

Technological Advances

The ships seen over Arizona, where did that sudden advance in technology come from?

Most of them came from researching genuine extraterrestrial ships that have been shot down over the years because of various political and other disagreements. One can, after studying this kind of vehicle, reverse-engineer it a little to get an idea how to make one. While you're in the process of reverse-engineering the drive system, other teams are doing the same thing with other systems. The teams can't figure out everything, but they are doing what they can, and you're beginning to see the results.

Now, we all know that invisibility has been coveted by the military for years. In the early years of the technical experiments, there were terrible disasters [the Philadelphia Experiment and the Montauk Project], so terrible that for quite a few years the research was almost completely underfunded. I don't want to say unfunded, because there was a tiny amount of research that continued, but only in areas where the researchers were unlikely to interact with other scientists and engineers, so it was very isolated and low-keyed.

But in recent years there have been greater "advances" in technology, and people from around the world, some of whom are in influential positions, have begun to acknowledge that there might be something up there (extraterrestrially speaking), asking, "what-are-we-doing-to-prepare-for-it?" (Use hyphens because it's a cliché in military circles.) Because of this there has been a groundswell of interest. How can we potentially defend ourselves in case there is a threat?

Now, *there won't be a threat*. But I can understand why they thought this way, living in a polarized world, and that's why the funding was greatly increased again to obtain invisibility and total silence in flight. When the concept of the stealth technology was accidentally mentioned by the President years ago, the military quickly identified it as a type of aircraft then being developed, suggesting that the President was referring to vehicles that are radar-invisible. But that wasn't it at all. He was referring to the development of systems that could create true invisibility, total silence, and something else that hasn't been talked about—an invisible-laser system. It wouldn't do you any good, militarily speaking, to have a silent and invisible vehicle that fires a visible laser that can be traced back to its origin.

A massive group of people worked to make weapons systems invisible. They couldn't do it with bullets, but they're having a lot of luck with compressed light. You might look at these achievements and say, "Well, the U.S. is going to have an undefeatable army at some point." But that kind of weapons system is so dangerous and subtle that it's like letting your prize bull, the one you've trained to walk gently and be genteel, into a china shop, while asserting, "This bull can walk right through this china shop without harming anything." It's a nice idea and looks good on paper, but it doesn't work out in practice.

Regardless of the best of discipline, one of those vehicles could be spirited away. It would not be too difficult—even though they broadcast a signature code, which is how so-called friendly radar systems can tell they're friendlies—to defeat that code and get in, fly it out and sell it to whomever you wished. You all know this; it's been the subject of movies for years. Real life is beginning to catch up with science fiction, and soon science fiction writers will have to get wilder than ever, because life's catching up with you guys. [Chuckles.]

Okay, so the lights seen over Arizona, the ones that were videotaped, were flown by United States military, its advanced technical arm, and has nothing to do with the secret government?

I didn't say that. What I said is that most of these are sightings of advanced military vehicles directly *associated* with the U.S. government. Many military people, even base commanders, won't know about it. After all, when you've got something supersecret like that, you don't tell everybody until you're ready, and then you tell only the people who need to know. A couple of sightings such as the one over Wickenburg and the one in extreme southern New Mexico near Deming were real extraterrestrial craft.

ETs Sampling Humans' Readiness for Contact

Needless to say, extraterrestrials themselves will be interested in this development. They do not feel threatened by it, or even vehicles from the alternative negative future, should that come to pass, because these vehicles cannot achieve interplanetary travel; that's a long, long way from what they now have. Several extraterrestrial races have come to observe. You might ask, "Why would they come close to the planet when they can observe from space?" They come close to the planet because they are basically testing the emotional fields of both the planet and, more important, the human beings on the planet. How do people react, how do they feel when they see something that *appears* to be extraterrestrial? How do they feel when they see something that is *truly* extraterrestrial? Are they afraid, anxious, nervous, excited, happy?

These things can be measured. Some of the measuring equipment is available even on this planet. The ETs are waiting to see when the mass of people feel excited and happy when they look up and see these things. And most people *do* feel that way, although there are still a few who feel nervous—and in some cases it might be warranted. Extraterrestrials are taking that sampling of people's emotions as a sign that the masses are ready to accept benevolent extraterrestrials and learn who they are, what they like, how much like you they are, and how they can help you (which they want to do).

They do not judge you, as you might hear sometimes, because they know that you have been raised in a situation quite different from their own. Even though some in the past have lectured you about becoming more spiritual, those beings are not allowed to come here anymore, because those lectures, however well-meant they might have been, did not take into account the vast differences between the societies on Earth and the extraterrestrial societies, which do not have any polarity to deal with, to say nothing of discomfort. Those beings are not allowed to come here, but beings who are more sophisticated and look more like you are allowed. Slight differences would not be frightening, and these beings will be coming pretty soon and will be reaching out to educators, journalists and average folks.

Who specifically is over Deming, New Mexico and Wickenburg? What are their origins?

The Wickenburg sighting was vehicles from the present Orion. The Deming sighting had to do with vehicles from Arcturus. There might be another one or two sightings from other extraterrestrial sources, so don't assume when you see something mysterious in the sky that it is always some advanced military vehicle. It might be from someplace else.

There are hundreds of people over Phoenix who saw this. One might wonder why the U.S. would decide to do this over a very large city [Phoenix TV news report Friday March 14].

Yes, one might wonder if it was the U.S. government in general doing this, but it isn't. We're not talking about the regular military. We're not saying that the vehicle took off from, say, Kirtland AFB in New Mexico; we're talking about a very advanced unit that is so secret that it's beyond cosmic secret. The average military person, including people of high rank, have no idea.

But what was the motive? I still can't understand big-city sightings like that.

Well, obviously, it's to see how people react.

The same as the ETs want to know.

Yes. The idea is, "What will people say and do if we fly over the city? Let's see what they do." I'll tell you something interesting. Several people who sent these flights out bet that most of them wouldn't be reported in the legitimate press, and if they were, it would be with some derision. That did take place in certain cases, but I don't think they really planned on how many people are out there with video cameras. They've become almost as common as regular cameras, and television especially tends to respect what can be recorded and shown to others. I think these military were surprised that the reporting was more along the lines of an actual news story than a put-down, which has been the case until very recently.

Hale-Bopp's Influence

This would suggest that something's changed, and I'm going to tell you what has changed. This is really an influence from Comet Hale-Bopp. It's an interesting thing. You must look up in the sky to see an astronomical phenomenon, so Hale-Bopp has several roles. Even if you don't look at Comet Hale-Bopp, even if you don't know it's there, even if you're living underground—[chuckles] which is very few people, but there are a few—it will affect you. It will tend to transform people's discomforts and uplift them a little. It will also tend to do something surprising: heal the wounds in early childhood most children in most societies caused by being made to look foolish. It's almost as if people in general are more comfortable with the idea of saying, "But the emperor isn't wearing any clothes!" [See Hans Christian Anderson's tale "*The Emperor's New Clothes.*"]

We have a situation now where Hale-Bopp is making a massive contribution—it has been doing so for the past several months, I might add. This last influence I mentioned is about transforming that deadly emotional shock wave that stifles children and causes them to remain stifled when they grow up because they are afraid to look foolish. This astronomical phenomenon is transforming certain emotional growth-stunters, allowing people to look at something without thinking about looking foolish and to say, "What was *that* in the sky?" They report it as if it were any other news story. Although the average citizen easily can do that, there's a lot of pressure in journalistic circles to put down certain stories—you know that. But it's fading and will continue to fade.

If it's not the sinister secret government, why is the SSG allowing this supersecret military arm that is part of the U.S. government to do this? Why are they even allowing the military to have these crafts? Do they have the capability of an Xpotaz ship? [See **Shining the Light II**, *chapter 12.]*

Oh, certainly not.

Okay, what capabilities do they have? Are they advanced Stealth bombers?

No! As I said, they have the ability to be unseen, to appear as a very bright light and to be unheard—no sound.

And they are not interplanetary.

They are not interplanetary. They also have some state-of-the-art weapons systems, though they do not intend to employ them in the home country. Why does the sinister secret government allow them to do it? It's not a matter of allowing them. We've been saying for a long time that the sinister secret government is gradually losing influence. If you're under attack, as they are, you're going to marshal your resources into areas where you can get the greatest return. From that perspective it does not pay them to interfere here. As a matter of fact, from their perspective they can use these incidents, because people will be up in arms about UFO sightings. They can use this attention on UFO sightings to stage a fake ET invasion. So they do not feel threatened by it at all.

You say they're under attack. Who's attacking them?

Well, I'm using that phrase in a different way. As people evolve, they become more their natural selves and are less likely to be enslaved in any way. An interesting sidelight of overpopulation is that, generally speaking, you have little choice about getting to know your neighbors, and wherever you go there are people in abundance. You either learn how to get along with the people, or you're going to be real unhappy. So it's simply an attitudinal change, a gradual evolution toward a worldwide understanding of basic human endeavors. This means that everybody is rather similar in their basic drives and needs and so on, regardless of their culture. This is causing a great deal of the suspicion that has been carefully nurtured by the sinister secret government to fall away.

Take the Gulf War a few years ago. It is one thing for soldiers of the U.S. to be trained to perform their job. But in past wars especially, soldiers were almost always given as much racism in their training as anything else. Now, however, the Army is reasonably integrated, and battles, especially future ones, will be fought more as a United Nations activity, not ruled by U.N. forces but like the Gulf War, where troops from many nations were all over the place. The troops were not given racist indoctrinations.

In World War II there was a tremendous amount of racist propaganda against Japanese people in general, but little against Germans. You had none of that in the Gulf War. You couldn't, because U.S. troops would be fighting alongside their Saudi allies. They couldn't tell these troops that all Arabs are monsters (which of course they're not). But in World War II they might have said all Japanese are _____ (fill in the blank). Even in the military, where the whole purpose is combat and control, command communications and so on, things are changing because people must cooperate with other people. The sinister secret government will gradually continue to lose its influence—steadily but gradually—as more people realize how much they are like other people and that their differences are differences of flavor and tone, not melody.

How long before we see some of this new technology filtering down into the regular military? How long before we'll have similar craft available to all the forces?

I think it really won't be that long. We're getting into an area now that I cannot discuss. I don't wish to speak of things before their time, so I won't give you a target date; I will simply say it's coming.

SSG Losing Its Grip?

Okay, so what is the update on the secret government? They're losing control, but what else is happening? How are they losing control?

By individuals becoming more empowered. Anytime you become more empowered, you stop giving away your power to anyone or anything and you let go of your cynicism. The sinister secret government is going to lose power because people are beginning to let go of the belief that only a military or paramilitary protective force can keep them safe from some terrible thing that might happen. The more people that let go of such fears, the less influential are the sinister secret government and individuals behind the scene who try to influence public opinion. The best thing you can do as an individual is to get to know your neighbors, even if you've been living in your neighborhood for a long time. Have a block party even if the family down the block is not your first choice for friends. The more people get to know each other, the more likely they are to be friendly and trust each other. If a crisis ever comes along, they are less likely to be suspicious of each other. Whenever the feeling of suspicion is fostered, it's easy to manipulate people.

Okay, has there been a dramatic change in the things you said last month, that the secret government would influence the police to make a wall between Mexico and the United States? Are they still as much into drugs as ever?

One thing at a time. In terms of the wall, that is still a strong plan. That's still in the works.

Are they still running drugs as much as ever?

As much as they can, yes. In order to stop it you'd have to make a really serious effort. I don't think people in this country have made a serious effort, like slowing down travel and interstate commerce. There'd be a price to pay. It couldn't be totally eliminated without the loss of all your freedoms, but it could be greatly reduced.

Do you see that, or will there just be an attrition of people using drugs as they evolve in consciousness?

I think it's going to be a little of both. I think what will happen is that the not-too-harmful drugs will gradually become legalized, such as marijuana. However, that will get caught up in the whole smoking thing. Those who plan to invest in the marijuana business are going to have to find some other way to package the product, because smoking will eventually become illegal. Be warned, smokers. Don't get hooked, because someday the government's going to step in and say, "Okay, that's it! That's the end." Now what else?

What about the prediction that seemed to have some statistical possibility, that the United States would break up into small groups of states like the USSR?

You know, that's still possible, but only economically at this time. I do not think that we're going to have the city-state thing like ancient Greece. The only reason would be economic, and even now there's a certain degree of that. That's not a serious problem. As a matter of fact, I think that it might have certain values because the world order is now becoming very well established in the corporate model (which I said would come first, and is in fact happening). Alliances between groups such as farmers or agribusinesses will become international. It's true that individual farmers do not have much clout, but certain types of businesses will become allied the world over, so there will be strong associations. I'm not just talking about, oh, the AMA or something that might be worldwide, but about business associations, economical groupings. Some of this might be useful because it will get people used to allying themselves with people other than those they completely understand. You might have very close professional allies on the other side of the world and feel very close to them even though you don't speak their language or understand their customs.

But that will help bring us closer to being one planet.

Yes. So there are some positive sidelights.

Comet Hale-Bopp Aftermath

What can people expect in May and June as a result of Hale-Bopp?

In the backwash of Hale-Bopp there will be a tendency to be more trusting, though not naively. There will also be a semi-euphoric feeling that comes and goes. By "semi" I mean that there will be times when you will wake up in the middle of the night and feel a sense of euphoria, then promptly go back to sleep—or times during the day when for no good reason you suddenly feel as if something wonderful has happened or is about to happen, and you're not quite aware what, so you go right on with your work and forget about it. That's a pleasant side effect. I don't want to tell you the mechanics at this time, but I will explain it later.

Hale-Bopp is having a highly effective impact on your world. You might ask, "How is this possible? It is millions of miles away." Yet you as an individual can look at it for five minutes (as discussed in the earlier homework assignment) and feel a tremendous transformation within you. But no more than five minutes at a time, okay? Then look at your hands and your feet to ground the energy for a few minutes. After that you can look back at the comet for no more than five minutes at a time. The effect of this tremendous blast of magnetic energy is so profound that it might possibly (over a 50% chance) pull you up to 3.57 in dimension temporarily and give you a feeling for that dimensional level. This will be a temporary thing, and it's not certain to happen. One of the effects is an occasional feeling of euphoria, feeling and anticipating something good. If you feel that, especially repeatedly, know that you are probably experiencing the 3.57 dimension at least temporarily. The more people who feel that, the more the planet as a whole will feel it.

Hale-Bopp Meditation

I like to talk to prisoners sometimes because they are stuck; so for those of you who meditate, meditate on what Hale-Bopp might look like. Some of you have seen pictures on television or in magazines or newspapers. Since most of you won't be able to see this, if you want to do the greatest good for the greatest number, including yourselves, meditate on it, and once you have a good picture of it, breathe it in—but only when you have a good picture of it in your mind's eye (or use a picture from a magazine or newspaper). Then look at it and breathe it in. Try to breathe in this picture when things are at their quietest so that you don't take in other people's pain. That is something you can do. Those who are shut in or cannot view the comet for any reason as it becomes more distant can do the same thing. The more people who integrate the energy of the comet, the more likely your and everybody else's life will change toward something benevolent.

Will we move up from 3.47 by May or June?

Will you move up permanently, you mean?

Permanently a degree or two by May or June as a result of Hale-Bopp?

That's real iffy. You know, the energy is now being put toward moving you up temporarily so that you can feel the value of where you're going. It's okay if you drop back down. So I'd say *maybe,* but probably not.

So it'll make a temporary difference, but . . .

It's important to have a temporary difference. I feel personally that it is more important to have a temporary difference than it is to make a gradual single-digit click, because you don't notice that very much. But if you make a sudden temporary difference, a radical difference, you will feel it. Then even if you do slide back down to 3.47, you will have a memory of something . . .

A goal.

A goal, yes. You can say, "Oh, I want *more* of that! Let's do that!" It will give you a taste of chocolate cake, and you're going to want more.

What's New with the SSG

Is there anything new to talk about? We haven't talked about the SSG for a long time. They were under Las Vegas the last time we talked. Where are they now physically?

You know, things have gotten to the point where I can't really say, because I can't play favorites. Regardless of what people have done, I can't single them out and say, "Here they are." I'll just say that they've moved to a more remote location and have left some underground facilities where they were, but they are unmanned.

The place where they used to run the planet from 300 miles down, with that special energy above, that's totally vacant now?

They have automated it, but they are not there.

Is Secret Canyon here absolutely empty now? At one point the terrorists wanted to take it over and it was destroyed.

They are not now anyplace where they were.

Let me put it this way. Is it safe yet for people to go out walking in Secret Canyon, or are there devices still there?

I think it's safe. I wouldn't go out strolling at night, but then it's not a good idea to go out strolling in the forest at night anyway unless you know what you're doing.

Okay, but they used to have the astral patrol and it used to be pretty deadly.

I do not think that's much of a factor now. You might run into something, but probably not.

They must be having meetings. We're only eight points away from being beyond their clutches. They must be doing something desperate or trying to make contingency plans.

Well, one contingency plan has always been to go to the Moon and operate from there if they have to. But that would not be a good thing for you, because if they are not on Earth, then they have no stake whatsoever in the future of Earth other than its being here so that the Moon doesn't spin off into space. So we would rather have them here than on the Moon.

All the Xpotaz are gone, right? All their allies are gone?

Yes.

They have a few Xpotaz ships left?

They have a few vehicles left. They are gradually getting to the point where they're going to need to have some replacement parts, but they still have some pretty lethal forces available. What will they do when they need parts? I don't think they'll be able to do anything. I think they'll just have to cannibalize other ships.

But the thirteen in the inner circle are still active? Is it still functional?

Yes.

Are the rebels back in the fold, what you called loose cannons?

No, they've been replaced. If you have an organization that likes to perpetuate itself, there are mechanisms for replacement.

Cloning?

No!

Bringing in another elder son?

Yes, just bringing somebody in.

How many have been drawn in?

Two. The other two are still loose cannons. One of them is unable to influence much and probably doesn't represent much of a danger to anyone, but the other one might get into some mischief.

So at this point we should just forget about them and focus on ourselves, do what we have to do and let them do their thing, right?

Absolutely, because the more that people become terrorized by the thought of what they might do, the less likely they will become empowered. Try to empower yourself in average, simple ways. Ask questions when you're not sure—it's surprising that one of the very first things students learn is not to ask questions, even in today's schools, which are getting better all the time. That's got to change. Students have to be reassured that if they ask questions they'll get answers and be encouraged to ask more, and that there won't be any intentional or unintentional punishment for it. Teachers must encourage them and do what they can to let the rest of the class know that asking questions is a good thing. That is empowering.

Jupiter's Red Spot

Here are some questions from readers. What causes the Red Spot on the planet Jupiter?

That is an exceptionally large portal. Yes, yes, there are swirling gases, but it is a portal that moves material from within the planet to the surface for more than one purpose. The basic purpose is to create a defensive atmosphere, to project the image that the planet is impossible to populate. (In all honesty, it *would* be difficult for human beings to survive there, if not impossible.)

The second factor, perhaps more important, is that this portal, which moves in an outward direction so that no automated vehicles could fly through it, can move matter from Sirius into this system. Most of this matter could be called rays, not unlike cosmic rays, that are intended to affect your Sun and gradually feed back to Earth enough energy from Sirius to stabilize Earth within this solar system. When you move a planet from one solar system to another, its chances of becoming unstable are very high—98%. This portal on Jupiter accounts for fully 80% (89% at times) of the stabilization of this planet Earth (which, in its current state, is from Sirius) so that Earth can function here. Some of the other planets in this solar system have mirror images of themselves in Sirius, too—for instance, Pluto, Venus and Mars, although not Saturn or Jupiter.

The Safety of Vaccines

Here is another question. Are vaccines on this planet causing mayhem? Do they have a hidden agenda in relationship to AIDS, and do they have something to do with the Ebola outbreaks?

We must remember that the motivation for vaccines is to alleviate suffering. Never forget that, okay? It might be that the current method of manufacturing vaccines needs to be changed. For a long time they have utilized dead microbes, attenuated or less virulent ones, and occasionally even live disease organisms, enlisting the patient's own immune system to combat the disease in the least harmful way.

But nowadays, because of the dimensional shift and the changing perspective that allows people to become more empowered, I recommend that the scientists involved in homeopathy begin to develop, at least in greater application, homeopathic vaccines. Starting in the past year and a half and continuing to accelerate for the next ten years, homeopathy will become increasingly effective even if you don't believe in it. This is because the subtle influences on the immune system will have a much greater impact than the more direct, confrontative approach of the average vaccine.

Are the vaccines actually *giving* you diseases? I can't say that, but vaccines are causing serious breakdowns in the immune system—unintentionally, for the most part—and you can't afford that these days. The immune system itself is gradually going away. As you become more integrated into your actual selves and more shamanic (if I may use that term) in your interactions with all life—understanding that all life is sacred and treating all life in a benevolent way, as you yourself would like to be treated—gradually the immune system will no longer be needed. This is a gradual process and cannot happen suddenly. So I'd say that the best counterbalance to the current system of vaccination is homeopathy.

I must admit that some vaccines, especially when given *in combination*—that's really dangerous—are having some deleterious effects on people. So try to get your vaccines individually if you can, even ones that have always been given together. Medical people, please consider giving vaccines in smaller doses, and less of the combined, okay? And look into homeopathy. I think you will not be sorry.

The U.S. Economy

Here's one with a completely different flavor. Is the Unites States going bankrupt and will there be new coinage to replace the money we have now?

Realistically speaking, as any person in business knows, the United States is bankrupt and is basically functioning on the good faith of its citizens and its creditors around the world. Good faith is there because your foreign creditors believe in your ability to produce. The U.S. is respected around the world for its production capacity, not just in specific locations, as you often find in other countries, but all over the nation. Creditors know that the citizens of the United States *are* the government, in terms of paying off the debt. When you consider your actual debt compared to your income, there is no doubt that you're bankrupt many times over. But since the U.S. (or any other government, for that matter) can print money, and since its citizens still believe in their country, then I'd say there is no urgent necessity to go out and stockpile silver dollars or gold coins.

Now, if you have extra money and you want to make an investment, being my good banker self, I will say to put no more than 7% of your investment portfolio into gold or silver, something obvious, not an ingot. Will the Treasury put out a coin that is equal to some kind of universal currency? If they put out a universal currency, it would likely be paper. Sometimes prototype coins might accidentally fall into places they don't belong and come into circulation temporarily, but I would say that the most likely currency to be promoted and utilized internationally—for economic purposes as well as simplifying the use of currency overseas by having the same kind on your European vacation as at home—is paper. Detecting counterfeits is easier for paper than metal. To summarize, your creditors and banks all over the world believe in the capacity of the U.S. citizen to produce, so they're willing to tolerate the towering debt, but you can't continue running a deficit. Gotta stop that.

Saturn's Rings

A reader wants to know if the rings around Saturn will eventually develop into a moon?

No, I don't think so. It's an interesting idea, but I do not think there's any likelihood of that happening.

What do the rings around Saturn do? Why are they there?

It's just broken rock, bits of a planet caught up in the gravity field of a big planet. If you look at some of the other big planets, you'll see similar things. As you get closer, you can study what I would call belts of gravitation, where such debris is caught. But I don't expect it to turn itself into a moon.

Okay, I think we're done for tonight.

Then I'll say good day.

15

Flash for Computer-Connected Businesses

Zoosh through Robert Shapiro
March 24, 1997

Since I've given fair warning to others, I'd like to continue. I do not feel it is necessary to take radical steps, but I want to suggest to all those who are manufacturing computers, hardware and software or are involved with them, including research, retail and wholesale that it would be wise to plan for increased security and protection for your employees and property. There are some religious groups that are now planning to disrupt or destroy anything having to do with computers. I'm not talking about computer viruses, but pure destruction. These people are beginning to consolidate the belief that not only are computers evil, but that whatever might cause individuals to have computers implanted in their bodies, such as the chip that is basically now ready, is also evil. Without commenting one way or the other about such matters, I'd say that now is the time for such companies to protect their employees and also institute levels of internal security by which they can ascertain whether people on the inside or the outside of the company are in a position to cause significant damage and/or loss of life.

You might wonder why I am warning people, because it is not my job to interfere with what human beings do. But I feel that I can, without interfering, give out timely warnings like this. This is my brief flash, such as it is, and I am hopeful that company officials can take steps that do not intrude on the life of their employees, yet still protect them and the company. I am most concerned for the area of hardware manufacture and less concerned about software, but I mention software because it is conceivable that those who would target such companies might consider a software manufacturer, distributor or even retailer to be an alternative target. However, their primary targets will be hardware manufacturers and potentially researchers. So universities who are involved in research would also need to be alert. I am not terribly concerned that this plot cannot be resolved. These are loose-knit groups that are not based in any one religion, but focused in concepts or ideals. It is not a political movement, but a religious one.

Can you be more specific? Are they going to attack the plants that make hardware and software with bombs and guns?

I think they will not use guns, as in bullets, but more likely attempt to gain access to small versions of missiles (obviously not computer-guided ones). Bombs are a distinct possibility as well as personal attacks on individuals known to be in the computer business. I'm not trying to scare people, but I feel this warning will allow you to make plans to protect yourselves, your families, your employees and your property.

I want to be very clear that you're talking about physical attacks and attempts to terrorize people who make computers, rather than somebody hacking into programs.

Yes, I am not talking about computer hacking or any kind of computer virus. I am talking about physical attacks that will require significant investigation. It will come in the form of terrorism from religious groups that will be formed the way cells are formed in some terrorist groups. It might be difficult to track down the perpetrator, and investigative agencies might find that deep cover would be the best way to go about it. I don't wish to sound authoritarian, but I do understand the point of view of these religious groups. Yet I think this tactic is mistaken. I would prefer to see them take a more political role, to object politically and to influence along political lines—promote candidates and so on. I think that this can be done, although it would be slower than you would like. But it can be done.

Okay. We'll put it out there.

16

5D Beings Reworking Atmospheric Flux

Zoosh through Robert Shapiro
March 25, 1997

Now I'd like to mention something that's been building, that is starting to factor in more and more—air quality. We all know that the oxygen on this planet is gradually decreasing in most places. More and more of the species that breathe in carbon dioxide and exhale oxygen are being paved over or perish from polluted oceans (plankton), and more and more individuals are alive and need oxygen. Obviously, you will have a certain reduction in oxygen. But now there is more to it than that.

As you know, you are all basically extraterrestrials—*all* human beings. With that thought in mind, to be here you had to have a body created from Earth stuff—Mother Earth's body, yes? You can't simply emigrate to this planet and live here, not only because of conditions here but also because of the atmosphere, the air you breathe. As the shift is taking place not only between the third and fourth dimensions but in the soul being of you all, you are beginning to become more your extraterrestrial selves and less your Earth selves.

For some of you, especially those who have reason to believe you're more connected to ET origins or perhaps have some genetic anomaly, the air you breathe will seem less and less satisfying. It is as if the air lacks what you need even though you can breathe a deep lungful of air. This does not refer only to oxygen, so it's a fine point I'm making here. Yes, you are affected by the decrease in available oxygen, and yes, as you begin to get closer to the fourth dimension, the planet is likely to have an atmosphere with more nitrogen in it. Because nitrogen is more of a preservative than oxygen and because people will live longer in the fourth-dimensional state of being, one would not be surprised that nitrogen will be more of a factor in the atmosphere.

For those who have close ties to the ET within your physical selves, oxygen-saturated atmospheres might not do it, but don't rush out and buy a tank of nitrous oxide [chuckles] to pump into your system. (We don't want to put you to sleep, nor do we want to change your voice.) I just want to tell you that it is an anomaly; it shouldn't be permanent. I expect that this will straighten itself out in the next three to five months. This is one of those situations that needs adjustments that you personally cannot make. You cannot even make a spiritual adjustment here. It is an adjustment that must be made from the future to the present (where you are now), and it must be done by others. It is being done, but it takes time. I just want to let you know.

Who's doing it, our future selves?

Individuals in the future, not your future selves. People now in the fifth dimension are reworking the atmospheric zonal flux (for lack of a better term, though that one's pretty vague) so that the change happens more quickly. If we can make the change quickly you won't need the gradual phasing in of the nitrogen atmosphere. Your bodies are not being fed as much oxygen as you need now. At the same time, those with strong ET ties (some of you have stronger ties than others) are experiencing a need for a more nurturing atmosphere, which you cannot tolerate at this time because of your Earth body. So basically you need to take it slow.

Should we get a bottle of oxygen and have it around or something?

Oxygen would make you feel a little better, but it won't have a lasting impact. I don't know what to say there. Maybe. It might be useful, but then again, you'd probably have to have a doctor's consultation.

The Central Arizona Hum

We had a call from a reader in New River, north of Phoenix, who has done some investigation and really needs your help. For the past year she's been hearing this deep artificial sound.

A hum?

That's right, a hum. She's discovered through people she's contacted that the hum is heard as far away as Mesa, and it's apparently the same as in New Mexico, because someone there had told her it was the sound of E flat. She checked it out and E flat is precisely what she's hearing, too. Every five or six weeks or so, it will stop for several hours, usually at night. A telephone pole outside vibrates from the sound. With a stethoscope she can pick it up only on the pole's southwest quadrant when it's louder. At those times a sign on the pole visibly shakes. Other people can hear it, and when it's loud, her husband hears it, too. She's asking what it is, and is it something that's going to ultimately cause her to move somewhere else?

Probably. This is associated directly with the Taos hum. It's a real thing, and it has been significantly reported. It is something that not everyone hears. Even in Taos, some people hear it and some don't. It can be maddening. Is it going to go away? Probably not. What is it associated with? Very much the same thing. In Taos there are underground vibrating devices that are not associated with extraterrestrials, but with exotic defense systems. They will allow for better communications where desired (I'm not going to be too specific) and will interfere with undesired communications.

Underground Government Activities

Is it associated with the sinister secret government? No, it is not, but it *is* associated with underground activities that are known to your government. I need to be vague here, because we're dealing with secrets. I'm willing to be reasonable with secrets, but I see no reason to bandy them about if there's no immediate need. Is she probably going to have to move, yes, I would think so. That is unfortunate. Obviously, there's not much point in moving to New Mexico, but it might be safe in Colorado, probably in the north. I wouldn't recommend Utah. If they're not experiencing it on a wide scale, they probably will be, certainly in the middle to southern area at some point. Sorry.

Is this something for the ultimate benefit of the population?

Oh, no. It is strictly for defensive purposes. Let's loosely drop it into the category of the military. That's all I want to say.

She asked if it is associated with the HAARP project.

It is not directly associated with HAARP. That project, as you know, has a lot of sinister side effects, and for that reason is perhaps one of the *most* sinister. When I refer to this particular hum, I'm not talking about underground droning noises, such as are heard in nearby Cottonwood or Clarkdale, but a very specific tone. In the past when this tone was heard in Taos, I referred its point of origin to Los Alamos, but it is broader than that now.

So I'd say it largely has to do with underground installations and the chances of its stopping in the near future are unlikely. If everyone heard it, a new technology would be developed, but since only some people hear it, then it has, as they say in intelligence circles, an air of deniability. It is unfortunate that it is terribly disruptive not only to human beings, but to plant and animal life. It will have a very serious impact on local ranching and farming, because it will bother domesticated animals very much. Rangers, watch out especially for balance problems in your animals. If you have to move them from place to place, take care.

17

Missing U.S. Warplane Chasing UFO

Zoosh through Robert Shapiro
April 21, 1997

C*an you tell us in detail what happened to the plane that disappeared nineteen days ago, when it crashed in Colorado?*

Well, this reasonably young pilot got a blip on his radar, and he wasn't sure what it was. Because it was a practice military mission, one is prepared for that kind of activity. But he saw it more visually than on radar. It was what they call a ghost image—there one moment and not the next. So he broke off to pursue it. I believe he did radio to the others that that's what he was going to do. I don't know if that's being withheld or whether that communication was not received. I can't say, to be discreet.

Then he pursued it to the Four Corners area, all the time being able to see it above and in front of him, moving at equal speed. It did allow him to catch up a little, occasionally exhibiting nonballistic characteristics, which is why he knew it was a UFO and not some exotic piece of military hardware. He lost it and picked it up again about a hundred miles west of Wolf Creek Pass. Then he lost the white object again in the mountains, while flying over snow-covered peaks. By that time the object had darted below him, under the left wing. It was hard for him to keep track of. He would slow down occasionally, but it would always pace him. So he wound up circling, trying to find it, and couldn't. I don't think that any other planes were scrambled for this object, so he was up there on his own. He spent quite a time searching and he experienced a problem with the steering, which is why some witnesses saw barrel rolls. He was having difficulty maneuvering. Now, prudence would suggest that he get away from the mountains, but sometimes when you see something and want to know what it is, you've just got to push forward, counting on luck to keep things together. Well, he was not able to clear a mountaintop.

I'm putting this out so that this pilot's relatives will know that this was not a suicide. This was a genuine attempt to identify a UFO, and it was also a fascination with the object, having seen it and wanting to get closer, which many pilots in similar circumstances might wish to do. Since the plane has been found, I want the people who cared about this person to know that he was not tired of life. I will suggest to those who investigate the wreckage that you'll probably find something governing the hydraulic systems on the right side of the plane to have been amiss. If he had not been over the mountains, he might have been able to make it back, or at least to where he could make a semicontrolled landing. The mountains were the problem.

Can you tell me anything about who the occupants of the lightship were, what they were doing here?

USA TODAY, Thursday, April 24, 1997

Warplane crash site confirmed

Metal scraps found on a Colorado mountain were identified Wednesday as parts of a missing Air Force warplane.

The A-10 Thunderbolt piloted by Capt. Craig Button, left, disappeared three weeks ago under odd circumstances.

Button, who is still missing, and his armed jet vanished while on a practice mission in southern Arizona.

Button AP **Story, 3A.**

Well, I think that they were actually observing military activities in central to southern Arizona. They weren't observing for any nefarious purpose so much as just to see your progress. This is not military progress, but here's an interesting example of what they might consider progress:The fact that the U.S. government and a few others no longer scramble aircraft to check out UFOs that are clearly extraterrestrially oriented (and some truly exotic ground-based radar systems can tell).

Rather than trying to shoot them down?

That's right. Nobody is trying to interfere with them or generally engage them. So progress doesn't have to do with how big the bomb is, how fast the airplane is, but what your reaction to the ship is.

Where were they from?

Well, let's see. The ship doesn't really have a home port. It's associated with deep space explorations, not unlike a scientific vessel at sea. I can tell you that the beings on board were made up of beings from the following sources: one from Andromeda, two from Zeta Reticuli, three from Arcturus and one from Sirius. The crew changes from time to time, but the makeup of the crew tells you that it's an unusual kind of a ship.

They must have felt badly when he crashed.

I think they were upset, yes. Significantly upset.

This printout is from the Farsight Institute [see reprinted bulletin on page 124]. They are remote viewers. In their open letter to the government of the United States, they say that they have extraterrestrial friends working with them and that the Institute can help the government vastly if the government will protect them. First, there is a group inside one of the intelligence organizations that has been tasked to eliminate them.

Understandable, yes.

Two, they obtained some new technology from these friendly ETs and three days after using it, an intelligence group came from a foreign ally of the United States. The next one that comes to demand information could be a terrorist organization, so they're asking to be protected. I'd like to know who their friends are, then about an atom bomb stolen from the Russians that is supposedly planned to be used in New York City.

New York City Bomb Rumor and Farsight Institute's Bulletin

Now, anybody with even partial exposure to security procedures knows that it is not as easy as people think to smuggle an atom bomb, to say nothing of dropping it. People of New York, don't worry. Now, in terms of the real potential for this happening? I would say that there's about a 1½% chance that this will happen within the next three and a half years—which is not to say that it won't. Airport security is getting a lot better so it would more likely come into the country by ship, especially in freighters disguised as something else. In terms of who would want to do this, I'd look towards the Middle East. It's safe to say that this kind of technology could be, and may well have been, purchased from the former Soviet Union, *not sold by any government official.*

They're calling it a tactical nuclear weapon

Well, "tactical" can easily go up to 20 megatons these days. I'm not going to say which Middle Eastern country these people are from, because I don't want to encourage any unnecessary wars. We're talking about a terrorist outfit that is not associated with the government of that country. But the government might turn a blind eye to them, as one might to a political foe in your midst, because you just have to learn how to get along. Don't feel like you're being attacked by a particular country per se.

Now, I do not wish to suggest or intimate in any way that these remote viewers are people who are unworthy of paying attention to. What

I do want to say is that they are taking what was always a military project in the U.S. to the public. But you have to remember, when it was a military project, it was just thrown in with the rest of intelligence, and when it was right, it was only partially right. Training in remote viewing has been done for military purposes and when it's not spiritual it is infinitely easier to make a mistake*. Even if it is spiritual now, anything that is remote-viewed these days is likely to be off by a factor of 8 to 1. I'm not going to explain the math, but I'll just say that it's like trying to be in a fixed place looking at a fixed thing while everything else is moving. In point of fact, you're not in a fixed place, nor is the thing you're looking at. Everything is moving at slightly different rates. So what they're seeing is a possibility, not a probability.

However, I do support increased security at airports and other ports of entry, especially overland routes, meaning Canada or Mexico. These are the areas where the United States is terribly vulnerable. A radical increase in security is needed at the Mexican border. This is not just electronic security but physical security. I will support the attorney-general's position on that.

I feel that although this letter is certainly well-intended, and one shouldn't dismiss them, the group that might be targeting them is not directly associated with the U.S. government—meaning people who work with the government, for the government or who receive a check from the government of the United States. I'm defining it specifically because I think that they might be under some threat, but it would be more associated with a sort of a rebel group within the intelligence services.

Is this the group we talked about before that was going to do the bombings? [See chapter 2.]

That's right. We've got rebel groups in the intelligence community that are working for good things and are still in the community, but this is a rebel group that is outside of the community. They're not receiving government paychecks, but they would seem very much like government officers if they came around.

These Farsight people are in some danger; there's no question about that. But I think they need to contact the government through more appropriate channels, probably not through the military, the FBI or some other judiciary organization, but through congressional representatives or perhaps the Justice Department. These days the Justice Department has just a little bit more capability for speed and more important, for referral. Very often agencies refer people from point A to point B. I think the Justice Department's ability is better here.

Who are the friends? Who are the ETs ?

I don't think I want to say. I'm sorry, but I think the people at Farsight have made that clear. Understand that they've taken this experience of remote viewing and spiritualized it a little. As a result, their contact with ETs is not what I would call physical. It is a remote experience, like telepathy. While I support their spiritual directions, in the long run I think they need to have some training by spiritual people to teach a degree of discernment. (Discernment in this case cannot be mental for them because they are using already that function.) The discernment technique will have to be physical, along the feeling plane. Even if it's spiritually and mentally oriented, if you look toward the spiritual and the mental exclusively for confirmation, it's not enough. You need to have physical, within-the-body feelings, certain discernment abilities to know whether something is true and what you are to do about it.

I don't want to sound like I'm pooh-poohing this outfit. I think that spiritually they're headed toward a good place. If they're going to ask for protection, they're probably going to need to contact the Justice Department. Asking the government at large is probably like sending a specific request to your local government information office. It'll get there eventually, but it'll take time.

I think that they're putting this out on the Internet so that if something happens, it's going to be "Well, we told you."

Yes, I agree. Of course, the other reason they're putting it out over the Internet is because one of the best ways to protect yourself is to go public. Another thing they might do is go to the press with it. But I don't think that the average press, the *Times* and whatnot, would print this material even though they have printed things about military projects in the past. This group is different. They have sometimes been indiscreet in terms of taking certain things public, but I hardly think it's a crime punishable by death. They're guilty of being mildly indiscreet at most.

To quote, they're referring to "events that you, the government, know are soon to happen with regard to human/ET interactions, or make it necessary for humans to understand the technologies that are associated with these phenomena." What specifically are they referring to?

I think they're primarily referring to simple technologies that ETs have to use to protect their energy bodies from human energy bodies. Human energy bodies are very complex because this is a complex school here: One might in the same moment be feeling happy, exultant, angry, depressed, and joyful. You might have all those simultaneous feelings, whereas an ET just cannot do that or even be exposed to it, because it's too complex. They need protection, which might have some side effects on human beings.

No. I don't mean that. They're saying that there appears to be an imminent ET-human interaction. Is there some landing expected?

ET Landings Depend on Your Choice to Accept Others

I don't think so. Sorry.

No?

Sorry. I know everybody wants that, but I don't think it's going to happen immediately, because you still haven't made your *choice!*

Of what?

Are you ready to let go of your differences, not only major but minor, from individual to individual and from country to country and everything in between and beyond? Are you willing to let go of that at least often (not sometimes), to begin with? You might say to me, "Zoosh, how can I prepare for ETs?" Are you ready as an individual to accept a person no matter how odd they look? For example, those of you who are a little older, are you ready to walk down the street and see a youngster dressed in their outfits of the day and not shudder and shake your head, but just be okay with it? Are you ready to see people who are different living in your neighborhood or to invite them to visit the neighborhood? Are you, purely and simply, comfortable being different or around people who are different? Are you able to accommodate that which is different in your life? To the extent you are able and choose to do that, then you will see ETs. If they came now it would force you to make up your mind, and because of their technology, their perception of life, they would be practically deified overnight by some people, and others would be terribly frightened because they are different.

Homework

No, I don't think we're going to see any major landings, certainly not in Times Square or in the plaza of CNN's major studio until you can do that. So practice—do some homework! In the next two weeks after you read this, sometime during the day note how uncomfortable you feel around different people. That's all. Don't blame yourself. Don't kick yourself. You don't have to rush over to different people and embrace them, saying "I'm sorry for judging you." Just notice how you feel. Another time, just notice different people around you and see if you can relax a little bit being around them. You don't have to let your guard down in dangerous situations; I'm talking about people who are simply different. See if you can relax. Try it. That's your homework.

Until enough people can do that, my friend, I do not think we're going to see the grand landings. We're certainly not going to see true ETs, who would perhaps be troublesome. We're certainly not going to see anything like *Independence Day* [the movie]. You know, that is strictly a figment of the movie's imagination, though I grant that there are some politically oriented groups that would love you to believe that ETs are to be feared. That can slow down your spiritual advancement. Some ETs can be frightening, upsetting unusual or strange—I can definitely grant that. But remember, especially those who've read *The Explorer Race, you are all ETs!* There's not a single human on Earth who doesn't have extraterrestrial genes and Earth-oriented genes. You are a mixed bag of ET gumbo, otherwise you couldn't really function in this Earth school. But that's another story. Read *The Explorer Race,* and *ETs and the Explorer Race,* and you'll get my drift. So is the landing imminent? No. Sorry.

All right, so what's happening in the cosmos? What would you like to report about this month for the magazine?

Mother Earth Increases Electric Energy

You know, there's so much going on always, but in terms of day-to-day experience, I will say that the electrical energy is very powerful now, especially between the hours of 2:20 a.m. to about 7:20 a.m.

A lot of you might think, "Oh, they're doing this, they're doing that," but it is Mother Earth. This is something she must do for herself. I've said before that all the electricity on this planet is part of Mother Earth's energy body, and because you are using so much of her energy body for your electrical necessities, she needs to produce more. Those of you who are living in areas whose soil has a lot of metal content (for example, ferrous substances) are going to feel it particularly strongly. That is not only in Sedona, because other places have red rock as well.

You're feeling electrical energy because Mother Earth is producing more of her energy body. She is replenishing it, making more electricity. Physicists might say, "There is only so much of this mass and more cannot be made." But you are wrong. Physicists know that magnetic energy radiates out of the poles. It is being produced, it isn't just going back and forth. This phenomenon is being caused by more electrical energy being created. You continue to use more and more electricity, because the world population is increasing, and the rest of the world is joining the age of technology. A vast increase in your usage of electricity means that Mother Earth will just have to make more. And if she ever needs some of what you're using when you're using it, you will suddenly and unexpectedly have a huge blackout over a wide part of the grid. (That's happened, I think, a couple of times already in the U.S., and certainly several times elsewhere.)

This is going to be tough on those who do not do well in electrical fields, but you can move places that are not overwhelmingly ferrous in makeup. (The beach, for example, has a lot of quartz.) Or you can try to learn how to deal with such energy or wear something that will protect you. I believe there's a company selling a form of Faraday cage to wear, with an inner lining of some comfortable fabric with perhaps aluminum screening sandwiched in between. Let's call this a jumpsuit. The side that faces the world will be some well-wearing material like denim, for example. You'll look like you're wearing a denim jumpsuit, but you're really wearing a denim Faraday cage. It will markedly reduce the effect (especially around the heart and most of the nervous system) of the impact of electrical fields that the human body is not meant to be exposed to.

Now, those of you who do not have trouble with electrical fields forget about it. It's not going to bother you. Those who do not live in places that are particularly ferrous, you're going to be okay for the most part, except for those who are particularly sensitive. I mention it here because there is something you can do about it, and that product is useful. It shouldn't be too hard to find through the Internet. A useful addition to the jumpsuit might be a hood that covers the back of the skull, up over the crown chakra. But not all of you might want to do that. I'm not saying to do it but to try it. There is a company making these, not with aluminum screening but a form of cloth screening is put through a particular process which would be much more comfortable. If you want to experiment with it, it won't be the most comfortable garment, but try aluminum screening just for fun, those of you who can sew.

What is the result of too much electricity on your nervous system?

The nervous system acts as a communication system within the body, and this energy will tend to stimulate most muscles and even the mind. So it will be hard for you to rest or go to sleep, but conversely, it might be easier to do physically creative things. So you might get up and do physical things, or even write or do something creative. Changing your creative time schedule so that you're working in the wee hours of the morning instead of in the afternoon, might work for those of you who are particularly sensitive to this. But this is mainly something that would stimulate the muscles, so your legs would be ready to run while you're trying to go to sleep. You'd not exactly have the fight/flight experience, but you'd be physically tense, wondering "Why am I tense? There is no reason I can find." You might be able to hang a reason on something, but that's probably not it.

There's no long-term negative effect on the nervous system, is there?

Oh, I'd have to say that there might be a strain in areas having to do with your cardiovascular system. This would probably not be good for people with heart conditions who are sensitive to electrical exposure.

People who have interactions between the fillings in their teeth might find it difficult. People who have metal implants such as steel pins that hold bones together or shrapnel in an old war wound, might have problems. In the long run this would be difficult for people with visual difficulties. If they wear glasses they need to have corrections much more often. (The optometrist might make money, but in the long run it's not a good thing.) Things that could be affected: some of the subtle mechanisms in the body, such as functions of the kidneys, the ureter, the bladder. There could be problems there.

How long is this going to go on?

Probably for quite a while, because Mother Earth needs to make vast quantities of electricity to replenish her energy body. It could go on for anywhere from three to seven, possibly even seventy years. Three years on the low side. It's possible that some individuals (in smaller circles) will discover a source of power that does not require electricity, and certainly within ten to fifteen years I should think that might be more widespread, allowing for the population explosion and the fact that vast areas of the world will be coming into First World technology within the next ten to twelve years.

This has a lot to do with your current world order, which is based upon the corporate model. There are circumstances in which corporations and the corporate model for government are going to accept a degree of Third World inefficiency. In the recent case of the Mexican strawberries [where some schoolchildren and personnel were infected with hepatitis], it was the way they were handled when they were picked. After paying out large settlements from incidents like that, the corporate structures of the world are going to say, "We've got to bring everybody up to speed, or we're going to have to funnel 20% of our earnings into an insurance fund. If we're sued all the time, that's essentially our profits."

Intolerance Backslid You to 3.465

All right, are we still at 3.47?

We actually backslid a little bit; we're now at 3.465 or so. There's a little backpressure right now.

From where?

Oh, I think it has a lot to do with intolerance. Tolerance is not enough. You can't just *tolerate* people; you have to learn how to be relaxed around people who are different. Right now there's a little more intolerance than ever, so we've backslid a little bit.

We've come back two and a half points?

Well, there's no guarantee that you're always going to be moving forward.

Lightbeings Here from the Ship near Hale-Bopp

I see. You originally agreed that there was a lightship with the Hale-Bopp comet, and then a month ago you said it was gone and I didn't follow up on it.

The lightship was coming with the comet only so close to Earth. Because of the proximity, some of the lightbeings would be able to work with people on the Earth, but the ship itself would not come close to Earth. That's the difference.

But they're gone now?

The ship is gone. Some of the lightbeings have stayed on. Roughly between 3500 to 5200 lightbeings at any given moment have stayed and are working with people here, which is a good thing.

In their lightbodies?

Well, yes. They're lightbeings, are they not?

So can they go back and forth to the ship?

No, they'll have to send a ship to pick them up. Theoretically, they could catch up, but it would take so long, why bother?

How long do they plan to stay here?

Oh, I think they'll stick around for at least twenty years.

Are they working with massive groups of people, one on one, or what?

Generally they're working one on one with individuals, but they don't always work with the same individuals all the time. Sometimes it's spiritual people, sometimes it's just folks.

In their sleep state?

Sometimes they'll work in the individual's sleep state, sometimes the dream state, sometimes the waking state. Spiritual people have spiritual practices that are open to such things, where the wakeful state is a possibility. Even some people who are deeply religious might see these beings within the context of a religious figure. They're okay with that if it can help you.

Do they have an agenda or some sort of a plan for being here, such as lifting the vibration?

No, they just are here to help you.

In whatever way they can.

That's right, in whatever way they can. But they're not here to help you to lift the vibration. You know, things like that are nice to think about, but *you* have to do that. If somebody else does it for you, what have you learned? Nothing.

If they're 32nd-dimensional beings, have they ever had a life on Earth or any interest or interaction with Earth?

I don't think any of them have ever had a physical life on Earth. I think only a couple, three maybe, have had a physical life at all.

They just want to help.

Yes. They signed on.

HAARP Project

Someone said that there would be some effect on the HAARP project from this vehicle, a positive effect for those who don't want it to continue. Will anything like that happen?

Well, I don't like to be the bearer of sad tidings, but I'd have to say that there was no long-lasting impact. You have to remember that projects like this are ludicrous even at face value. It's like, "Let's see if we can punch a hole in the atmosphere just because we can." Think about it. That is the same rationale as, "Let's take a big dose of LSD just because we can." What's the difference? That's potentially self-destructive or even beyond. I grant that they're trying to learn something, but you don't shoot off your left foot to see if you can learn how to use only your right foot.

I must not have said that correctly.

No, no. I'm talking to the readership here. I'm not talking to you only. Understand?

We are not for the HAARP project.

I know you're not. I'm speaking to the readership.

Well, they're not for it, either.

Well, just a darn minute now. Do you think that everybody who reads this magazine has read it from the first issue?

No.

This is an interesting statistic that you don't have and can't get, but most of the people who are reading this magazine right now have read at most two or three issues.

Really?

Yes, because your readership is expanding. When it expands suddenly and quickly, it goes out to people who might not have seen it before. So you need to understand that we need to talk to people as if they haven't read all of the past material.

Okay. I was hoping that something bad would happen to the equipment.

Nothing that can't be fixed in a week. I encourage people to do things, as other entities do, but I also encourage you to not be attached to the outcome of what you do. You do things and hope for the best, but don't assume that you're going to knock out the project forever or that it's going to be too expensive to fix. No spirit of good conscience is going to show you how to destroy the project, because in order to do so, people would be killed, hurt or maimed. If any spirit is telling you how to destroy something, say, "Thank you very much," and ask for somebody else. (Just a little basic reminder there.)

Is the alternate negative future stressing humanity? Is that why we've moved backward?

Expand Your Creative Potential by Embracing Others

No. I think you've managed to do it on your own, in terms of wars and unnecessary strife. Although I say "unnecessary strife," I'm not amongst you dealing with the things you're dealing with. That's why I want to give you homework that is not particularly threatening, yet allows you to expand a little. This whole thing with prejudging people on the basis of experiences you've had with someone who looked like that or because of something people told you about them, is limiting your opportunities.

I'm thinking of the people who pray, hope and wish for good things to happen in their lives, but who keep away from wide groups of people due to fear. I know that 90% of the reason they're not getting what is being asked for is because they will have to interact in some benevolent way with people they are avoiding. When you ask for something, as you know, you very rarely get it by a direct route. It might be through a third party or from something that you do. You know how discovery works, but you are limiting your creative potential based upon narrow human-to-human contacts. I'm not saying you have to go out and embrace everybody. I am saying "Don't assume that everyone is ___" (fill in the blank).

You need to seek out someone wise to talk to and ask him/her how to do whatever you need to learn, and I'm not just talking about old Uncle Zoosh here. There's a lot of wise men and women out there to talk to. Ask, "How can I do this?" or "How do you do that?" Pay attention. Who's doing something well that you admire? Ask them to tell you how they gained that ability, or see if they can help you to begin to do it. If they're too demanding of you, seek out another teacher. If they just tell you what they do and can't explain it any further, say thank-you and go on. The main thing is, people who are doing something you admire might be in your own family, in your immediate neighborhood or people you see every day, but they have this one particular thing which they can do very easily. I might add that almost *everybody* has at least one thing they do easily, that everybody else struggles with. That's why you're here together—so you can help each other. (That's my old lecture.)

If they do that, it will expose them to people of different races, religions, beliefs, looks, all that. Is that part of what you're saying?

What I'm saying is, pick out something that you admire, whether it is making money, getting along with other people, being successful or knowing how to break the tension in a situation, making everybody else laugh and feel that everything is okay. Ask how to do that. In other words, seek each other out for wisdom. All the traits that you would like to have, some other being on Earth has right now. If you want to understand true Earth wisdom, you need to seek out—in this case—Earth individuals.

Oh, you're saying to quit looking to the stars?

Don't look only to Uncle Zoosh and other entities. Acknowledge that there are some people who can do things or have things that you wish you had. Then ask them how they did that. You don't have to follow every word of what they say. You do what you can, maybe just a little bit. The main thing is, you need to help each other. This is one of the things that ETs will look for on Earth and see if you've progressed. How much are you helping or hindering each other? When ETs come to see how you are doing, they're not looking to see if you've built a new atomic bomb. They're coming to see how you're *helping each other*—the children, older people, the sick and the prisoners. If the situation has improved, then they will say that you have progressed. If the situation has regressed, they'll say, "Huh-uh, got a ways to go yet."

So you're saying it's simpler than . . .

It's so much simpler than it seems, but it has to begin with each individual. I understand that this magazine at this time does not go out to every individual, but others have said similar things. To the extent that this knowledge can go out, let it go out, and maybe a few people will talk about it and put it out in other ways. You don't have to sacrifice everything you own or everything you stand for to help each other, but there are times when just a slight delay of two minutes means you can help someone.

Maybe you decided to leave five minutes early for work because you don't want to rush so much when you arrive. Your little girl comes up to you and says, "Daddy, will you help me tie my shoe?" Normally you might say, "Oh, ask your mom to do that." But you know, she's not asking you to tie her shoe because *she* can't do it. She wants you to be there for her, to do something with her and not be short with her. Just bend down and slowly tie her shoe, and she'll be talking to you about other things. You listen and take time. Remember that no matter how hard you work to gain benefits for your family so your children can get ahead in life, you won't do those kids any good if they don't see you and learn to love you, and learn to be your friend by your being *their* friend and loving them as parents.

Now, you've heard this 150,000 times from other people, but I'm reminding you, because these are the ways in which you will advance. "How can we get to the fourth dimension, Zoosh?" By doing the things I'm talking about here. It's what you do, how you do it and who you do it with. It's the little things that come up every day. I'm not asking 2% of the population to sacrifice 100% of everything they are to do this. I'm asking you all to contribute in some way *every day* to the betterment of others. Donating money isn't it. If you want to donate money to causes, that's fine. But it doesn't let you off the hook. That doesn't fulfill the Zoosh homework, okay?

Now, I'm not going to check up on you. I'm not going to go around with a clipboard and put a red check mark by your name if you don't do it, but the next time you wonder why it's taking so long to get to the fourth dimension, just remind yourself of the time you were standing in line at the supermarket and that lady was in front of you. She looked nice, and maybe you've seen her at the store before. You always say hello, and she says, "Hello, how ya doin'?" But perhaps you notice she's got a new hairdo or coat you haven't seen before that looks attractive. If it's all right, if it's proper, you tell her, "What a nice hairdo you have today! That coat sure looks attractive on you." Simple things like that. Little things can brighten up a person's day more than you'll ever know. Remember that.

Say it when it's true and when you mean it. You know, it's an interesting thing that very often people will be polite and say nice things, but if they don't mean it, it actually injures the person they're talking to a little. So say what you mean. You know this one—say what you mean and mean what you say, and that will actually compliment the person. Okay, that's my lecture for today.

Farsight Institute's 22 April 1997 Bulletin

The following was taken directly from The Farsight Institute's Web site at http://www.farsight.org/science/overlay.

To Whom It May Concern: It is with considerable excitement that I am able to announce to all of those who are interested in our work at The Farsight Institute that we have made an important new discovery that affects all of the work that we do. Last week, we diagnosed a serious problem that we were having with regard to the accuracy of some of our remote viewing sessions. Before I discuss this problem, let me offer some background. Previously to last week, we learned how easy it is to alter a timeline. After remote viewing the future, it is possible to change one's behavior so as to create a new timeline. We discovered that the timeline that one departs from still exists, since the past, present, and future all exist simultaneously and can be remote viewed transparently without restriction. We also discovered that it is possible to remote view alternative timelines, all of which really exist, and that it is possible to shift from one timeline to another. There is a default timeline that exists if no action is taken with respect to information that is obtained with remote viewing. However, it is even possible for the remote viewing process itself to change a timeline, particularly when deep mind probes are executed, and individuals are influenced on the subspace side of their existence. In general, we have found that remote viewing the future is more difficult than remote viewing the past due to the fact that future is still undetermined, and it is possible to re-direct the evolution of the present in infinitely possible ways. Moreover, the default future timeline is only weakly weighted in a remote viewing session. If we want to specifically remote view the default timeline, we need to specify this timeline explicitly in the target cue. Otherwise we risk viewing an alternate future timeline by mistake. Remote viewing the past is easier since our past time stream is more heavily weighted as the default timeline. While it is possible to remote view alternative past timelines, it is not so easy to do so by mistake.

We have long known that the monitor in a remote viewing session could influence the results obtained by a remote viewer through a process known as telepathic overlay. That is, the thoughts of the monitor are picked up by the remote viewer and interpreted as data. Moreover, the thoughts of the monitor can actually influence the remote viewer by redefining the target cue with regard to alternative future timelines. It is for this reason that we long ago made the decision to conduct all of our professional sessions under Type 5 conditions, which means that neither the monitors nor the viewers know the identity of the target until after the session is completed. With this instituted as official Farsight policy for our professional sessions, we believed that we had the problem of accurate targeting solved.

As mentioned above, last week we discovered another serious problem that had potentially drastic consequences with regard to the accuracy of our remote viewing results. Indeed, it is only because we now have so many highly trained professional viewers that we were able to reliably locate and diagnose this problem using a cross-section of professional sessions. We discovered that the thoughts and preconceptions of the person who designs the original target cue can cause inaccuracies in remote viewing. Moreover, this is true even under double-blind Type 5 data conditions. Apparently, the subspace mind of the remote viewer knows immediately the full conscious intentions of the tasker (who is the person who designs the target cue). These intentions become the target, and we now believe that these ideas redefine the target along an infinite continuum of possible future timelines. We now call this "tasker overlay," and we realize that we need to control for the potential for bias in our sessions due to this phenomenon.

Quite honestly, we diagnosed this new problem of tasker overlay ourselves, but we did not solve the problem ourselves. The problem was solved during a communication with an outside agency (a group we call our "Friends.") It was told to us that we need to specifically declare in the original target cue a statement that requires the remote viewer to disregard all preconceptions that the tasker may have. Specifically, we were told to include the following words at the end of all of our target cues that are used by our professionals: "OMIT TASKER ENFORCED PERCEPTUALS." We have tested this new procedure and have found it to work satisfactorily. We intend to use this new addition to all of our professional cues from now on.

But here is the problem that we face now. We do not know how many of our previously posted sessions may have been tainted by tasker overlay. Thus, we feel morally and ethically obliged to inform everyone that all of our Type 4 and Type 5 data must be considered conditional until we can determine the extent of monitor or tasker bias that may exist in these sessions. Truthfully, we feel that the controls that we used to collect our professional sessions were satisfactory to avoid massive problems. But we still need to check all of our prior results.

Thus, we want to notify everyone that we are immediately instituting a full-scale research investigation to determine the degree of monitor and tasker bias that may exist in our published research. We are dedicating all of our professional resources (we have approximately 30 professional viewers) in this project, and we expect to have the answers to these questions in about two weeks. We will post the updates to our previously published work soon after we complete our research. But please note: It is important to emphasize that we do not now know of any mistakes in any of our previously published reports. It is just that we are now aware of a newly discovered potential problem, and we are checking our work to see if that problem affected any of our prior work.

We are dedicated to developing this new science of remote viewing. This includes telling people when we make mistakes, if and when we make them. This also includes explaining to people what we learn about the remoteviewing phenomenon while we conduct our investigations, and the implications of this new knowledge to the remainder of the scientific field. We hope most of you understand that mistakes are made in any new scientific endeavor, and remote viewing is no exception in this regard. Nonetheless, we want to reassure everyone that you will not have to wait long for us to determine the extent of any potential problems with our prior research. Indeed, in many cases, we are quite certain that the possibility of tasker bias is virtually nonexistent. For example, the "atom bomb terrorist" sessions were conducted under Type 5 conditions with no conscious expectations on the part of the tasker. Nonetheless, we will check all of our previously published results, and we will get back to you in just a few weeks. We hope all of you enjoy this learning process in this new and exciting field as much as we do.

Sincerely, Courtney Brown, Ph.D.
President—The Farsight Institute

18

Flash to Health
Professionals

Zoosh through Robert Shapiro
April 22, 1997

All right. Speaking to health professionals, doctors, nurses, health administrators, I recommend strongly nationwide testing for tuberculosis. I think you have something to be concerned about here in the States. Once upon a time nationwide testing for tuberculosis was common, at least in the schools. I feel it is necessary again. You might be a little appalled by what you find. There is a degree of this disease creeping back in. Please do not think that just because it seemed to have been eradicated once upon a time it still is.

Private doctors, make certain that your patients are tested once a year. People who run clinics, make it part of the regular patients' annual physical for a time. I feel the threat has become significant enough to say something about now. It will ride a slightly higher crest for the next five years, but if you get on top of it now you can probably once more make it of very minor concern.

Is this a natural situation?

I feel this is largely the result of unfettered immigration across the Mexican border, which is bringing in people who, although they are not bad people, do not have the exposure to the health care readily available in this country. There has been unfettered crossing for a long time, and although it is not as extreme as it once was, it is beginning to cause serious health problems amongst many individuals. This is not only for the southwest U.S. I recommend that the entire continental U.S. be looked after in this way. It is perhaps not so important in Alaska and Hawaii or even in the other nearby states, Canada and so on, but in the southwestern and western United States it is essential; even in the southern U.S. it is important.

19

The True Purpose of the Mayans

Zoosh through Robert Shapiro
May 18 and 29, 1997

Well, what would you like to talk about tonight? [Long pause.]
This calls for an oral response; I will not respond to brain waves. [Group
laughs.]

*The Mayans, their link with this part of the land [Sedona area] and their belief
system—do you have any knowledge about that?*

You're asking about the link with this part of the land and their belief
systems, so I guess I can touch on that lightly in about five words or less.
[Laughter.] Well, I will simply say this: The ancient Mayan peoples
were half Earth beings, half extraterrestrial beings. That's why they're
not here anymore. They didn't just turn to dust, with their spirits return-
ing to the stars. How many books or articles do you read, or how many
pictures do you see about "the great rescue," about these ships coming
and taking people up? These people were the last people to be "rescued," but it wasn't actually a rescue, you see.

Shifting the Magnetic Poles

They came here to do something quite interesting, a most amazing assignment. Their job, in concert with others they would never meet on
the other side of the world, was to put the magnetic field of Earth into
imbalance. It was a requirement to speed up the process by which the
Explorer Race would come into the remembered wisdom of creationism,
which involves the physical self interacting with the feeling self and the
spiritual self (always being the observer, the mind was not involved at
all, but was in the audience). In order to speed up the process it was

necessary to create a certain dire adversity. So it was their job, through the use of ceremony, rite and applied mathematics and physics, to create, force or even drain the magnetic pole of the Earth and twist it to some extent so that it would go through the middle of the Earth on a separate axis line. Their assignment sounds appalling, but if you think a little deeper about it, you can see how clever it was. If you are going to get people to change something for the better (what is the old saying?), the squeaky wheel is the first one to be greased. Human beings tend to respond to emergencies before they respond to that which is mundane or part of their regular work or activities.

So they were here to do that job, and they accomplished it. They were not able to move the entire pole to run through the Earth on the new axis line, intersecting the original pole, but they were able to bleed off enough energy from the pole so that it is now wobbling, and that has been enough. It has proved to be enough, because it has thrown the Earth slightly out of balance, which means that from that point on the Earth was unable to be solely (pun intended) responsible for the well-being of humans.

Before that time Mother Earth was very responsive to your needs, but after that she could be only intermittently responsible and other times have to look after herself. Mother Earth was not beset with this as if it were a terrible burden, but was open to going along with it, because it was explained to her and she clearly understood that in order to accelerate the growth of the human being into the responsible position of Creator, it was necessary to throw you into the arms of consequences. In this way you would have to respond immediately to many things more than you used to.

Before the Mayans were there, anyone could go out and ask for rain when it was needed. One would do it with his/her heart and love, saying, "We need rain. The peoples need rain." (When they said "peoples" in those days they meant everybody: plants, animals, stone, Earth, humans—everybody. It wasn't until recent years when it changed to mean different groups of humans.)

The Mayans were wholly successful in their job, and they left what people have come to call a calendar behind to suggest when you would be able to begin to let go of as much duty as you have been pulling, as they say in the service, "to respond to your own and the consequences of others." Look at the last symbol in the calendar. It is quite obviously a spaceship, okay? It's not a diamond. It's not a lemon. It's a spaceship. This illustrates when the spaceships started coming more regularly, which they are also doing now and will continue to do in the future.

Gradually the burden of decisions that human beings have had to make in recent years, especially the past three or four hundred years, will gradually ebb away from you. Mother Earth will be able to move her pole back in tightly, and you will have learned your lesson. Does a human being learn a lesson in forty, fifty, sixty years of life? No, no. You are all here, you are a cumulative Explorer Race. Are only those people alive today the Explorer Race? No. Anybody who's ever been here in modern times, say the past forty or fifty thousand years, is associated with the Explorer Race in some way. This involves three, four hundred years of accumulating decisions having to do with major things. "What do we do with this water? Do we dam it up, or just let it flood the place?" These are major decisions, not just, "We have only a couple dollars. Do we get butter or eggs?" So in the next fifty, sixty, eighty years Mother Earth will begin to remove—this is happening now—a lot of these decisions you have to make. The waters will travel in predictable pathways, coming out to flood only every once in a great while for the sake of purification, not of the people but of the land itself. So it's all part of an intention.

The Mayans were wholly successful, and when they had achieved their success, the ships associated with their extraterrestrial origins, coming from a distant star system, picked them up. They returned to their natural bodies or went on the ships in their human bodies, and soon discarded those garments. Before the ship left, the Mayans were in their lightbodies. All of the human material was gathered. They went to a quiet place and took the human material out again—what they had worn—and lovingly put it back on the Earth to honor Mother Earth for her great gift of providing the vessel by which you can learn creationism.

You know, Mother Earth is a spiritual master, a material master and a teaching master. She's a dimensional master and she's working on quantum mastery. (She is really quite well along with that.) "Quantum mastery—what's that, Zoosh?" It's the mastery of consequences. When you come here as a soul, also known as an immortal personality, you don the garments of Mother Earth. You are encapsulated briefly in Mother Earth's body, which means you are exposed to all the lessons and have the capacity to assimilate wisdom associated with all the levels of mastery that Mother Earth has. That is essential. How could you possibly become a creator if you are not a master of consequences? That is why, even as a child, baby or toddler, you are faced with consequences all the time.

Someone who's had a lot of ET lives and finds him/herself in the life of a little child is quite shocked to have so much responsibility so early in life and so close to being totally helpless. The people who surround you do not readily recognize your language of feeling that can be translated to some extent to basic thought, meaning a feeling of hunger. A receptive person would suddenly feel hungry for no reason while looking at the baby. If you're inexplicably hungry, you'd think, Oh, baby's hungry! But the people around you might not be that open, in which case they might get a word—"food." Feelings do not readily convert to language, but they will convert to simple words. Even then most people don't get the message, and baby is annoyed because human beings do not come with a book of instructions (whereas, I might add, beings do on almost every single other planet). Here you're not born with that, because here you have the gift of ignorance whereby you can create and re-create yourself. As a result, you have the opportunity to experience what life will offer. So the Mayans did an excellent job.

The other part of your question is, how does it relate to here [Sedona]? There are underground lakes, rivers and also a water route that directly connects from the area the Mayans occupied to this area and a couple other areas, too. One area is Tibet, and there's one more, but that's a secret. That is why sometimes people here will have dreams of sea creatures that have evolved to freshwater creatures and of pink dolphins because they have the capacity to swim here and did so in the distant past. There used to be some big lakes here; that's obvious from some of the stone formations. I don't care what you hear, the place is not going to flood in your time, okay? (Compliments to those who have said that, but don't hold your breath.)

Pink dolphins exist not too terribly far from the place that the Mayans were known to have occupied as well as places in Central America where the Mayans traveled. The Mayans had a job to do and they did it. But they had a lot of spare time, as it were, and they made it their second official job to go out and meet as many different peoples in the general region as possible.

Draw a line from the southern tip to the northern border of the state of Texas, then put a dot about three-quarters up from the bottom and draw a horizontal line across. They went that far north and throughout Mexico—what is now called Old Mexico—and Central America, all the way down into Venezuela and in some cases, into northwestern Brazil. They gathered knowledge and wisdom, and to some extent they imparted knowledge and wisdom to peoples who could gain from what they had to offer. They had a lot of knowledge about the seasons, so they had a great deal of physical knowledge. They were able to pass on to people this knowledge so that they could have some level of predictability in their lives, which in the old days was considered of significant value.

With regard to the Mayans, how did they travel?

A reasonable question. Well, they obviously didn't travel in the family limo. They got about physically. To some extent, where possible, they would travel in the sea via boats. But for the most part they traveled on land. They utilized a well-known travel method. Even today this tribal method is so simple that it is almost ridiculous. In those days a life cycle would be over in around thirty-five years, so they knew they'd need to be going great distances in a short time. They had to get where they were going and return, so they ran. If you look at some of the more ancient cultures still in existence, you will notice that not only do the people often run, but they will have ceremonies about running. It is surprising what an agile, fleet-footed person can do: how far he can go in a day, a week, or a month by running. It is quite astonishing. That's how they made it, not by any fancy ET stuff. No they honored their Earth selves when they were here.

Running is now a sport, but it was always intended to be a ceremonial rite. There are stages of feeling that can be reached only by running. Sometimes when you run you get exhausted, and if you push yourself on a little bit farther, you suddenly find yourself running by rote, as it were, without thinking about it, without noticing it. All of a sudden you realize you've gone five miles and you don't even remember having run that far. That state of being is as close as a human can get to achieving nirvana. When you are doing that which requires no conscious attention and your mind is at one with all life, you experience the totality of being; that's nirvana, you see. Of course, because you're running, you are rhythmic, and you achieve nirvana through rhythmic acts. Even the older gurus will tell you that if you want to take the fast track to nirvana, find something to do that's repetitive. Make the same motions all the time. Running is now largely misunderstood, but the long-distance runner knows what I'm talking about here.

One thing further, then. In their time of passing over, how did they go, because they took their physical bodies with them?

No. The only time they took their physical bodies is when the ships came and got them. Other than that, they would pass just like you do. You come to the end of your natural cycle and your body says, "That's enough. No more," and you exit your body. What exits, a light? Yes. What else? You see it as yourself. You look down and you're kind of a version of yourself, only usually younger, in your prime, and you go on. Suddenly it's like a big weight was removed; you're light. The personality that you know yourself to be is totally present, but not burdened with any cares or woes associated with Earth life. Oh, you might still love family members, but you won't have the burden of grief or any of that. The Mayans would die the same way.

There's so much material out there about the Mayans. I'd like to explore what you have said a little more.

The Mayan Mission to Speed Your Evolution

The Mayans were a peaceful people, but they were really a people with a mission. That's why I felt it was important to reveal that mission, since they left behind such cryptic messages. That's why I feel it's important to reveal it now.

Can you give me a time line, in terms of our calendar? What year did they come first and where did they go?

It's a little difficult, but I'll give you a ballpark figure, as they say. They became aware of their mission really about two or three thousand years ago. They were able to accomplish their mission in unusually short order, because when you really think about it, that's a tall order—to change the poles.

The magnetic pole or the pole of the rotational axis?

Not actually the magnetic pole, because that could be measured. Their mission was to torque the pole that goes through the Earth, intentionally unbalancing it. This wasn't done capriciously, but to speed up your evolution as a people and to test you to see if you were ready. Now your scientists are aware of a lot of problems. And spiritual people are aware of a few more, not the least of which is the problem of the ozone layer and Mother Earth's general condition of imbalance—to the point where the steps she needs to make to correct her situation could be detrimental to the surface dwellers.

Once you as a surface civilization can develop a spiritual science (a more complete science, or a science that has a god), and apply it, you can move that torqued pole and shift it back into its natural north-south position. (The magnetic pole is more of an energy pole.) And when that takes place, several good things will happen for Mother Earth. When that pole was moved by the Mayans, Earth immediately lost a significant amount of her energy to duplicate her body parts, if I might be that vague.

So when you as a civilization can click it back into place, she will be able to make a lot of corrections. One correction she will make, by the way [chuckles]—which is by way of saying, "Be aware, miners"—is that she will develop a very dense subsurface layer that cannot be penetrated by the most advanced laser-drilling devices, even those that are on the drawing table, those that people are imagining. This is necessary so that

Earth can reformulate her crystal and mineral veins, which, as I've said before, are all a portion of her functioning body. She will probably develop this layer closer to the surface than deep in her crust. She can then rebuild herself and no longer be susceptible to damage done by mining.

I think that spiritual scientists (complete scientists) are going to be able to do this. However, it will require a concept or model that science can produce. Science can produce a very clear picture of what's wrong. They don't always get the whys correct, but they usually get part of the why. Correcting what's wrong is where they've fallen short because, generally speaking, those who correct what's wrong do not utilize the complete picture of who and what Mother Earth is and how she functions. It would be as if an engineer working on a bridge were to make a wrong repair. He might not only fail to solve the situation, he might do harm.

This is what's been happening even in a lot of the best-intended ecological repairs. They have not been complete because they haven't involved a spiritual connection between those who did the repairs and the person (or patient) who received the repair, as in a doctor-patient relationship. We need to have spiritual people who can talk to Earth as a being, not just mentally but on the feeling level, so that they can physically feel what Mother Earth is feeling and the repair can be done in concordance with what feels best to her.

Now, this is something that falls more under the heading of a shamanic or even a priestess function. Several sensitive people can be so in touch with the Earth that they will know, by moving something this way or that way, which way is right through their empathic connection with Mother Earth. This is essential for shifting that energy beam back into its proper north-south axis as well as for any work done on Mother Earth. As an aside, and this would perhaps be most important for people whose soil is susceptible to earthquakes, such and in Japan or Afghanistan: When you are working with a good engineer and scientist, if you can get a spiritual person—a shaman, a mystical person—who can empathically feel the right place to put a footing or foundation that feels right to Mother Earth, you will not have to go as deep; or you might use a new type of foundational method that will be much safer. You will be able to put much more weight on that foundation and still be comfortable for Earth.

I'm challenging the engineers, the mystical people and the scientists to get together and begin exploring this on a simple level, such as laying the foundations for a house. Typically, foundations of houses and buildings use a square pattern. In the future you might find that foundational patterns might seem to be square, but you might also have some unexpected diagonal lines. I suggest that you experiment with it, not just saying, "Let's try this because it sounds interesting." But make sure you have a mystical person or a shaman there who can actually feel in their physical body the feelings of Mother Earth and thus know where and how deep and so on to put the footings.

All right. You're saying that the Mayans had to wake up to their mission, so they came as spirit beings and were born in human bodies?

The Initial Setbacks and Help from Neighbors

No, no, I'm not saying that exactly. What I'm saying is that they were here for a long time establishing their civilization. They knew they were extraterrestrials. They had come here in very advanced vehicles, but what was bizarre, was that most of their advanced equipment was damaged or destroyed upon landing or else would not function in the Earth environment, which has an oxygen atmosphere. Oxygen is very damaging to some materials. Also, the advanced devices and the vehicles that dropped them off with plenty of equipment either wouldn't work or couldn't be worked by anybody who had been trained on them. For a long time they didn't know what to do. Then they said, "Well, let's make do with what we've got." They knew they were supposed to build something.

They were supposed to build the shapes that the Mayans are famous for, but they originally expected to use very refined stone-cutting equipment and so on. It was not exactly laser technology, but a little more advanced than that, which would allow very tight fit—tight to the point of appearing to be welded or fused. They couldn't use that technology, so they had to adapt to Earth wisdom. They were fortunate; they had visits from other people in the region who told them how they did things. They showed them smaller versions of what they did. The Mayans had medical knowledge, they had stories, they had wisdom, they had practical knowledge of what's safe to eat and what isn't and so did the other people.

So the newcomers had a good relationship with the peoples who lived near them. But for the first 500 to 1000 years or so they were basically unable to build the structures they had come to be known for. As time was beginning to shift a little and curve, they found that they were able to utilize some of that original equipment they had brought—not the larger pieces, but the smaller pieces. They learned that they could do it if they functioned in group harmony, not only musically speaking, but empathically united on the physical and spiritual level—you know, a lot of physical union.

True physical union is not sexual, though sexual is a perfectly legitimate physical union. True physical union means that you feel a benevolent feeling in your physical body—warmth, for instance—and other beings also feel that feeling. This is not only protective, but when more than one being feels this, it begins to amplify almost exponentially. As I've said before, when two beings are doing this, it has the effect of three beings. With three beings, it's five and so on. So when they had ten or occasionally twelve beings doing this (they were able to get volunteers amongst the stone people), they were able to use their small portable equipment to cut the rock, though the artistic cuts were done in the traditional way of carving stone, and they were able to build the structures for which they are now known.

I mention this in some detail because I want you to realize that it was very much like being astronauts stranded on a planet, thinking that they were fully equipped, only to find out that the equipment they brought wouldn't work under the conditions of the planet they had landed on.

Where did they arrive from?

Let's see if I can say that now. I'll just say this: It was not Ganymede, but near there.

Three thousand years ago were there civilizations on some of the smaller asteroids or moons or planetoids in this solar system?

Well, I don't like to say civilizations; I'd rather say more like . . .

Outposts?

Outposts—that's a good word.

Where did people come from before the outposts? Who were the Mayans?

I don't think they were associated with outposting. They came here for a specific reason, only they didn't know the reason.

Did the Mayans come from the Pleiades or someplace? What is their origin?

As I said, they came from a place near Ganymede, which is a star system.

Thank you. There's a moon in this system called Ganymede.

This star system is at quite a distance. The people who come from this area always have one basic thing in common: They are explorers. The real reason that those people who became known as the Mayans came here is that it was their job to seed the explorer experience here. It was also their job to stimulate, somewhat through enigmas, by what they left. You know, you can leave little bits of yourself behind and no one will ever know, but if you leave massive monoliths and so on, people are going to wonder who you were.

Seeding Exploration for the Explorer Race

So their job was really to ground the entire explorer phenomenon. One tends to think in this age of exploration that exploring as a general human custom is something that has always gone on, but that's not so. Go back even 400 to 500 years in many civilizations, exploring wasn't being done because people were just trying to get by and in many cases exploring was taboo in one way or another within the culture. You could go this far and no farther. You could explore your immediate area—the area of your village, perhaps—but you didn't go any farther because it was dangerous for one reason or another.

Now, when the Mayans came here it was their job to invest this energy into seeding the crop of exploration, of curiosity—the burning curiosity that people are used to these days, that causes people to go to great lengths and terrific risk to explore something. That did not really exist two or three thousand years ago.

That was the Mayans' main reason to be here, though they didn't really know that. Their secondary reason was to build those structures, which they initially thought were going to be landing pads. (Not for rockets, by the way. The vehicles were beyond that.) Later they came to find out that this really wasn't the intention at all, and that these buildings functioned much more as purposeful enigma.

I might add that what the Mayans built has in most cases been flat on top. They did not build the structures that are found on top of their structures; I think that a good anthropologist would confirm that. But they were known for creating a science of their own time.

Now, most of these people left (I will tell you the percentages). They were one of the original liftoffs. But a small group of about a thousand people stayed behind. They stayed behind for various reasons: some had married into other tribes, some had become indispensible to the nearby people because of their medical or spiritual wisdom and some just loved the place. But the bulk of the people, about 90,000, lifted off. The 1000 or so who stayed behind added to the gene pool here on Earth and their wisdom affected the wisdom of other tribes.

I realize there has been a lot written about the correlation between the Mayans and the Aztecs. I'd have to say that the correlation is much less than supposed. The Mayans were very peaceful. If they needed to protect themselves, they used defense systems, but their defense, was not anything violent. They could seem to be not there—invisible. They could blend into the surroundings so that only a person of the same energy of that moment could see them—para-invisible. They had these passive methods of protecting themselves.

The Aztecs are known more for their dramatic qualities. They were not what I would call direct enemies of the Mayans, but they didn't grow out of the Mayans, either. They were beings who attempted to become more influential than perhaps was originally intended. This did not have to do in any way with the average, day-to-day Aztec but with certain ambitious leaders. (As any of you know today, an ambitious leader can totally change the external appearance of any group of people. Many people around the world today think of the U.S. as an aggressive country, but you don't think of yourselves that way because your leadership has allowed that image to prevail.) I would mainly like to loosen the ties between the Mayans and the Aztecs. There is no direct link.

How many beings came in the original landing?

Originally there were about 10,000.

So the 90,000 were . . .

Just the natural expansion of population.

So they did the regular reincarnational thing, then. They lived, they died.

No, not regular. In a regular reincarnational cycle one goes here, one goes there. These people continued to reincarnate within their own tribal group. Thus they were able to do something that is not normal to the rest of the population—they were able to remember their past lives and accumulate their experience on Earth. They could remember experiences one thousand years later (it could be a hundred or fifty, sixty lives later), pooling information from previous lives so they could be tremendous weather predictors. They would pretty much know when it was going to rain. They could guess when there might be an eclipse and so on. Therefore they could be of invaluable help to the other peoples who surrounded them, because the other peoples had a normal reincarnational cycle, meaning sometimes here, most of the time other places.

So of the thousand Mayans who stayed, how many of those were of the original landing?

None of them, of course. Think about it—the original landing was several thousand years before.

I meant the same souls.

No, none, which is not surprising when you think about it, because those who come who want to be here on the great mission are going to want to go back and talk about it.

So the Mayans went back home with the full memories of their experiences and are living on Ganymede?

They don't want me to say yet.

These beings went back and they're living on their home planet with full memory of what they did here.

Yes.

Are they part of the Explorer Race?

They were the initiators physically of the whole sense of exploring—not to suggest that there weren't individuals who didn't explore thousands of years ago, five, six thousand years ago. There were, but not as a general trait amongst people.

But are they considered part of it, in the sense of who is the Explorer Race?

Yes. They're part of it in the sense that they initiated the energy, in the sense that they put it into the Earth. And with some of their descendants, put it into the bloodstream by marrying into other tribes.

But as the Explorer Race goes on to become the Creator, are they part of that?

No. They're not part of that which will go on to the stars and become the Explorer Race.

What have the Mayans done here specifically?

They landed in what is now known as Central America. That's why in some cases you have ruins associated with the Mayans far from where people expect to find them.

Which is in Mexico, right?

Yes. People expect to find most of the Mayan ruins in Mexico, but in recent years there have been many Mayan ruins found in Central America. There is even some controversy among scientists whether they could possibly be Mayan ruins because it is so far. But they migrated.

The Mayan Calendar Stone, Pacal Votan and Quetzalcoatl

What they're famous for is the calendar information. They brought the calendar and changed while they were here, right?

Yes, they actually brought the calendar complete and they reproduced it. As you know, if you reproduce something on paper, you can't count on it to stay there. So they reproduced it very large in stone. One could say, in looking at the last symbol, "Might that not simply be the ship that's coming to take them home?" This is an interesting idea, but it isn't the case.

If you look at the calendar as being cyclical, every (depending upon how you count it) three to five thousand years it repeats itself, so you can see how that might be possible. But I would say, just touching on that theory for the sake of honoring others who have considered it, that the calendar was intended for our times. It was cut out of stone and made so large in order to catch people's attention. [Chuckles.]

Pacal Votan is said to have written some of these lost books. Was he one of the original souls?

No.

Was he one of those who stayed?

I think he was one of the beings who was trained by one who stayed. Pacal Votan is someone who was very enamored with the mystical. The beings who stayed would have been very advanced mystically. And while they might have been simply interested, they would more likely have been enamored with what is Earth and the people of Earth.

Where does Quetzalcoatl come into it, the Feathered Serpent?

Quetzalcoatl is really more associated with (and please do not jump to the wrong conclusion) the Luciferian trait of applying tools to a problem. He has to do with impatience, a desire for hands-on control and a quest for divine guidance. But if you ask, "Is Quetzalcoatl associated with a more advanced being?"—no. I'm applying the idea of the Luciferian trait here because Lucifer, as you know, was the original being who unintentionally stimulated separation by giving the people tools. It's not that other civilizations don't use tools—and tools are not Luciferian in their own right—but when Lucifer gave the people tools, they did not need them. If someone gives you something new, you might use it, then proceed to forget how to function without it. This is what Lucifer did, kind of by accident.

Was there a being named Quetzalcoatl?

No. This is a term of honor. Sometimes people refer to God by another name because "God" is so holy. This was a name given to a being whose name was considered by the people of the time too holy to be spoken. If I were to say the name you would say, "Huh?" It's not a name that you know. So Quetzalcoatl was an honorable term applied in the tongue of the time to what I would say is closer to a Martian deity— roughly speaking, a god of war.

So it has nothing to do with the Mayans.

I don't think that there's any direct connection at all, no.

It's carved all over Mexico, though.

I think you'll find that it has to do with a warning. If you looked casually at many Native American things, you would see a symbol that looks like a swastika, but it isn't, in terms of the Nazi swastika. It's the original symbol that has to do with directions, whereas the Nazi swastika is twisted and turned. It's carved all over to warn the people to beware of those who would encourage them into battle and violence with their brothers and sisters for personal reasons. For example, today someone might "drape themselves in the flag" or in a religion because of their own personal agenda to make it appear that they are a sacred, politically correct person. I'm sure anyone who observes the political scene can grasp that.

What year did the 90,000 leave?

Roughly 1500 years ago.

Instead of 400.

It has to be roughly, you understand, because time was even more curved then. There was a short period with the Mayans where time was very steeply curved, in the sense that they were able to do a lot in a short amount of time. They were able to see a lot in the future. It was like a very brief window. Allowing for that, it was roughly 1500 years ago.

And the 1000 who are the ancestors of the Mayan-looking people now—did they stay, or were they picked up later?

They were not picked up. They stayed because they wished to. They were of great service to other tribes around them or had married into other tribes. They felt they couldn't leave. They felt an allegiance to the people of Earth who were there. They wished to carry on with those people so they stayed not unlike explorers and settlers anywhere. But when they made that decision, they no longer maintained that reincarnational cycle. They then joined the normal reincarnational cycle, where you would usually reincarnate elsewhere.

But you still see groups of people who look like . . .

Yes. Especially within female Mexican citizens and in isolated places, you'll find visionaries, mystical people. It's prominent in Mexico to a lesser degree, but distinctly so, in Colombia, because the Mayans meandered about in Central America.

Changing the Pole Energies

At what point did they start and when did they complete changing the energy of the poles?

They were told about 700 years after they got here that they would need to do this to accelerate the Explorer Race's experience here.

Told by whom?

They were told by their teachers. It was explained to them very slowly why. Once it was explained to them, they were able to accomplish it in about thirty-five minutes.

[Laughter.] All right!

This gives you a little idea of how tremendously advanced they were, mystically speaking. One might set one's sights on doing something scientific that would seem to take an appallingly long time, but mystically, things can be done much faster if you have the cooperation and desire of all the elements concerned to commit to the project, meaning that the energies wish to commit to it, that Mother Earth in a given spot wishes to commit to it. That's why I'm telling scientists that if they can align themselves with heart-centered mystics, they'll be able to accomplish a great deal much faster. And they might pick up some worthwhile traits for themselves while they're at it.

Just think about that: thirty-five minutes!

If someone had that ability now . . . of course, there were 90,000 of them . . .

There are people who have that ability. It didn't take all 90,000 people to do it.

How many did it take?

Three. Not because they had the specific skills, but because it was the luck of the draw. Everybody wanted to do it, but it took only three people.

And it could also be undone in thirty-five minutes by three people who knew what to do?

Yes. These people had interacted a lot with the land. Everybody had different jobs, but a lot of the people had jobs with the land, so they knew right where to go, how to hold out their hand over the land, connecting the land and their bodies, and ask the land (meaning not only the land on the surface but straight through to the other side of the planet) whether it wanted to be involved in something like that. When they found a spot where they felt the warmest and most empathic energy from Mother Earth, they stood around in a triangle and essentially invested that energy there.

Are there buildings in Central America thought to be Mayan that are built on the same principles of mathematics as those of the Giza pyramid? And were those buildings built by the Mayans or by others?

They were built by the Mayans. You have to understand that the mathematics involved in these buildings is essentially . . . it's extraterrestrial, but I'd rather just say it's ancient. The nice thing about mathematics is that its principles lie basically unchanged, except when adding new discoveries. You don't really take anything away; it's a matter of discovering something new. (As an important aside, zero as a number is not zero, but a circle, meaning complete. For any mathematician or numerologist who wants to play with that, understand that zero is the circle, a symbol for completion. We'll talk more about that some other time.) The main thing is that when one discovers principles about mathematics, you add them to the body of wisdom. That's why a civilization can develop mathematics to a fine art when it is undisturbed for millions of years.

We do not have those exact principles now . . .

No.

... in the scientific community, because if we were to use them ...

Well, that's true, and also because you haven't had the time to develop it. Any civilization that tends to be as self-destructive as your civilization is not likely to develop that time. The intention is that you begin to revere and enjoy life enough that you will have the time as a civilization, not just as a reincarnational being.

Indian Mystics Who Assisted the Pole Torque

Directly opposite the Mayan area on the globe appear to be India. Was there a group of people there doing the same thing?

Not exactly the same thing, but something similar. In India there is a great deal of what I would call spherical wisdom. In practical application the zero is understood there and applied as a sphere. It is true that there is a great deal of suffering in India, but spiritual enlightenment is perhaps much more easily accommodated there because there is an energy in the land, an accumulated energy in the people. We might say that India has a state of mind (I'd rather say a state of heart) that allows that.

All the time that this was going on in the Mayan country on the other side of the Earth, in India there were a great many circles of mystical people who gathered. When the three Mayan beings were standing in a triangle getting ready to ask the energy to go through the Earth and come out the other side, in India there were three sets of twelve beings sitting in three circles that touched each other but didn't interlock, in a triangular shape. They were meditating deeply with an energy of welcome, love and perpetuity.

Did they know what they were doing?

They didn't know why, but they knew that it needed to be done then. You see, one of the most important principles of mysticism that any mystic must know is that it is not important to know why you are doing something that needs to be done, but to simply do it. The why is almost insignificant. If one stops to consider why, you might miss the moment in which something needed to be done. So they didn't even consider the why.

It wasn't a particular race or group of beings, just a group spiritually advanced enough to know they had to do this?

Yes, and they had some knowledge of each other.

The Mayan Calendar

So how do we look at all these people putting all of this attention into wanting to change the calendar. What was the Mayan calendar meant to tell us? It ended on August 15, 1987.

Theoretically ended. Understand that the calendar didn't end. There was a final symbol in the calendar. This is the most intriguing part, which is what scholars have looked at and said, "Why is there so much space for other symbols but there are no more symbols?" Think about that if you look at it. It's because *you* are intended to write the ending. That is clearly indicated by leaving the space. It didn't end with that final symbol; it began.

A new beginning.

A beginning in which the individual could advance the application of spiritual expression through the integration of creatorship responsibility and consequences. Normally, as you know, creatorship is associated with massive beings of one single temperament or personality, not many millions and billions of beings of individual personalities.

There are many people who now follow this calendar, which has thirteen months of twenty-eight days. Was part of the original purpose that people change to this calendar?

No. I grant that it is an interesting calendar, loosely based on the lunar calendar, which I think is perfectly legitimate. The calendar you're using now is basically used for business reasons, really no other reason. I think the lunar calendar is perhaps more realistic, more appropriate, because it puts you in alignment with heavenly bodies. For that reason I support it. I'd rather see people associated more with the lunar calendar than with the esoterica associated with the Mayan calendar as now applied.

CB Weapon Smuggling, What Can Be Done

We've been getting a lot from the Internet about chemical/biological weapons being smuggled in. Is there anything you want to say about that? Are we facing a chemical warfare situation?

I will say this: As you know, your country is, even in its current state, perhaps one of the more trusting and open countries. Citizens coming back from abroad are not automatically frisked. So it is possible, with very little effort, to bring dangerous items into this country. That's going to change, I might add. There will be much more scrutiny at the borders in the future. The potential exists for something like this happening as a terrorist act, *not* brought in by foreign nationals, but planned citizens of the U.S. The chances are about 8% at the moment and will climb to about 10% in about a month and a half, then fall off sharply.

Because this possibility exists, this is what I'd like certain individuals to do. I'd like mystical people to do what you do to encourage any organisms involved in the human beings or plants or animals to become benign. I would like and recommend that homeopathic people pull out remedies (there are homeopathic remedies for these things) and arrange them in the shape of a six-pointed star. (Make certain it's not in the shape of a five-pointed star, not that the five-pointed start is awful; it simply works as a six-pointed star.)

This homeopath should be someone who's beyond the hobby level, who can really work with the basic ingredients. Then work with a mystical person (unless the homeopath is also one) to encourage the spreading energetically of the substance within the homeopathic treatment all around and over the surface of North America. (Let's not recognize borders here.) That's what I'm going to recommend.

I do not think that there is more than a 10% chance of this happening, which means that I think that there's a 90% chance it won't, but the risk is sufficient to acknowledge. As I said, the great risk in this country is not what comes in at the borders (although there is some risk there), but what moves around freely. You can drive from Arizona to Colorado, New Mexico and New York and you're not stopped at any borders and frisked because it is the United States. That's important, and I think it ought to be maintained if possible.

Then who are these people? They're home-grown terrorists?

I don't want to call them terrorists. I'd like to say this: There's entirely too much information available now. Years ago when the atomic bomb was first utilized, the means of making it was not particularly secret. Of course, you couldn't go down to the corner library and get it, but you could get a diagram and roughly see how to make it.

Well, they pulled that out of circulation, though it was there for a while. Now with the success of the Internet one can not only download information, but can obtain information that I have to say would be better left in the hands of adults.

You have to understand something about youngsters especially, and it might be hard for some of you adults to remember this. When you're young, especially thirteen to eighteen, there's a tendency to not really think that there is a tomorrow. You can plan ahead, but it's very easy to get caught up in the experience of the moment. You're very impressionable at that age, and you might also be very curious. You might be interested simply for curiosities sake as to what might be in a poison and what effect it might have on people and what might be the ways to cure or prevent it and so on—curiosity. But if you're just a little off or if you're with people who are off—more likely with adults who might manipulate a youngster very easily—you might be inclined to do something that you wouldn't ever think of doing after you grow up.

It's pretty easy for a youngster to become suicidal, not with a death wish and not just a risk taker, but to feel depressed, to not see what the future is. That's why it is important for adults to sit down with young-sters and encourage them, letting them know that the future will come, that they will have a life and they just need to get through what they're going through now.

So this 10% possibility has to do with these thirteen- to eighteen-year-olds?

I'm not saying that. I'm saying that they are at the greatest risk of be-ing manipulated to be involved in some way in something like this, not unlike the recent guerrilla warfare where children, sometimes even younger than thirteen, were utilized in war because they are so young, not really thinking about the future. They're 100% in the moment.

I'd say to any officials involved in this: Pay attention to what's coming into the borders, yes, but also pay attention to what's moving around in the States. The biggest hazard with the Internet is too much knowledge. Most of the Internet is a wonderful thing, but there is a teeny portion of individuals on the Internet who are giving out information that is really catastrophic in its nature.

The Three Crystal Skulls

Could you tell us something about the crystal skull?

The crystal skulls we're talking about are three original crystal skulls, of which the Mitchell-Hedges is one. I'm not going to single out other people and say, "They've got a real one; they've got a false one," but I will say that the Mitchell-Hedges is one of the three and the other two haven't been found yet. This is not to suggest that crystal skulls being toured around by different individuals don't have some value. But I will say that the ultimate intention of these three skulls is to link your planet with one of the original seeders of the human race, and those individuals are lo-cated in Orion.

The skulls do not represent an imitation of the human form. They do not even reflect images associated with humanity. They are primarily in-struments that are intended to gather information and broadcast it to a central receiving point.

I'm not going to say where the other two are because they'd be so easy to find, it's ridiculous. But I will say that the other two are both on the surface. The person who has one of them doesn't know that he/she has it, and the other is so cleverly disguised that it is almost like a picture that looks like one thing, but when turned looks like something else. The reason these skulls are on the surface is because the information that is to be broadcast to Orion is intended to be broadcast from Earth's sur-face—meaning that their interest lies in the surface population.

These three crystals skulls originally had full skeletal structures as well, and they were here for a very long time. But about two and a half years ago they were transported first to Sirius, where their knowledge and wisdom was downloaded, and then moved to Orion, where they originated. The crystal bodies were intended for gathering information by sampling the emotional or feeling condition of the human race, the plants, the animals and the surface stone. But about two and a half years ago they became saturated and were no longer able to receive anything or even turn what they received into impulses. They were filled up. They won't be brought back for a long time, possibly in six hundred years, when the surface population is less and you have migrated out to the stars. The skulls themselves can actually impart information, but they're primarily intended to retrieve and transmit it. You might ask, "What is so important that these objects are to transmit? Is it thought?" No. "Is it facts?" No. "Is it an accumulation of wisdom?" Not really.

What they are sending is the prevailing *feeling*. I'm not talking about emotion or physical feelings. When the mass of the population, plants, animals, rock and humans is attuned to the same general spectrum of feelings, then the first message goes out. (It went out a couple thousand years ago.) As the feelings become more focused, meaning more specific, then the second message goes out. (That went out about fifty years ago.)

Now we're waiting (if you don't mind my including myself here) for the feeling to be synchronized with the physical feeling of love/calm. Love, as you know, can be love/passion, but in this case we're looking for love/calm, all right? In this case, the stones, the plants and the animals all have a capacity to achieve love/calm soon—I mean simultaneously, of course.

Many human beings can do this as well, but in order for human beings to do this (and this is the big confusion over the past many years), they must get past the intellectualization of love. Now, human beings might define the word "calm." You can look it up in dictionaries; the general meaning of "relaxed or at ease" is pretty universal. But then you look up "love," and the definition depends upon the dictionary. Some dictionaries might have mass amounts of information after the word "love." Other dictionaries, having perhaps a more pointed purpose or having thrown up their hands at any attempt to define such a thing, will have a briefer description. But ultimately the human race for the past one hundred years or so has been caught up in the confusion of the mind. Whereas love, as recognized amongst natural beings—meaning stone or Mother Earth, plants, animals—has existed as a single feeling, not as a thought at all.

As a matter of fact, it is not possible to *think* love. Oh, you can think the word or the definition, but it is not possible to think love, because love is a feeling. So without further ado, it is time to feel the feeling. Feeling is an experience, yes? Most people experience it as a blissful feeling, as a wonderful feeling, as a tingling feeling. That is all very well and good, but I want to get to the heart of the matter, and this is the heart of the matter: You can all do this *right now.*

Exercises in Feeling Love

Put your feet on the floor, because the floor is closer to the Earth, and Earth understands love very well. For some of you this will be a snap. Others who cannot produce it at this time can practice it at home. When you're practicing it, you can cross your arms over your chest; that's fine. You can hold your hands facing your chest, but don't turn your palms away from your chest, because that is done for protection. But putting your palms toward your chest, that's support, nurturance.

I'd like you to generate or look for a physical heat that you can actually feel anywhere across your chest or in your solar plexus or abdomen. Go ahead. If you feel the heat, go into it and feel it more. All right, relax. Those of you who have felt that heat, that is love. It is something you generate or notice on your own, that is within you. That is loving yourself. Anything else—tingling, thoughts, I-can-love-myself mantras and so on—perhaps these prepare you to love yourself, but that heat is the actual feeling.

Now, those of you who felt the heat in your abdomen or solar plexus, don't try to push it up. Let it be where it is. Those of you who didn't feel anything, practice—you'll get it. The thing about this feeling is that it's exactly what the crystal skulls are waiting for, because the animals can feel that. As a matter of fact, it's a universal greeting amongst animals, plants and stone because it does not have to deal with the limitations of language. It is a feeling by which all feeling beings can experience. Those of you who would like to do it, approach a tree, a mature bush or even a big rock and bring up the heat. Don't send it to the rock or tree. Just say, "Greetings," or, perhaps more appropriately, the natural greeting—"good life." "Good life," says you, because that gets to the heart of the matter. And notice something. (I'm not going to tell you what you might notice.) Find the right tree, bush, rock or wild animal. Try this with the wild animals, because they are pure in consciousness and are not confused about how they must behave as a pet, and see what happens.

So the crystal skulls are waiting for the surface population to have that feeling simultaneously at some point, which is why I'm doing my bit to spread this idea around. Feel free to spread it around if it feels good to you.

Understand that this is not something that you bring up and project to others. "What's this Zoosh is saying? Don't send love to others?" That's what I'm saying. This is your own love. Most of you, in the greater you, have no capacity to understand individuality. You don't have the capacity because in the larger you, you are many more things and you feel totally connected to all beings at all times and love is the natural element. But when one is in creator school (which is where you are now), one must learn about responsibility. One must also learn about consequences. The lesson of individuality is to learn to feel and to be the sum of all of your personal creations. Within that context you see things perhaps a little differently. I don't want you to hold your love in. This heat—which is the physical representation of love—radiates naturally. You don't have to go over to a fire that's burning and say, "Send that heat out," because it does it on its own. We also know, as a human being, that love naturally radiates out. How do we know this? Because you have all had the experience.

Let's say that you go into a room where there might be one person present or perhaps many people, but they are not looking at you or don't see you. Yet if you suddenly feel good, very wonderful, you know they are feeling love or something akin to it. If, on the other hand, you enter a familiar room where there is one person or many and you suddenly feel uncomfortable in this room and haven't felt that way before, then those people are feeling something uncomfortable. You, as a good human antenna, picked it up and responded to it because you have an instinctual body, which is made up of the spirit of the physical self and of the feelings, not of the mind.

The mind is the student and will always be so in your experience here on Earth. It is not the teacher. Giving your mind teacher responsibilities is a big mistake because it has to use arbitrary methods of establishing right and wrong. It has to use rules. But the physical self knows what's right for you in any moment, what is love for you.

Let's say you are walking somewhere and you are not quite remembering how to get to where you are going, but you are walking in the general direction. You're not quite sure, and you're thinking, There are three trails here. Which one goes to the place I want? I can't remember. Three trails, but which one? I don't want to go out of my way on the wrong trail. Your mind cannot know on its own.

How do you know? You use the instinctual body, which is made up of the spirit (known as inspiration in this case). It is made up of the physical self, giving you the means or the avenue of expression. It is made up of the feelings. So use your magic wand. What's the magic wand? Your left hand. That's authoritarian. This is receiving, possibly also giving. So since you are interested in being stimulated as to which is the right path, you know that when you feel the heat it is love, yet you can also use the heat to make decisions.

So here you are at the crossroads of three trails. You walk up to the first trail, moving from the right to the left because that's the way life goes. Then aim your hand outward, asking, "Is this the best way for me to go?" Or perhaps because we are doing a homework assignment here, "Is there love for me to go this way?" And you see what happens in your chest. Do you get warmth? Good. Make note of that and wait there for a while. "There is love this way, yes. This is good for me." Then you go left to the next trail and point your hand, "Is this way love for me?" You notice a little warmth, not a lot, but a little bit, and you say, "Okay, not as good as the other." Then you go to the next trail and ask, "Is this the path for me? Is this the love direction?" You get very hot and you say, "Oh, *this* is the path!" And you walk down that path.

I'm not going to give you too much, but I want to expose you to the true potentials you have, because the instinctual body does not require a logarithmic mind, meaning that it does not have to retain information. It does not require disks that hold gigabytes. The instinctual body acts and reacts according to the needed wisdom of the moment.

So when all three crystal skulls are tactically located on the surface of the Earth and simultaneously send out the same signal, it does not mean that all human beings have suddenly come into love all the time for themselves, but that human beings are feeling that warmth and love, plants, animals, stones and Mother Earth. When the crystal skulls do something, everyone near them will hear a distinct sound. It is not an unpleasant, piercing sound, but it will be a distinct hum. Some people will see pink, depending upon which skull they're looking at. Because of the disguise of one of them, some of you will see the color and not know why you're seeing it. Some will see pink, some will see green and some will see gold.

The Last Step in Creatorship

When that signal is received on Orion, it will be broadcast to all points in this universe as the final alert to all beings that you, the Explorer Race or creators in training, are almost ready to take your last step in that creatorship, which has to do with going out to the stars, bringing your knowledge, wisdom and—yes, ignorance. Why? Is it stupidity? No.

Ignorance is a gift because it allows you to re-create. Ignorance does not come from some terrible place. Creator gives you the gift of ignorance when you come here so you can find yourself and redefine yourself. But ultimately this gift is so you can re-create yourself. Beyond this school you have your accumulated wisdom all the time and it works for you. It is your wisdom—that is what you do; you never do anything differently. Why should you? You do what works. But when you are here you do not have your accumulated wisdom, so you must reinvent and re-create yourself. You then have the opportunity to make mistakes and learn, sometimes acquiring new talents and abilities.

Future Changes

Zoosh, would you talk about the changes that humanity can expect in the next ten years?

Does it have to be precisely ten years, or could it be a little more or a little less—thirty, forty, fifty? It's like this: You can't set your calendar, much less your watch, by the time these days. It's an irony that people will spend a king's ransom for the most accurate clock. Five minutes after that clock is built, it is off time—even though people will say it's exactly right—because time itself is changing. It's changing for the better, meaning that it's changing into your natural sequence of time. Your natural sequence of time is immediate. Linear and sequential time is foreign to you, but it is required in creator school so that you can experience responsibilities and consequences. After all, if you were living in vertical time, which is your natural state of being, you might not ever know a personal responsibility for a consequence, because the consequences of any act when you are in your normal lightbeing state of existence are *shared by all beings.* Thus you cannot experience a personal consequence. There's a very important distinction, very important.

So what could be expected? What is coming largely has to do with the change in being. That's why I'm trying to give you exercises like the warmth you feel in your chest, because that's *home.* Many of you have at one time in your life, perhaps many times, said, "I want to go home now. Where's home?" Has anybody ever said that? You say that because you know that this is not home; it's school. That's why life here doesn't last very long. An embodied life on some other place could easily last 2500 years, but never here, because the Creator does not require you to be in school more than a hundred years or so. He says, "That's enough. Send them home."

So time is shifting into being more homelike. That's where I'm trying to shift you—into experiencing that feeling of heat. That's love, yes, but it is also home, because that is the feeling you have when you go through the veils to the other side. You have heard from people who have made their trip and returned. More of that happens these days because people need to be reminded that life goes on. They describe that they're overwhelmed by the feeling of unconditional love. It's true. Unconditional love is absolute and is interpreted in the physical world as the heat in the chest or solar plexus—that warmth that is calming, nurturing, enriching—yes, loving. So that is how time is changing.

Time is changing into being more physical, more feeling, instinctual and spiritual. But time is moving away from mental paradigms or measurements of itself because that is false time. Really, time is very simple. Sequential time was always intended to be simple. It's night; it's day, period. That's time. If you want to build up a little bit on that, there are the seasons. If you're a farmer you need to know that very well.

This idea of what I call commercial time, marketplace time or economic time has become entirely too pervasive in your world—Monday, Tuesday, Wednesday—that's not time. It's very easy when you get caught up in false time to forget about real time, which is day, night and the seasons. And when you get caught up in false time, you become very easily distracted from your truth, your home, your love, which is the heat that is felt by all natural beings. Getting caught up in unnatural time separates you that much more from what is real and true. So time is shifting and providing you with physical evidence so that you can feel it and use the apparatus of your physical self to understand night, day and the seasons.

The coming years will be agitating, upsetting and unsettling for some because all that you have been told is arbitrarily true—dogma, propaganda, in some cases even apparent wisdom—is going to be hurled unceremoniously in your face, as if to say, "If this is true, prove it!" What you're being forced into, in a good way, is Mother Earth basically saying, "If that calendar really is time, and if night, day and the seasons isn't time—prove it!" How is she proving it? By doing things with her weather—flooding, rain when you least expect it (and that's the "dry season"). So when is the dry season? Is it a calendar time? No, it's a time according to people's senses. What are senses? The mind? No, feelings. Do we tell the seasons from some calendar we make that basically divides time into seasons? No.

As you get more connected to Earth, you will know when it is going to rain. How is it that Earth knows where to put the rain? Is it a decision like, "Three o'clock Tuesday, time to rain?" No, that's not it. It is because her body—dirt, rocks, soil—surrounds and nurtures plants that grow wild where they are welcomed. Her body *requests* the moisture and Mother Earth sends it there. *That moment* is the rainy season.

Human beings have the ability to know this, and the more you get in touch with your true feelings, the more you will know when it's going to rain, regardless of what the well-intentioned weather person says. So how do you know? It starts with the foundation, the feeling of love within you. That's why I gave you that homework.

I've given you a hint about how to make decisions using that, because ultimately it is in your nature as human beings to make decisions based on your feelings. Is it love to do that? Feel the warmth. Point your fingers; love to do that? Uncomfortable feeling, no love? Rephrase the question or ask some other time. This is how human beings were intended to make decisions, which is based upon your instincts—instincts accompanied by physical proof.

This is why the mind is constantly looking for physical proof. The mind looks at something that someone says is true, and your mind says, "Prove it." How can the mind be absolutely satisfied to know something is true? The mind has the capacity to *feel* what is true or what is love for an individual in that moment. If someone absolutely convinces you beyond any words that you can argue back that something is true, you might give up, saying, "I guess it's true," but you don't really believe it. (Because there are many, many common, everyday things that are love for everyone, you don't have to ask, "Is that love for us?") If you have a feeling, "Is that love for me? Is there love for me in that?" If the heat is there, yes, there's love for me there. You see, what's coming in the future is your natural state of being, so you might as well begin to practice now. That's why I'm giving you this homework, so that when the future comes you'll be ready!

20

Jump-Starting Humanity's Awakening

Zoosh through Robert Shapiro
June 20, 1997

T his is a time now that you all must know about. It is an extreme time. It will cause the average person to realize that since extremes are both volatile by their very nature and potentially benevolent in their outcome, one must be aware—even vigilant—about such occurrences, though not necessarily for everyone in the same precise cycle. (Let someone draw a picture of a sine wave [see figure 1] to show a cycle.) To put not too fine a point on it, it will be a time of extreme highs and lows, not for society in general but for individuals. You might feel very cheerful, even euphoric, and within the same hour possibly low and upset.

Figure 1. SINE WAVE
Actual Energy—Magnetic Resonance

I want all those of you who are aware of having the condition of manic-depressive illness to know that the lack of sympathy you've gotten over the years will be changing. Most people have had no idea what you've been going through with this condition. But now everybody will have an idea, because they're going to experience it, albeit without the accompanying long-term depression. With everybody going through extreme highs and lows, those of you who know you have this condition will find yourselves laughing up your sleeve a little bit. I'm not saying that you are all going to be manic-depressive, but that you will have this extreme situation, and this is in effect now [June 20, 1997]. It will build for another three or four weeks, sustaining itself at that extreme position for perhaps two or three months [into September], then gradually decline over the next seventeen months [November 1998].

This is what I recommend: If you are making any commitments or promises, even mundane day-to-day promises, write them down, because in the very next hour, certainly sometime during the day, you will have either totally forgotten those promises or commitments, or they might seem uncomfortable. So make commitments and promises with care. It is probably not the best time to make long-term commitments unless you are really sure that this is something you want to do. And "sure" means that no matter whether you're up or down, you still want to do it. Then it would be all right.

There's a reason for this extreme situation. It is not just the capriciousness of life, as it were, but what I would call the jump start. This jump start is intended to cause the last wave of people who are waking up to be able to do so a little quicker.

This intensity, which is pulsing on and off, affecting some people one way and other people another way, will not always come through on the same frequency. As I indicated, it is like a cyclic sine wave. But what's really happening is that every time there's a pulse— this is one pulse and here is another, equal pulse [draws two pulses, figure 2]—you have something that looks like this [draws figure 3] ad infinitum, a varying degree of pulses whose only common characteristic is a sort of cyclic sine wave.

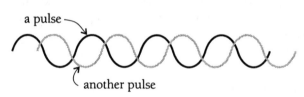

a pulse

another pulse

Figure 2

How would you define the pulses? Frequency? "Energy" is such a vague term.

The sine wave is a reasonable way to describe these, although the actual pulses have to do more with magnetic resonance.

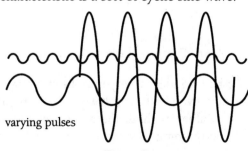

varying pulses

Figure 3

Let's call it magnetic resonance [adds titles to figure 1]—"sine wave, actual energy, magnetic resonance." In order to get that last group to wake up, we have to goose everybody at a slightly different time and way, but we must use the same energy because ultimately, the function and readout of the cycle look the same even though people are being prompted in different cycles. That's why I've drawn it as a sine wave even though the actual graph would look more like this [draws three lines to illustrate figure 4]. But the sine wave is easier to understand. The actual wave would be like this, but it's a two-dimensional image, whereas the wave is four-dimensional and cannot be drawn.

The main thing is that this urgent prompting is intended to wake up the last wave, and while they won't wake up completely, they will begin. You see, for a while there has been sort of a panic in sinister secret government (SSG) land. They know they cannot stop the spiritual awakening on Earth,

Figure 4

but they did not realize how *soon* it was coming. After all, here's old Zoosh talking about thirty-five, forty years and so on, and they have said, "Oh well, we've got time." But they don't understand that to get all these relatively unconscious people to become conscious, the people have to begin now. There's a gradual upturn in the graph of their awakening over the next thirty to forty years, every year a little more, hitting an average. Their panic has caused them to fund a lot of projects that are intended to keep humanity as dense as possible.

21

The SSG's Last-Ditch Moves to Prevent Humanity's Awakening

Zoosh through Robert Shapiro
June 20, 1997

Now, I'll mention a few of the projects because they are so blatantly in the public eye. For example, movies that are about evil aliens. The movie coming out soon, the Men in Black, suggests that Men in Black are really heroes to save you from evil aliens, when we know this is quite the contrary. Although, the film is tongue in cheek, it is appallingly bizarre that anyone would even suggest that idea.

Other projects are also being funded, not the least of which is drug addiction. I'm not saying that people who become addicted to legal or illegal drugs are relieved from responsibility, but certainly it would not be so easy for so many people to become addicted without such backing. Look at the former Soviet Union (Russia), for example. It wasn't more than a few months after the so-called freeing of Russia that crime was overwhelming. It was not that there wasn't crime before, but nothing like this.

People there are now addicted to things they couldn't even get before. They had been relatively innocent, in terms of exposure, having supposedly lived behind the Iron Curtain. But in reality the curtain worked both ways. It kept out benevolent culture, but it also kept out malevolence. With that so-called curtain removed, the people were suddenly exposed to things they were very naive about, and now you have thousands of desperate addicts over there and an economy that is pretty flat broke.

This is not an accident. The sinister secret government financed a lot of these projects to addict people. They even influenced television programming; television is hardware, but the programs are the software. Television itself can keep you dense if you don't look away from the set at least once every ten minutes. But the average person stares at a television set for perhaps forty or fifty minutes at a time, being bombarded by subliminals. Even the flash rate of the hardware is unsuitable for the brain, tending to make people less receptive. It is an interesting thing to note that if a loving couple, for example, sits and watches television for two to three hours, they are more likely to get into an argument or have less love between them than if I they had gone to dance or for a walk in the moonlight. This is not true yet for movies, but they have subliminals. Television is proven to be a more effective influence, because movies have a constant source of light illuminating the screen, and there's no blinking. It turns out that with subliminals . . .

It's a hypnotic effect.

Yes. The subliminals' on-and-off signal, even at that rapid rate, is much more effective than the steady light of the movie screen, even a five-second subliminal in a movie.

What about projection screens?

Projection screens are not as bad because they require a fairly strong light source. So if you're going to watch TV, it's better to watch projection television. I want you to realize that even with all the things the sinister secret government is doing to keep you dense, they cannot stop the last wave from beginning to wake up—and the last wave represents the mass of the people. It's important to recognize that this doesn't mean that those of you who are working, praying and doing ceremonies and rites to create a benevolent atmosphere can now stop what you're doing. But it does mean that there is help.

I want you to be aware that even though things will seem to get worse before they get better, this is a last-ditch effort by the sinister secret government to control you by any means necessary. They're not above starting a war. They're more reluctant to start a war these days, however, because they realize that when wars happen, stuff is destroyed. They don't care about people, because to them people are a means to make money—a platform, in a sense. But they don't want stuff to be destroyed, so they're disinclined to encourage a war. The might start skirmishes, small, short-lived wars, but not wars that destroy cities. They don't really want to do that, so they'll try to avoid it.

When you say the pulses have to do with "magnetic resonance," what is it resonant with? Where is it coming from? What is the energy?

The energy source has largely to do with Mother Earth, who is in her own right a magnetic body. Look at the way she spins, stays in orbit around the Sun with other planets and so on. This is not just physics; a lot of it is magnetics. Mother Earth is functioning as a go-between here. In the larger sense, all of you—the Explorer Race and people beyond that—are doing this together. You as the Explorer Race have only to allow; you don't have to really *do* anything.

This is understood, because you are so distracted. People on other planets don't have to be distracted. They can give this their absolute full-time attention, and they're not *doing* something so much as coming together to create an intention. The intention is that whatever distractions you are suffering here will be swept aside by the magnetic energy now radiating from Mother Earth and the Sun.* (You see, the sinister secret government can't do anything to stop the Sun.)

The Sun's rays are bouncing off the inner portion of Mother Earth's body and radiating outward to all portions of her body. As you know, all portions of her body means the plants, the animals, the people. Anything made up of her physical body will be affected by this magnetic resonance. This resonance is not only good for Mother Earth, but it is primarily intended to allow you to move beyond the distraction of greed.

Greed and Impatience: Afterlife Consequences

Greed is something that is immediate. There is no patience associated with it. Greed is "I want it now, I want it all, and I'm not going to wait for a second." Greed does not allow for consequences (and there are *always*—consequences) nor does it accommodate any level of sharing.

It is an interesting thing that when sometimes people who desire money, for example, say, "I'll share it with others if I get it," it doesn't necessarily draw money to them. They're concerned about being greedy, and I honor that, because they do not wish to fall into that abyss. On the other hand, for those of you who *do* want money, ask for what you *actually* want that the money can buy. That way you will not have to worry about that abyss.

For those who wish to accommodate greed, understand that there are consequences. If you want it all now and you're not going to wait another second and you're willing to do whatever it takes to get it as an individual, you will always take some of whatever that is from other people who were meant to get it, which means that you will necessarily incur some complication—either in this life or, more often in the next life or

---

* As of last November, Earth's resonance—Schumann frequency had reached 11.2 Hz, up from October's 9 Hz, rising from its long-time steady 7.8 Hz.

between lives.

It is very easy and seductive to become involved in what looks like a short way or a fast track to something—even a fast track to spirituality. "Oh, I'll take this drug," or "I've taken LSD and it opened me up spiritually." But if any drug opens you up spiritually, it will affect only this life. It will not have any effect on your soul in lives to come or lives that will expand. Thus it is not a natural growth.

It is the same thing with greed. If you take what was meant to go to others, then you must deal with that in lives to come. I'm not talking necessarily about karma. I'm talking about the fact that in between lives you will have your life review.

Let's say you are an individual who was desperate for money and got it by any means necessary. It is very possible that you will have harmed other people, intentionally or otherwise. If you did, you will have a long life review in which you will feel the harm they suffered. Although you might, as a physical person, now think, I can take it, you *can't* take it in the life review after the end of your physical life.

At the end of your physical life you will experience total love. When during your life review you feel the pain you have inflicted on others (because you must do this to learn), it is far more difficult and you will feel much more wounded, more suffering, than you would during a physical life.

Religions have tried to symbolize this to mankind for a long time. It has been difficult because religions have established dogmas, however flexible, and they're stuck with them even though times have changed, at least in terms of communication. But this is what religions were aiming at all these years—to tell you that there is a payment to be made, and the payment does not stop with that life review. After you do the review, even if you have another life to go to, you will often have to act as a guide to those individuals you have hurt. Let's say your cycle ended before the cycles of those people who were going to get some of that money that you got instead. You would have to go down there and be a guide for those people even if you had never been a guide before. This means that right after your life review you would have to take time off *before* you go to whatever life you will live next. This is true—it's not movies or fantasy. If your actions affect the children or even the grandchildren of those people, you will have to remain as a benevolent spiritual guide and learn about being a guide *while you are there* to support them in any way you can.

Now, this is actually not a punishment. It is a reward, but it forces you into a moment-to-moment exposure to the consequences of what you have done. I'm bringing this up, not to preach at you, but because it is a time of consequences. I'm not suggesting to the affluent that you are greedy, not at all; I'm not even suggesting that those of you who desire great riches are greedy. I am simply saying, ask for your *own* wealth to come to you.

Say, "I need my own money to come to me now. I need my own wealth to come to me now, and this is what I want to get with it: peace of mind and a new car" and what-have-you—go ahead. But to do other things to get wealth—especially manipulations and even stealing—is where consequences will come into play. These consequences apply not only to the individual who robs—but also to those who commit so-called white-collar crime. Know that if you become involved in this, you will have to pay the piper. It will not be a terrible payment, but it will be something that must be done *first*.

So you could say that you will need to learn about consequences.

I've said for some time now that this is a school for which consequences are available. I do not expect you all to be gods, but I expect you to learn as best you can. No one is expecting you to become creators here and now, because you are in the school of hard knocks, a place where you must learn. But try to embrace the learning the best you can, and that will support you.

That's great! So you're not talking about someone who wins the lottery, or someone who just goes bankrupt and then plans to run his life better after that. You're talking about someone who deliberately intends to defraud or to steal.

That's right. I'm talking about people who are really manipulating the books, people who are acquiring wealth they know is not theirs. But I'm also talking about people who, for instance, have fifty million dollars or, if you like, five hundred million dollars—more money than you or your family will ever need—but are still desperately acquiring money. They have to take a look and ask, "Is this greed?" They can't just rationalize it and say, "Well, it's fun." They have to really look at it and say, "Is this greed?"

The Ultimate Joke on You and the Secret Government

Okay, we haven't talked about the secret government for a long time. Is there anything dramatic? They're still all on the planet? They haven't taken off in any ship?

No, I refer to them tonight because this is what they're up to now. In terms of running and hiding, no, they're not doing that. They're still not ready to give up their real estate, if I can put it that way, and they're going to hang on until the last second. But when it becomes necessary, they think they will be able to flee.

To where?

Wherever. The main thing is that there is no way for them to flee the effects that are happening to all human beings. So even though they think they are protecting themselves from the wave forms that are helping others to wake up, they will wake up *in spite of themselves.* The ultimate joke is really very much intended. Do you want to know the real joke of it all?—when you are all awake again you will not be angry at these people and they will not be jealous of you. You will all just sit and look at each other and say, "I can't believe that you did this." Or, more likely, people will say, "I can't believe *I* did this. In such-and-such a life I swore I would never do this, yet here I am in this life doing it."

You will all have a big laugh about it. There is not going to be any big revenge. Revenge is only accommodated in the life cycles of people when they don't remember who they are. The minute you remember who you are, you realize that everything that happened to you, no matter how inconsequential or monstrous, happened for a reason. Very often it makes complete sense—and when I say "sense," I don't mean mentally. Of course, it *will* make sense mentally. You will understand it. This is not to say it's karma. It has to do with something you just couldn't understand any other way. I'm not saying it's okay to do evil things to people, just the opposite. But when you remember who you are, immediately evil things stop happening, because then you no longer accommodate such things in your life. Revenge becomes an idea, but not an experience.

But the SSG must go through something similar to the examples you just gave. What they've done is far beyond someone who has been greedy. So they must have consequences to face at some point.

The SSG's Wakeup

Yes. The interesting thing is, when they wake up they will not wake up as people do here—gradually and slowly processing it. It will probably happen in a split second. When *you* wake up, you have the chance to do this and that, to make changes in your life. But when *they* wake up, they will still be in the environment of discomfort created by who they were before, which will be uncomfortable to them. This is not intended to be a punishment, but for them to feel the consequences of their actions.

Thus they will feel those consequences while they are still alive, and then they will be taken where they will gradually go through the process of waking up again. First they will experience the pain and discomfort. Very quickly after that they will sleep (for lack of a better term), followed by a very gradual period of waking up and exploring all the consequences of their actions to all of the people, plants, animals, stone, elements—everything that was affected. They will remain physical during this period of probably eighty years of experiential time. This will take time. They will be rescued—resuscitated, as it were—but they will learn.

When you say "they," are you talking about the thirteen leaders of the inner circle, about the five hundred or the outer circle?

I'm talking about the inner circle.

Only the thirteen?

Yes, because the outer circle, remember, do not realize who they're working for. It's very tenuous. Most think they're working for some wonderful cause, and they're willing to do nefarious things to further this cause as is the case here sometimes (certainly in the past). Look at religions, for example. How many religions were involved in conversion by the sword—the antithesis of the purpose of the religion. Things like the outer circle are affected by things like that. And I'm not saying that religions are involved in the outer circle per se.

What about the ripples of the inner circle of the SSG as it moves out into the Mafia and organized crime, drugs and the rest? These people are all going to wake up?

Yes, because as it is said in that book, "The last shall be first, and the first last" [Matt. 20:16]. Simply coming here requires it. That's part of the reason most ETs have left. Waking up will be required no matter who is here. For example, even if you were born on another planet, you would still have to go through it. Physical proximity is a factor, and this wakeup will stretch out (in the examination, the consequences and so on) to roughly 200,000 miles past the Moon.

The ETs and the Wakeup

So the miners on the Moon who come from other star systems and galaxies will be affected?

Everybody. A lot of ETs who might otherwise be here and who are most likely benevolent to people will have to pull back, because they cannot tolerate the extremes of emotion. There is no technological means to prevent the effect, even at the highest levels. When it begins to happen, there will be no way to avoid it, so just before that there will be a very fast exodus of all extraterrestrials who happen to be here doing something, even if it is benevolent. They'll have to get out. It won't affect spirits, but it will affect anybody in a physical body.

But there are so many beings in physical bodies who are coming to the Moon and then hauling away material that's mined there. That will all have to stop?

That will have to stop; otherwise they will be affected. Interestingly enough, there will be a few beings who will *want* to experience the effect. They'll be volunteers, almost study projects. Here on this planet you would call them graduate students, who work on projects to see what it feels like. There will be a few outposts of similar studies like that involving volunteers who want to see what it's like. It will have a very minor impact on benevolent extraterrestrials, but they will require a great deal of training even to tolerate that minor impact. Other than that, certainly all commercial operations on the Moon will have to cease.

Timing of the Wakeup and the Time Bubble around Earth

At this moment there's no way to know in our time when that is going to happen.

No.

It depends on how we act every moment?

The timing has to do with when the inner circle of the sinister secret government is forced to wake up. I'll tell you what will cause that rather than give you a date. At some point they will try to flee the planet, though I won't say how.

Well, they have a superfast lightship . . .

I'm not going to say how at this time, but I will say that regardless of the means they use, they will not be able to flee the effect I have discussed—even if their attempt to flee does not put real space between them and the planet. Their fallback position is to flee in time, but that won't work because there is a time bubble around this place now. It's too late for them to go back or forward in time and escape.

What would they choose?

Most likely they would go back, because from their perspective they could alter things in their favor the further back they go—which is what they want to do. You know, that kind of greed knows no bounds: rule the planet, rule the solar system, rule the universe. This is because the satisfaction of a victory lasts only a short time, and then they want more. Greed is such a good teacher because the greediest individuals do not have much satisfaction with their newest acquisition. It's something they've wanted, so they go for it and go for it . . .

It's addictive and they have to get more. The more they get, the more they need.

Yes, that's right. And if they are wise at all, they will eventually realize that what they acquire does not give them satisfaction. The satisfaction is in the *attempt* to acquire it, but the moment they've gained it they need to get something more. It is self-destructive and most certainly, as you say, addictive.

Were these thirteen beings ever part of this game on Orion? Were they part of the Empire or the Black League?

No. Remember, these thirteen beings are not immortal. They are living their lives . . .

But do they have past lives where they experienced . . .

No, because if they had, they would have learned that! All of the beings whose mantle is passed on to them and who become inner-circle members of the sinister secret government have one thing in common—*they haven't had the opportunity to learn what a lot of humanity learned on the Explorer Race circuit.* They *must* be a member of the Explorer Race to come here, but most of them are new members when they're born, therefore they will not have learned that. If they had learned those things by going through those cycles on Orion and on to other planets and so on, they never would have become involved with something that is ultimately so self-destructive. Because no matter how much you think you're in control, you're still absolutely addicted to more and more power, more and more money, more and more property and more and more control. Even if you get it, you want still more because it is ultimately not enough. It doesn't satisfy you.

SSG's Overseers and the Wakeup

What about the SSG's overseers? How are they dealing with this? Have they already been already vanquished, or are they going to have to go through this wakeup?

They must go through the wakeup, and it will, interestingly enough, affect them in a much less dramatic way than the inner-circle members themselves. Because they have some off-planet roots, they will get support, however benevolent, from the place where they were born. For example, let's say they are from the past on Orion. They will get support from the present Orion. Energy will be directed toward them to ease their way and to allow them to understand the lessons, to learn what must be learned and to grasp what must be grasped in the least painful way. It is the inner-circle members who are Earthlings who have to go through every bit of it. But anybody, any ET, even a malevolent one, is not going to suffer as much, because that ET will get support.

This suggests something, does it not? It suggests that the individual who corrupts others is actually less evil than that which is corrupted! When you are of the Explorer Race, especially older souls who've been in the Explorer Race for some time, individuals have a depth of wisdom that goes far beyond their mental capacity in this life. Let's say there is a malevolent ET trying to corrupt an Earth person—and you and I know that malevolent ETs number less than a hundred on this planet. I'm not trying to make excuses for that person, but from his perspective his agenda is self-serving for himself and for his people, meaning his immediate circle of people or his government body or what-have-you. These beings are loyal to a cause, so they are, in a sense, soldiers.

Earth School for Quantum Mastery

But the person who allows himself to be corrupted, if he has had other Explorer Race lives, will allow himself to be corrupted *against his better feelings.* I'm not saying the corrupter is less evil, but that the person who allows himself to be corrupted even against his own feelings must deal more with consequences than the malevolent soldier-ET. This is because it is understood by all souls that when you come here you must learn consequences, because no creator-to-be (which you all are) can possibly function as a creator without being a total master of consequences. This means that you have to be, at a minimum, a *quantum master.*

What we have here in this school is a number of things *designed* to be thrown at you all the time (even the sinister secret government) to test you. What you do in these tests makes the difference to all beings who are here, who are ultimately going to come together and be that Creator someday. That is why you must all do it together.

I see how it's more complex, yes.

It is interesting to think about this, because it allows you to look at things a little differently. It allows you to have perhaps a more philosophical look at some of the corrupters. We know that the corrupters' effect is evil, yet if we as individuals, spirit beings and people (if I can identify with you for a moment) on Earth choose to allow ourselves to be corrupted against our better judgment, then ultimately we must take the test again. It doesn't mean we haven't passed the test. It means that we haven't performed in the test the way a creator would. A creator would expose him/herself to malevolence, but would know better than to be involved in it personally. This is how it is possible to recognize that your Creator here on Earth, who seems to allow such terrible things, is allowing them because you are being tested in quantum mastery—the mastery of consequences. Yet even though these things are here, the Creator is not affected by them, because It is a quantum master and more.

You mean the Creator?

The Creator of this place, this universe.

Our Creator, right?

Yes. One might wonder, why does the Creator allow such evil and terrible things? But the Creator *must* allow them if you are being tested; yet the Creator Itself is not affected by these things.

And that's the key. We, as part of the Explorer Race, are not supposed to be affected.

No, that's right. You are not supposed to fall into line with it. To the extent that you do and allow yourself to be influenced, you have to take the test over again. This is why uncomfortable things seem to happen over and over again until you no longer fall into the trap of becoming that which you have beheld—becoming the evil. Rather, the evil will come to you and be all around and about you, but you are filled with the love of the Creator and do not succumb to it in any way, nor does it affect you. You are not harmed by it; you do not even feel uncomfortable. It is like being an allowing creator, a white and gold lightbeing, and pink light, if you will. You have self-love and unconditional love, and you can be exposed to evil because it does not affect you or corrupt you or, most importantly, influence you. That is why I say that the corrupters are less the problem than the corrupted.

Right, because they don't have the high standards to live up to that we all do.

That's right, and they are included here to test you.

The Crime Bosses

Now, where do the Mafia and these crime lords come in? Are they new souls also who fell into temptation?

No. Very often, crime bosses are old souls. Yes, it is ironic, because the criminal families that are not associated directly with the sinister secret government do know the effects of what they are doing. Regardless how they've been taught as youngsters, if they know the effects of what they are doing by being in that "business" (they would have to turn a blind eye not to know), it is very possible that they are old souls and highly involved in the Explorer Race. This does not let them off the hook, though, and they will experience many things in their life reviews.

They are not young souls. As a matter of fact, practically none of them are. Pick just about any crime boss from among the young and the old and some who have passed over, and the one thing they all have in common is a constant state of internal conflict. I know you'd like to say that their conflict is between good and evil, but it really is more between yes and no. That is as close as most of them can come between doing what's right and what isn't.

You have to understand that they're already living by a different philosophy of what's right, so you can't compare them directly to you. But there is no crime boss who does not experience a constant state of inner conflict, even when he has "retired" (which you don't really do in that profession). Many people have inner conflict sometimes, but these people have it *all* the time. They can make the decisions they do only because they are constantly distracted.

Whereas the inner circle is not distracted. They are committed; there is no other option. This is their life?

That's right.

22

Zeta Cloning

Zoosh through Robert Shapiro
June 20, 1997

I *want to skip to another topic, depending on what you say. From a spiritual point of view, is cloning humans a bad thing? The Zetas do it.*

No, cloning does not have to be a bad thing. You know, in the past the Zetas cloned beings for a very good reason. From their perspective they were highly justified (even from my perspective) because they had, through various genetic experiments, found a physical self that could tolerate all the extremes. This means that when they refined that physical self in recent years, they knew that their primary work, their life's work, would not happen on their home planets. They knew that having a body that would be comfortable on their home planet was not sufficient, because they would be traveling and involved in experiments and trade and what-have-you, which would expose them to many different energies. They would need a body that could tolerate such things and survive on a minimum of resources, so they cloned small bodies for themselves so that they would need fewer resources. Once they got the body right, they continued to clone it.

Once that happened, they didn't say, "Okay, now you're one of us." No, no. It was a very sacred thing. They had upright machines that sort of tilted against the wall and looked like half a test tube sliced down its length. You could see the being gradually forming within liquid. Once the body was formed and the liquid drained off, something that looked like glass but was really a form of liquid crystal opened up, leaving the body standing on a platform, not speaking. The eyes were closed and did not communicate. It was physically alive but not present.

This would be the tube with the body inside [draws]. There was a second group, sacred seers who numbered three, four or five people at most. Next were members of the general population standing in this forum. The sacred seers performed a ceremony to invite the soul personality, as a gift from Creator, to inhabit that body for its cycle of life. Then

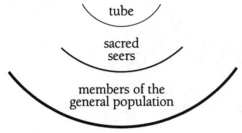

they performed ceremonies such as releasing smoke from something burning. They might create deep sounds like a chant and move their hands about. They performed ceremonies appropriate to the sacred seers of that time, which would not always be the same. There was a degree of latitude. The back row was pulled from the general population at the moment—whoever happened to be handy. They were Zetas who were present to welcome the soul.

The sacred seers performed their ceremony, then the body would begin to move. The soul personality would move into the body, the eyes would open and the being would look around. Then the members of the general population would approach the tube and help the being out of it, befriending him/her and introducing him to Zeta beings. It is a friendly accommodation. So it is very benevolent for the Zeta clones. Cloning does not have to be an evil thing if it is done in such a benevolent fashion.

What age is the Zeta at that moment compared to an adult human?

It doesn't relate, because their bodies do not age. The aging process is really a gradual crumbling, as it were. When they're at the end of their life cycle . . .

They look the same as when they're born.

Yes. Their heart just stops. But they get a warning. They will know when they are going to cease roughly three days' Earth time ahead. The sacred seer (or two or three) who brought them in in the first place usually knows at least a month (experiential Earth time) beforehand. It is not their job, however, to tell that individual if he/she is involved in a delicate job or one where someone might need to step in and immediately assist. If he/she is on a long-range job, the sacred seer would go to the Zeta council and say, "This individual is going to cease to exist within a month, so we'll need to have a replacement handy."

The body will cease to exist.

Cloning Humans

Yes, the soul will go on, as you do. This scenario springs from your question whether cloning in and of itself is evil. No, it is not. It depends on how it is done. The big hazard here on Earth has been in determining which features to retain and which to eliminate, because the physical Earth body has been chosen for purposes far beyond what current science can understand.

For example, science does not really understand what the thymus gland does. It has a purpose that involves not only the body's endocrine system but, even more important, your physical body's interaction with the auric field. When science discovers its God and becomes a sacred science, it will be able to deal with that. But it is not sacred science now, and as a result this is not a good time to get into cloning Earth people. Currently the temptation is strong to say, "Let's just eliminate these certain features" (not to say that those features will be easy to eliminate). "Let's make that our goal, because we don't see that they have any benefit."

Like the appendix.

Of course, the appendix is ultimately intended, as I said some time ago, to gradually grow to the surface, creating an orifice that is only occasionally opened to dump out toxins that can't be dumped any other way. This would allow your physical body to live a minimum of another 250 years. Thus the appendix is growing.

What happens if a particular person who is ensouled wants to be cloned?

To perpetuate his existence?

Yes.

It won't work.

Can the soul move into the next body?

The soul does not have the same objective as the ego or the conscious mind—that is the great fallacy. The soul has no interest whatsoever in moving into a cloned body, however familiar it looks or seems.

It learned its lesson. It's done.

That's right. It's done with its Earth life and knows it's going to go on. It's not going to want to stay away from embracing the Creator again. If someone told *you* that if you kissed the Creator you would move into a cloned body, you know what you would do—you'd go kiss the Creator. You'd do that and then go on. But the soul has no interest whatsoever in moving into clones, nor can it be forced. There are some beings who think it can be forced, but it can't. The moment the soul begins to exit the body, it is on its own. It cannot be affected by any technological Earth means, even any malevolent magical means. (Malevolent magic is just a tiny portion of magic. Most magic is benevolent, but there are some people who think it can be done malevolently through magic—but guess again!)

Well, see, it's hard to get into the higher perspective here and then go back to the lower view. For instance, will the HAARP project be activated? Is that an "ain't it awful," after we've already looked at the higher point of view?

We've looked at the higher point of view, but that doesn't mean that people are excused from politically attempting to raise consciousness about such things that are very corrupting. Material mastery means that you understand how things work so you can work with them benevolently. It includes the politics of consciousness, which means that you do what you can from your level to convince others of the most benevolent way for all beings. If what you're doing is marching in the street with a picket sign or standing on a street corner saying, "If the HAARP project goes into effect, the end of the world is near" or "Revelations has spoken—the end of the world is near," it is all right, because it depends on who you are and the ultimately benevolent effect you have on those who hear you.

People who were considered insane in their own time have often been considered greatly gifted in later times. For example, Leonardo da Vinci was considered to be absolutely insane in his own time, but is now considered by many to be the greatest genius of all time when it comes to his art form, which was revolutionary. So don't underestimate the guy who stands on the street corner yelling that the world is coming to an end. You don't have to agree with what he's saying, but he *is* speaking to someone.

23

Bringing Heart Energy into the Northern Hemisphere

Zoosh through Robert Shapiro
June 24, 1997

T his article says that things are changing in the Antarctic. Can you say something about that?

There are wild magnetic energy fluctuations in that part of the Earth. Those who would go there with long vision (which includes feelings and the ability to touch and so on) might find it less accessible for a time, because it is actually a protection for you. The fluctuations relate to the project you are working on [see chapter 18, "The True Purpose of the Mayans"]. All of you on Earth are getting ready to stabilize the poles, even encouraging the energy to come out of the South Pole more rapidly, flowing in a 360° pattern toward the north. This will allow the Northern Hemisphere to become more balanced in the heart, as the Southern Hemisphere is.

The restriction is actually a good thing; if you were to saturate yourself even remotely with this much magnetic energy, it could affect your thought process.

So is there too much magnetic force at the South Pole and not enough at the North Pole?

No. The feminine energy is concentrated more in the south and the masculine in the north. A lack of understanding has caused many people to believe that the poles were going to shift, but it won't actually happen that way. Instead, through various means the energy will simply become more. The masculine can impose itself on the feminine, but the masculine *always* receives from the feminine. So we need to have more feminine energy generated at the South Pole come out and flow upward.

It comes up into the Northern Hemisphere from the South Pole?

That's right. Picture the Earth as a grapefruit, with the stem on the bottom. The energy comes out there and flows upward, apparently against the laws of gravity. Gravity does not affect magnetic energy in its normal state.

Was this excessive magnetic energy at the South Pole caused by the distorted axis?

No. The energy is being generated on purpose to bring heart energy into the north, to balance the two hemispheres and to bring all of Earth into greater heart energy. This is being stimulated largely unconsciously by all human beings, and in a very few cases by certain beings in meditative circles in Tibet, Iceland, Siberia, Denmark etc. So the majority of the initiations of this southern flow, this created energy coming out of the South Pole, is being stimulated largely by what's happening in the north.

Are these groups doing it consciously?

They know what they're doing, yes.

What is the possible percentage of heart energy for a human now, and what is the average? It was 11% the last time I asked.

The possible is 80%, but the average in the Northern Hemisphere is about 16%, in the Southern Hemisphere about 28%. The farther you go into industrialized areas, the less heart energy there is, especially in the north. So for those who live in the Northern Hemisphere and want to bathe in greater heart energy, take a vacation from your industrial surroundings and go to Australia, New Zealand, South America or Africa, someplace well into the south that is also a comfortable vacation spot. Spend two or three weeks there. Remember how you feel; write it down. When you go home and no longer feel that good, look at your notes and remember the feeling, then generate it on your own; let your body memory generate it.

You can't really generate much more heart energy than is in the latitude you live at?

Most people cannot. The occasional highly spiritual being might be able to do it, but most people cannot generate and hold it while they are conducting their life. But warmth in the heart helps a lot. A northerner vacationing in a benevolent place in the south might feel that warmth in the heart without attempting to generate it. If it's someplace you want to be, you're happy to be there.

The people in the Southern Hemisphere are generally more inclined to make decisions on both the feeling and the mental level, without trying to suppress the feelings. So just living in the Southern Hemisphere gives you a tremendous advantage over those in the Northern Hemisphere during these times.

So what are we doing here?

Living, working. [Chuckles.]

24

Authority and Rebellion: Lessons from Creator School

Zoosh through Robert Shapiro
July 14, 1997

Authority is a whole issue for many people here on Earth—those of the religious world, those of the spiritual world, even those who like to be told by someone authoritative what to do so they can be sure they are doing the right thing. Why do people seem to crave hierarchical frames of reference? You might ask that, because on other planets it is foreign. People are not rebellious on other planets, yet they do not seek the voice of outside authority. One finds that there are many independent people here on Earth, many of whom have done great things—who have heard that something is impossible, yet go out and do it. There are many famous stories in the area of technology, but certainly philosophy, medicine, healing and all kinds of areas are famous for people like this.

Why do so many cling to the experience of the voice of authority? *It is part of your experience as the Explorer Race.* It is the challenge. It is not exactly the gauntlet flung in your face, but the challenge put to you by Creator. I will tell you exactly why; this is Explorer Race material. Creator knows that when you get to be Creator, you will have many skills, opportunities and desires about what you might wish to do and how you might wish to provide for beings. However, the biggest challenge you will face as a creator is to be looked on as an authority, to be considered a great god to whom the people are nothing but little beings compared to you.

When a creator allows itself to be deified in that manner, it will immediately lose all perspective of its true responsibility. And a creator's true responsibility is always to pass on its skills and abilities to those citizens, to those beings for whom it is responsible—in other words, as the native mystical people say so well, to pass on the stick, to give you what the Creator itself is composed of. Creators who are deified and allow themselves to be deified might just as well put themselves in a tiny little box and close the lid, saying, "This is my world, and I'm happy with it." It is necessary to understand this, because the challenge for you as the Explorer Race is to see past this.

You can go anywhere all over Earth and find some of the most beautiful religions and philosophies that can be found anywhere. You will also find some that are not so beautiful, that are in fact hateful, meaning that they say terrible things about other people who are not a member of that religion or philosophy, or hateful things about other religions. The minute you hear that from any religion, no matter how well-intended that religion or philosophy is, you must know that that religion or philosophy is flawed. And if it is flawed, it is not what you are looking for if you are a member of the Explorer Race who is literally attempting to cocreate with Creator.

Your true Creator would never judge any single one of you in any way. He/She would never say, "I am this wonderful being, and you are . . . who?" Creator would not speak to you in such a way, but if you look around you will see rebelliousness toward authority, and sometimes it seems annoying. Children become rebellious toward their parents when they are teenagers and so on, and while this is annoying (often for teenagers and parents alike), it is *intended.*

You might ask yourself why the hormones in the body of human beings actually cause the youngster to become more rebellious around the age of adolescence. The psychologist will say, "Certainly, the child needs to create its own identity so it can be separate from the parents" and all that, and while all of that is true—I'll go along with that—there are actual chemicals in the physical body that are forcing this. Creator has deigned to see that these chemicals would be in your body, because the Explorer Race human being here on Earth is raised in such a way that he or she would be a follower absolutely marching to the beat of the same drummer all over the Earth if there weren't something to pull you up short and say, "Wait. Look. Stop. Maybe there's something else."

Adolescence is not a hellish experience, though it might seem like it sometimes for parents and teenagers. It is a gift from Creator, saying, "Wait—look—stop—see—think—feel—consider—do" in exactly that order. The reason is that Creator does not want you to be only the extraterrestrial loving being that you are in other places. This is finishing school. Although you won't go from here to be a creator, it's *finishing* school—and the first few grades of any school (as anybody who has ever been to school knows) are the toughest.

These are the first few grades of finishing school here on Earth that you're going through right now, and it's the toughest, because nobody tells you what to do or how to do it. You don't know what's the "in" thing to do, what the other kids are doing. It's like going from grade school to high school. You don't know what's expected of you, and you're nervous and upset and afraid you're going to make mistakes, and you do.

Here's what you need to know: The experience, the desire, the addiction to outside authority is meant to draw your attention to the fact that there is something within you saying, "Wait, stop etc." You are intended to create in this life. You are not intended to create things that destroy, that hurt, that maim yourself or others, though it happens because this is a polarized world. You must learn absolutely that you have responsibility and that what you do generates consequences sometimes far beyond that which you intended. In a world like that, you can always tell you're in creator school.

I'd like you to recognize that there was this desire to hear the authoritarian godlike voice, whether in the form of a wonderful, benevolent, loving being or the form of a despotic being like Hitler or Stalin (as he was certainly in the beginning and in many ways right through to the end; I'm picking out these men because they are men who are well-known and -understood in your times, not that there aren't others now). If you are a follower, you might very easily follow the beautiful, loving words of some wonderful being, but you might also follow the words of Hitler and believe that what he says is true because it makes you feel good. Doing what he says, since all of your neighbors and friends are doing it, must be a good thing, yes?

That is exactly how most of the German people got caught up into this thing (ruling out the whole economic thing, if you understand where they were in their social history). I'm not saying they were monsters. I'm saying that they were like you: They wanted someone to tell them what life was about in a way that they could love and adore that being, whoever it was, and see the truth in it even if it was a total lie. I'm bringing this to your attention at this time because this issue is up now. It needs to be understood by you all.

I'm not saying that Jesus or the angels or Archangel Michael are bad people, not at all. What I'm saying is that if they were here, they would put their hands on your shoulders, look you right in the eye and say, "You are like me. There is no difference except that you are in school, and it is my job to help you through this school." They would say that.

They wouldn't say, "Follow me and I'll show you how to live." *Never!* So when you hear someone say that, even if it is old Zoosh testing you from time to time, you say, "Wait a minute, Zoosh, I want to go my own way."

We want to shine the light behind the scenes and expose certain things so that people can be conscious and aware of them. The more people who are aware of them, the less likely those things will be influential. We also need to remind people that there is something going on in the larger picture. How can organizations like the sinister secret government be successful? *Only because people are looking for the voice of authority outside themselves.*

There is electronic mind control on this planet. I read something today that says that there are eight layers of it. Can you talk about how the control works, how it affects a human—the body, the mind? Is there anything we can do about it?

I'm going to talk about what to do about it first. It's true there is mind control, but it's not the kind of mind control that puts thoughts in your head, though people who are experimenting with these programs are trying very hard to do exactly that. It's more like something that tends to stifle certain creative elements within you, tending to set a mood more than shove a concept into your head. But they cannot have any direct effect on the feeling body, which is why it's necessary for people to come into more awareness of the instinctual body, as Speaks of Many Truths* talks about and will teach about at length—your gut feelings.

While gut feelings might be different for different people in different circumstances, they're still very important. I'm not going to say that you should follow them in all cases, because sometimes your gut feelings are based on your anger, your resentment, your rage and so on. But your gut feelings are an example of what the feeling body can do. When you have angry feelings in your gut, as it were, yes, you need to do something, but it doesn't mean hurt yourself or somebody else. It means to do an anger exercise like Zoosh or others have talked about, something that is constructive—constructive violence, as I've mentioned in previous books. [See page 12 in the September 1996 issue of the *Sedona Journal of Emergence!* for an exercise on negative energy.]

Now, because your society is so overinvolved in the mind, in controlling the mind and regulating it and so on, most of the research that goes into mind control is geared toward adapting electromagnetic energies to

---

* Speaks of Many Truths is a Native American in southern Colorado who communicates through Robert Shapiro from his own time (around 1575, when he is in his sixties, which is very old for his time), using what he calls long vision. He is currently giving information for a book that explains how to attain material mastery with certain shamanistic techniques. The book will be available in spring 1998.

the median brain waves of average people. ("Median" means they'll take an average, a spread within a certain brain-wave pattern, and broadcast that energy, attempting to create effects such as sleep that this natural pattern might create for you. It is possible to broadcast an electromagnetic signal that would tend to encourage someone to go to sleep. If you're not sleepy, it might make you just a little more relaxed. If you tend to be drowsy, it might make you want to lie down and take a nap. People who wish to control you use brain-wave patterns in an attempt to influence you. You were saying that there are eight layers?

I'm asking.

You're saying that someone has received and put out this information, which is very useful. But understand that all of these levels or layers, to the extent they exist in any given place at one time, are invariably built upon that idea of people wanting someone to tell them what life is about. They're built upon the philosophy, however false it is, that *people want to be led.* It's as simple as that. Certain individuals believe that people want to be led (and they can give you a lot of history to show that this is true even though it isn't, though it certainly appears to be), and that is why they utilize such technologies.

Control through Subliminal Technologies

On one hand, such technologies could be used very benevolently and beneficially to create health, such as creating a certain signal that would tend to dissipate disease, discomfort, unrest. For instance, in a prison it would be possible to broadcast a signal that would tend to keep the prisoners *and* the guards and staff calm, enabling them to interact together comfortably. It would be so comfortable that after a while these people would simply have a big wall and function independently within this walled fort. They would be given things to do for themselves. They wouldn't need to be in cells; they wouldn't be violent. It is possible to broadcast such signals that do not harm individuals.

So mind control started out in a fairly benevolent way. It started out as something that might be passive security—not chain-link fences or barking dogs or guns, but something that sits fairly gently upon the land. It would tend to create a mood in those who approach whatever you want people to keep away from, some mood that would cause them to turn away without injuring them in any way.

Secret Mountain, Secret Canyon?

Yes, those of you who have been living in Sedona or other areas where there are government installations or installations not associated with your government, will have a pretty fair idea of what this is. It was not such a terrible thing because people were not usually injured. Generally it would simply keep people away and not harm them. It's like a toy, you know. You give a child a toy, and if it is a ball or something simple, the chances of their hurting themselves or other individuals are minimal. If you give a soft toy to a child, it won't hurt itself or others too much. But if you create a challenge—if it is an instrument or toy that has multiple potentials and you set it on one level of the dial and give it to a child—it's like, "Oh, this is wonderful," but the child soon wants to know what the other levels do.

That's very much the kind of instrumentality that individuals discovered who were not only in security groups but, more important, in groups that research these security devices. "Oh, if we put it on this setting, people might just become stimulated. They would do their work better, work harder, produce more and be satisfied with a job well done." I don't have to tell anybody in manufacturing that this would be a wonderful thing for the manufacturer—if not necessarily for the workers, who might ultimately work themselves to death. But the seduction (that's why I'm trying to make this clear) of this kind of instrumentation is such that anybody who has this kind of technology *might* use it benevolently—but they might also use it in any productive way even if that production is malevolent.

I don't have to tell you that it was gradually discovered that you could influence people with it, that you could use methods that would keep people addicted to certain things. We all know that years ago subliminal messages were projected onto a movie screen: "Buy popcorn" and so on—that famous business. In those days it wasn't particularly successful, but subliminal messages had not become as sophisticated as they are today. Some people wanted it outlawed in this country; other people said, "Well, it doesn't seem like it's really causing any harm." People in the background lobbied to make it legal but not talked about, because it might be used for military or defense purposes and thus ought to be kept secret. It happened exactly like that, the way I'm speaking it. It really was kept in the background, and of course, one of the levels of mind control, as you all know, is subliminal messaging.

On TV and in movies?

On TV, in movies, in print.

Print?

Subliminals in Sound and Print

Yes, it can be done in print. Certainly on radio. It can be done on CDs and so on, anything where you have a medium upon which a signal is imprinted. It's highly complex, but it tends to use the signal that is believed to work, and to some extent does. I'm not going to give any improvements on this technology (I'm treading carefully) that tends to open the mind to outside influences. The technology first gives that signal digitally (it works best digitally, but I'm not revealing anything new) and then implants the idea.

So the violent songs go right into the head?

Not necessarily; if you go in person to hear a band and it is using acoustical instruments and singing, not electronic instruments, that is entertainment. But not if there's anything electronic. It could be consciously inserted electronically by individuals who are curious or who want to try it, considering certain individuals' influence in electronics in general (the sinister secret government has some influence there). Generally speaking, if you hear a musician on the street playing a guitar, it's safe—stop and enjoy it, no problem. But if you hear any form of recorded media, it is possible, though not in every case (probably not more than 15%), that someone has inserted a digitized signal believed to open the mind, then put a message through.

The message might not be the music at all. It would probably be like this: You start the tape or the CD, and slightly before the music begins there is a little blank space, as it were, a little quiet spot. It might have to be measured digitally; it might be so quiet that you don't really hear it, and the music seems to begin right away. But there's a little space. It is possible to broadcast a signal and follow it with the message even before the music comes on.

The Successful Influence on U.S. Voters

For instance, here's one that's been very successful: "What's the use of voting? It doesn't count, anyway." Now, you might go out on the street with a microphone and a recorder and ask Mr. and Mrs. Average Citizen as they come by, "We're interested to know whether you vote or not, and why or why not." That's all. Allowing for the fact that a lot of people would be shy or ashamed to say they don't vote, eventually you'd get some people who would be forthright and say, "What's the use of voting? It doesn't really count anyway."

If you hear that once in any one of those surveys, you'd hear it many times, but you'd represent it only once if you were a journalist. That belief has been implanted pretty successfully, although it has not been successful entirely in its own right. There are other reasons people might have for that conclusion. Certainly there are historical reasons and cynicism [see *Shining the Light IV*, chapter 44].

But there are successes that you ought to be aware of. It's interesting, you know, to go to a Third World country where voting is new and the people want to vote. When the opportunity comes to vote, 97% of the people vote if there are no restrictions. They vote if it's the last thing they can do, understand? Their motivation is strong. It is true that as time goes on it might pale a little, but you don't get turnouts there of 15% or 12%.

A lot of people will say, "Well, I just didn't have the time." Or they'll seem to have excuses. But this "What's the use of voting; it doesn't really matter anyway" has been pretty successful. This has been implanted by the sinister secret government. I might add, however, that it was implanted right around the later fifties (the mid- to late fifties) in this country as an experiment by people who thought it could not possibly influence people not to vote. They were particularly interested in the demographics. Were they young, middle-aged, old? They thought they couldn't possibly influence the older people from voting, because these people cherished the vote and so on. They were surprised and shocked that it had a significant influence. That's really what got subliminals going to the extent they are being used now.

In the case of voting, you're talking about print, radio, TV, movies—it's in all of them?

Yes, the media. It is more difficult in print, but it's possible. The main technique in printing is using the white space. Pull away to look at a page (this can be done on a computer these days), then remove the print and look at the space left over. Does it suggest anything? For instance, you might have the rough suggestion of a question mark, something like that. If the article is about why people don't vote or "let's get out the vote; the candidates are worth voting for," you might pull back and see a question mark. That's a strong subliminal message. I'm using that only as an example.

On the other hand, you might look at the spaces between the letters, which is sometimes used. Remember that the brain, at its deeper levels, does not require that print be sequential and logical. The word can be backward, upside down or diagonal, as in the type of puzzles that people sometimes like to do. The mind will easily be able to assimilate it even if the word is jumbled.

I'm not saying that you should cease and desist all contact with media. If you pay attention and concentrate on the words, especially if someone in your home is reading to you, it's not a problem. But this is something to think about; I'm putting it out there because I think it is worthwhile. It's true enough that you can certainly broadcast signals from satellites and justify experimenting with electromagnetic fields on the general populace by saying, "Let's just see if it works. We're not going to *do* anything with it." You might believe it when you say it, not realizing that there might be others who would be happy to do something with it. When you're doing research like this, *always remember who is paying for the research.* It's truly there now, so let's come back to what you can do about it—unless you have questions about it.

I wanted to know other levels. There's microwave, satellite, media, ELF waves . . .

There's all of that, but don't forget one of the most important levels—in fact, the most influential level of all—the person who has in some way become convinced of the validity of the subliminal idea "What's the use of voting? It doesn't matter anyhow." If people have been convinced of that, they are the final and ultimately most influential layer of all. If youngsters go to high school and are about voting age, and if somebody they trust or feel good about says, "What's the use of voting? It's never helped us," they could be influenced. They could be influenced ten times more than any subliminal message could ever impact them even in a cumulative way.

Because it's like a voice of authority?

It's a voice of authority or voice of someone they care about or trust saying that to them. If that person says it to them—I'm not talking about teachers, but other people—that is the most damaging level of all. I want those of you who think this (What's the use of voting? It doesn't matter anyway) to examine it, not trying to figure out whether voting matters, but to examine whether you really believe what you're thinking. Could you have assimilated that from someone? Consider other beliefs that fall under the label of some kind of cynicism—or, most important, beliefs that relate to addiction, such as "once you get on it, you can't get off." I'm not saying that you can get off easily, in the case of addiction, but you *can* do it.

Subliminals Used by Manufacturers and Government

What are some of the other messages?

That's one of them. I wanted to put that one out there because it's so common. The most regularly used ones would be for products. Here is a typical message that might go out: A product is shown and the message impacted there might be "good for you," regardless of what it is. People like sweets. I accept that. [Chuckles.] Years ago people who sold cakes and stuff to children would say that they were good for the children because it gave them energy at a moment when they needed it. They would say this forthrightly, openly, you know, no subliminals. Scientifically you could prove that that was so. Nowadays people do not say that openly, but it could still be proved. Yes, sugar stimulates your endocrine system and you will have energy as a result.

And then you'll crash?

Well, you might, and you might have other side effects. Aside from that, manufacturers are not evil, but they were given a tool they could use, and it worked—for many (10-15%) of the largest manufacturers, especially. You know, when your company gets so huge (I'm talking about international companies where people tend to become more faceless), the idea of using such techniques can be justified by the bottom line rather than by morals or values. In a smaller manufacturing company you're more likely to look at morals and values, but the usual value in the larger corporations tends to be the bottom line.

Here we get to a point I made before about the Explorer Race. I told you that your first world order would be based on the corporate model. That is so at this time and is becoming more apparent to you as time goes by. Business conglomerates have replaced what used to be the neighborhood bank. They have names you've seen in magazines but never thought you'd see in your town. As things like that happen, you become more aware that there's some vast corporation out there. Knowing this, you must strive to the best of your ability to be someone with a face. With the larger populations you have on Earth now comes the necessity (and I agree with this) for homogeneity, meaning that people must be able to get along in some way other than strictly tolerating each other. There have to be common causes you hold dear, I agree. Yet it is all right to keep your individuality within that homogeneity. If everybody at your school has to wear a uniform, you can wear a little pin on your lapel (even if it's only the inside when they don't allow pins). Be an individual *and* get along with others.

So we've got manufacturers and the secret government. Who else is using these techniques?

Authority Figures

Well, I don't want to isolate manufacturers. Certainly governments might use them. This is much more the case in other countries. Countries outside the Third World might be inclined to use this technology because electronic media in general are more available. Other countries might be more inclined to keep the messages more direct, using authority figures—the president, the council, even the policeman in the neighborhood—to say certain things. They've been told to say it to the people to keep order or they've been convinced that these things are true. Very often they *are* true, but sometimes they might not be, and are simply an attempt to influence people. People might be told, "You should be happy to be in this country because in" (fill in the blank with the name of another country) "it's impossible, the people are awful and you'd hate it there."

That is particularly useful in Third World countries that are up and coming. In this country you might have an elected official who talks about some country being a menace (in the recent past especially). Now that the corporate model is coming in more, you don't hear quite as much about the "Red menace." One might ask why not, because there are still countries that practice communism. It is because the United States is embracing economically, with as much fervor as possible, the largest communist country in the world [China], yet at the same time rejecting, officially hating and attempting to corrupt or do whatever it can to harm one of the smallest communist countries in the world—Cuba.

The Challenge of Organized Crime

When I say the United States government, I do not mean most of the workers in the United States government. I'm talking about official policy behind the scenes, secret policy to some extent. The secret policy behind the U.S. government is to "get Castro out of Cuba," which is their way of saying "get communism out of Cuba." The people who were influential in Cuba before Castro (although they talked about Batista and all this stuff) was in reality organized crime. The United States has been in league with organized crime behind the scenes (not up front, not your day-to-day elected officials) ever since World War II. You could say there was influence before then, but the bulk of it happened as a result of World War II, which I've talked about before.

Organized crime was particularly influential and helped save a lot of lives when the U.S. and the Allies had to go into Italy and Sicily. So the U.S. made some agreements behind the scenes—not the government or people you have now, not the President of the United States, certainly not the senators or the congressmen. They didn't make an agreement to cooperate with organized crime, but agreements were made with certain individuals (I'm not going to name names because descendants still exist today) in organized crime families that "if you do this for us, we'll do that for you." Even today there's a certain amount of this still going on.

I'm going to tell you something about organized crime that's ironic. Organized crime is now a highly corruptive influence. However, it was actually intended to be something else. Those who have been affected by or involved with organized crime cannot see it now, but ultimately it will turn into something else as it expresses itself on its higher level—the adventurer; the artist that goes the other way because although the way the whole crowd is going is okay, they're missing something; the inventor; the creator.

You might ask, "Why does Creator allow such influences?" Is it because Creator wants to taunt you or challenge you? Creator would never taunt you, but Creator would very often challenge you, sometimes seemingly beyond your capacity to react. Organized crime, even disorganized crime and highly organized crime (as in the sinister secret government) are all here so that you would learn how to change yourselves and ultimately how to change what you need and want. The human being is a sponge, to use your term. It is intended that you be a sponge so that you can *feel,* because ultimately it will be through your feelings that you will trace the means by which you can change all things. We will soon go into this at length at some point.

It might seemingly be an impossible task if you are a police officer, for instance, but even if you are an individual police officer or something else, you can utilize what I call benevolent and ordinary magic. There is nothing too strange or fantastic about it. It is what I call a *living prayer,* where you ask for something, make certain gestures, run certain energies and then it happens (I don't want to go into that right now because it's out of context)—things change, people change. The reason Creator allows organized crime and so many awful things here that you suffer from is that ultimately *you must learn how to change what cannot be changed any other way.*

Applied Love

What will you do if you are a creator and discover that one of the worlds you haven't been paying much attention to (you've been busy with your favorite projects), something you created a long time ago, now has people fighting other people and doing terrible things to each other? You ask yourself, "How could this have happened?" Do you go there wrathfully and destroy the place? Certainly not, absolutely not. No true creator has *ever* destroyed anyone or anything—never forget that. Instead, you put your attention in that area and work with the people and their guides and teachers to help them remember the benevolent magic, which is love—the application of the energy of love. Then things change in time.

How could you possibly be a creator if you react to a circumstance by saying, "I am your true god. How could you act this way?" and smash things or destroy the world. No creator who has ever been with you at any time on this planet has ever done that. I know that I'm flying in the face of what it says in the Bible and in religious documents in many places. (If Mother Earth is offended by your behavior, which might be your behavior to each other, she is certainly allowed to exhale her waters upon the surface, and Creator will sit back and allow it.) What I'm trying to tell you in a roundabout way is that God is not jealous, authoritative, superior, judgmental—none of those things. God, true Creator Itself *and* the creator in you, is love only, certainly in application.

I'd like to get a little more explicit. Obviously, love will mitigate mind control, but what specifically should people do? When they feel a thought isn't theirs, they should see how they feel? Can you give more things they can do?

Yes. That exercise that has been given about the warmth in the chest and in the solar plexus—I've probably said that many times and Speaks of Many Truths has said it also—include it [see box this page]. One of the most important things is the foundation for training the instinctual body. It's homework, in any event.

• Practice feeling love as heat in the chest. (You can use your hands over your chest to help focus energy.)

• When you can hold this warmth, add the feeling (not visualization) of gold light.

• Keep practicing back and forth until you can feel both at the same time, and hold it for at least 10 or 15 minutes.

• This is alchemy, and can transform any discomfort that arises for you. You will feel ecstatic, it is the closest feeling to the Creator energy that you are.

(For the full exercise and commentary, see page 383ff in *Shining the Light IV* and a simpler version of the Heart Meditation in the following chapter on page 198.)

That's the most important. If people, no matter how desperate their situation, can have that feeling within them, they can improve their lives. Just by feeling that, they will potentially improve the lives of others, not by radiating it toward them, but because love and warmth naturally radiate. That is one of the most important ways.

Sacred Recognition: Seeing Creator in All Things

There are other ways. Another is to pick out any portion of your body that you like and thank that part. Remember that Creator is responsible for the shape of your body. Yes, your soul is responsible for some of its details, but ultimately Creator is responsible for your body and how it looks. Would you despise Creator by despising your own body?

I think everyone could find a part of their body they feel good about, even if it's their hands, you know, because you can touch things that feel good. Thank that part of your body, and when you're thanking it, know that you're talking directly to Creator. It's necessary to begin to look at your world with eyes that see it as something sacred—that a tree is someone, that a blade of grass is someone, that an ant is someone, that your next door neighbor is someone, that your wife or daughter or husband or child or son is someone and that you are someone. It is essential to begin doing this, because to the extent that you despise yourself or others, that you hurt yourself or others, you are spitting in the eye of Creator.

Now, I'm putting it to you point-blank like that because I know that many of you are strongly religious or philosophical, meaning that you believe in many of the valuable principles that religions espouse. Many of the principles are valuable, such as treating others the way you would like to be treated. That's wonderful, yet how often do you despise your own bodies or the bodies of others? How often do you get angry at that old tree stump when you bump against it? You could say, "But, Zoosh, that tree's been cut down for years and years; it's not alive anymore." It is alive. *Everything* is alive.

Homework

If you can understand that everything is alive even if it's been manufactured into something else, then you can begin to see the Creator in all things, in all beings. Ultimately that's why I want you to find a portion of your body to which you can say thank you. Stroke it, pet it lightly with some other portion of your body, gently pet one hand with the other, saying, "Thank you very much," stroking it as you might stroke a dog or a cat or a lover. That way you officially recognize the beauty and love of the Creator, which is absolutely you as well as the mass of Creator Itself. You must begin, because to continue self-despisement or destruction of the self only leads you back to the beginning.

So no matter how impossible a situation looks, ask that it be changed into a situation that is more benevolent to you. Fill in the situation, saying (you can talk to God if you want to), "God, this is the situation." If you're not a believer in God, you can ask the universe (whatever you want), "Can you change it into something more benevolent for me?" Or some might want to say it this way: "I need to have that changed into something more benevolent for me." Those of you who are working with groups can say, "We need to have that changed into something more benevolent for us."

Now, I can't guarantee you that that will work. But let's say that a family—Mom, Dad and the kids—is suffering, maybe living in a car or forced to move out of a nice house into a little cramped apartment, just toughing it out. Get together and say out loud, or have everybody write down, how it is for you now. Then everybody reads what everybody else wrote about what the situation is, the problem. Afterward you all say together, "We need to have this changed into something more benevolent for us." That could work.

Begin by saying this for yourself, because ultimately your responsibility is you. That's why you are in a physical body; that's why you have a survival instinct. Don't turn a blind eye to the way things are physically. You are created the way you are for certain reasons. It's not an accident that you can't stick your head into a tub of water to drown yourself. The body, even if you become slightly unconscious, will pull your head out of the water. Your body has a built-in survival instinct because *your body is your teacher and it's trying to show you the ways of the Creator.*

Remember, by the time you get here to this planet you will already have had many lives. Your soul has its deep conscious memories, and some of you will continue to wage war or have enemies or lovers with those you've been lovers or enemies with in other lives. But that can all change here, because your body is made up of Mother Earth's body, and she is a wise being indeed. Her body was created by this Creator in whose domain you live.

It is intended that physical life show you, yes, your responsibility; yes, your consequences; and, yes, your rewards—by utilizing the physical self, by honoring your physical self, by learning how your feelings work so you can work with them for your own good and the good of others. In the coming months either myself or Speaks of Many Truths will talk to you about this in more detail so that you know how to function with the instinctual self, as Speaks of Many Truths might say, or with the vertical mind, as I might say.

25

Unification of Heart Threads Begins

Zoosh through Robert Shapiro
July 22, 1997

I've been talking recently about people getting connected. In the past I've said that on other planets people are connected to each other—all beings connected to all beings—because they are benevolent, and the warmth and love is there for all beings and it is safe to be open. Yet here on Earth, in this school for the Explorer Race, it requires a different system. You can't suddenly just open. You can't have your love—your actual total, complete love available for you—poured into you so you can open to all beings. You can't do that because everybody has his own levels of discomfort to comfort and this ratio there varies from individual to individual. However, there is a system now functioning where for about the past few weeks everyone has freely been sending out threads to everybody else's heart. ("everybody else" means on this world). All humans are sending out threads to all other humans, animals, plants and stones and Mother Earth. These are not the same threads you have to spirit; those are intact. This is something new, and they all connect with each other's hearts just a little bit.

This is why some of you who are sensitive have been feeling discomforts for no apparent reason and equally those of you who are leading a more difficult life have even been suffering. At times you will feel a little better for no apparent logical reason. This is because the unity between all beings must begin on a gentle level to prepare your physical and spiritual bodies for such levels of unity as will evolve over time as life and society become more benevolent here. I'm putting that out now as a brief message because I want you to understand that this connection between life and life forms is guaranteed, yet it is necessary to begin slowly.

This is different from a spiritual meditation or group that gets into a benevolent state and unifies their heart and love energy. This is a beginning of a unification as you are, essentially a test to see if you can ignore the pain and suffering of somebody else. Now, it is obvious that you as an individual cannot alleviate all pain and suffering of all beings all over the planet by yourself. But this is what I'd like you to do; I want to give you some homework. It is simple homework and, as I like to say, it's cheap and simple, so maybe you'll do it.

Heart Meditation Exercise

Sometime when you are focused on your heart or doing a heart meditation or a loving meditation by yourself (we don't want to include this into a group activity without the group's knowledge or permission). When you are focused in the heart and can feel the heat or the love or both, I'd like you to do simply say out loud while you are feeling it (it's a bit challenging, but you can do it), I'd like you to say, "I give all beings permission to be of love, to be fed, clothed, healed, and comforted." That's it.

I want to keep it simple, and you can add other things you feel might be appropriate. Don't say anything like, "I don't want people to feel . . ." —you can't do that. Encourage them to feel and say something benevolent, because manifestation works on *what is* and what is desired. It does not work on what is *not* desired, at least not so well.

A Momentary Interruption

This is a comment for this moment tonight. Scattered energy happening right now is causing some interference in this process at a level of about four on a scale of one to ten, which is really significant in channeling). This is being caused by changing, retrieving, moving into the future, retrieving from the future, moving into the past, retrieving from the past, and generally exchanging and retrieving—sort of like little bubbles of future to past, past to future, present to past, present to future and so on. This is going on all over the world, I might add. In areas such as this where you've got more red rock on the surface, it is a little more pronounced because it is amplified even though it is muted in this particular area of Sedona because of so many people coming and going. It is not associated with anything sinister, but is largely caused by the need to pave a road from the present to the past and the future, and from the future and the past to the present and so on. (It sounds like the same thing but really isn't.) The resultant side effect is a lot of scattering. For instance, you can sit down and watch a television program and then you'll want to read something. Before you know it, you can't pay attention, understand? So all those with attention deficit disorder: *Everyone* is feeling your feelings right now.

Are you saying that all humans are connecting to their past future, paving roads for themselves?

Yes, this is really a human thing. It's not really an animal or a plant thing. Their life goes on. It's what I'd call a shakedown period; there has been so much change in your present—and even the cycle of time is changing; we know that—that the past needs to become more aligned with your present. So past lives are being shifted and changed, to the extent that what they were then affects who you are now. It is all intended, however, to happen in such a way that it does not overtly interfere with your current life. However, there is a little bleed-through effect. It's as if a computer were overloaded with information, at least on the borderline, and cannot function predictably as it normally would. It's overwhelmed by too much input. So it's very hard to follow thought; it's even hard for muscles, tissues and nerves to work. That is why during times like this, which usually last for a few days at the most, it's very important to pay attention where you put one foot after another. Even though you don't have to worry too much about accidents, there's a feeling as if you're functioning so much someplace else that it's very difficult to stay conscious in the present moment, yes?

Yes, yes. Wild dreams.

Yes. Crazy and unusual, bizarre dreams.

Yes, not cosmic, just weird.

Yes, and different from anything normal. That is the reason the channeling is plodding along tonight and you're having a hard time paying attention to what's being said. It's the distractions to other places.

Are we also we assimilating other dimensional parts of ourselves?

Yes. That falls in neatly as well. It is very complex within a physical world like this to assimilate all that and continue with life as if everything were just fine.

One more question —there has been talk forever about the economy falling apart. I get bored with it, but now it's surging up again. Are we looking at something in September and October? Is the economy going to become unstable?

I don't see it, and I'll tell you why. We're really developing a world economy here. You're seeing right now and for the past few months the beginning of the world stock market and world investments—this kind of business. Initially, at least, it's going to be very good. It will lead to a more conscious way of doing business. People are going to realize that if one large segment of the population is suffering, not only do things need to be done to help these individuals, but these people are not producing, they're not involved in the abundance of the world.

I said quite a while ago that the first corporate world order would start out very businesslike and somewhat recalcitrant, but would gradually turn into something more conscious. Corporations need to unify entire businesses, and when you put the world on the level of a corporation, that unification must take place in a form that is not only accepting and allowing, but also vitally encouraging, supporting and, yes, nurturing.

So I'm not expecting anything catastrophic. I do understand that there are problems with the dollar and so on, but look at it this way. Because the world is now financially quite well interlaced, especially since the changeover in the Soviet Union, and will be much more so in the future, that other parts of the world cannot afford to have anything catastrophic happen to the United States economy. You'll find that the economy will continue to grow somewhat, and there hasn't been a whole lot of trickledown to a lot of sectors of the economy, I think it's going to change.

The United States needs to learn what products it can make efficiently, not just competitively, compared to other countries. All countries will eventually specialize in certain things. It will be like a big corporation, you know: one part of a corporation or business does the accounting, another part the selling and so on. It'll be the same all over the world, economically speaking. To a great degree that will create economic parity amongst all nations of the world, with everybody doing what they do best. This will be partially based on cultural influences, certainly geographic influences, and will gradually create a more benevolent society where people need everybody else to be working well for the machine to be well-oiled and functioning.

Thus the corporate model is gradually beginning to change into something more benevolent.

Granted, I'm one being, but I do not see any catastrophic economic problem coming up in the near future. There will be, you know, blips here and there, but I don't see, for instance, the United States and other countries of the world allowing the former Soviet Union to fall into some kind of a horrible depression without doing something. Quite the opposite. The people over there want to work and they're willing to work. It is really a minor problem of currency that will get worked out. It's going to be fine.

Speaks of Many Truths on Assimilating
Past, Future and Other-Dimensional Selves

Zoosh talked about the fact that we're assimilating our past, future and other-dimensional selves.

Assimilating, but I think you also have been doing and learning what will normally be passed on to your other lives as you come to the end of your natural cycle, when you will have completed all your work in that life. But what is happening here is that apparently you are working on so much more than one would work on in a normal lifetime that you now are in a time in which you are passing on that knowledge and wisdom while you are still alive. It is possible, certainly for some of you, that you will start some whole new direction after this time passes, because you are no longer working on something that benefits these past lives or future lives. So there might be a chance for something new or some new level of wisdom.

26

The Angel of Roswell

Zoosh
July 25, 1997

My question is about the image I sent to Robert, the alien angel of Roswell.

It's an interesting thing, in that this being was not in and around Roswell before the now-famous crash. The being came to the site after the crash on the basis of a distress call from the occupants of the vehicle. She was at the site for a long time, even after there were no more life signs from the vehicle's occupants. She remained on the scene, although this is not normally the case, in order to smooth the energy out.

The culture that crashed there does not believe that the departure of the soul from the body is the end of their responsibility, whereas most cultures on Earth believe that the Earth body is something of Mother Earth. This culture believes that one's entire self is associated with one's being and one's responsibility. Because their ceremony could not be done during the passing (unexpected passings are especially unusual in that culture), it was requested that this entity remain until she could conduct the rites of passage for all parts of these beings.

She had to transform herself into something that would adapt to anyplace on Earth and also protect her essence. She would have to go places other than Roswell in order to sanctify the remains of these beings. Thus she has been all over the Earth in order to do that, not only in the United States, but because in a supersecret operation some of the remains had been transferred overseas for a short time, she had to go there. She is able to do so at will, you might say, but will does not factor in. Now she has done this with all of the beings and is involved in her own passage.

This is where you picked up her image. In order for her to pass back to her point of origin where she resides until she is called upon, she needs to let go of all things Earth (as Earth exists in this galaxy). To do that, she phases through many different colors. When you saw her she was phasing through the color green, which in Earth terms is a healing color; but where she's from, green simply applies to oxygen planets that would have a nurturing atmosphere for plant and animal life—oxygen breathers exhaling carbon dioxide. That's when you saw her.

If you were to see her as she is now, red is the next level of her phasing. This is the release of life forms on Earth, for whom red would be a significant color, humans and animals and so on. You can watch her go through all of these colors if you wish. I understand your perception of her as the angel of that place, because when you originally saw her she was just beginning to release all forms of life associated with Earth that she had come in contact with. You would have seen her releasing not only extraterrestrial presences, but also flowers and trees and desert plants, cacti and rocks, stone, sand—everything associated with the area.

The passage of all of this material from her would have made her look like an angelic energy. She's not physical, but an energy whose primary job is to respond to the distress calls of any beings in distress—not unlike an angelic being might respond here to a human—is more in the realm of the angelics. She's not an angelic for people on this planet, but for others.

Over the next time period you will see her changing through different colors, because she's still here. At some point you will see her in an environment that you can tell is not Earth. When you see her there, you will probably be seeing her in her home, because that's where she will go after Earth. However, she will be called upon to go elsewhere.

Right now on Earth you see many images of angels, yes? But these are false images, however lovingly made, because angels do not have wings and never did. If you were to see angels, they would appear rather like people—humanoids with the light emanating from them that's associated with benevolence, love and also whatever is associated with the planet on which they're working. Angels are seen with white light because that is unconditional love, but they are also seen simultaneously with gold light because that is associated with this planet. Were they to go to another planet it might be a different color, but the white light would underlie it all.

This being would normally not come to Earth, but that is because she is so far away and on call to other beings. She would like to see angels depicted on Earth as they really exist.

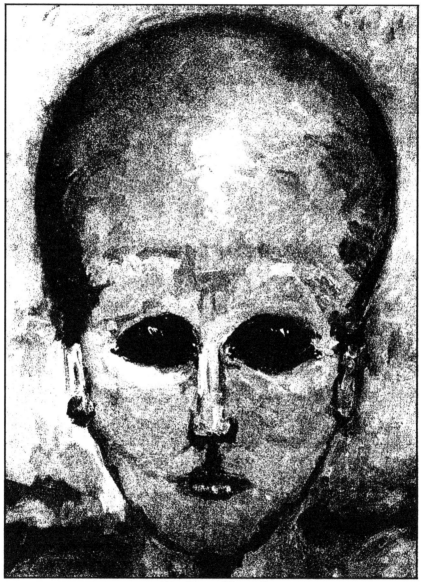

Alien Deva of Roswell
Full-color 11" x 17" posters are available by calling 800-860-1844.

People have had temporary experiences on the other side and have come back to describe the beings, and you will always find that they do not have wings. While that is a delightful idea, it is carried on well past its time. It might be interesting to have pictures of angels as they might come when a human being is in distress, emanating that white and gold light, looking rather human themselves, but not, of course, with wings.

Most likely you won't see them with feet because angels are really sort of leaning through an aperture in the fabric of your world. Although they might have something that resembles feet, they usually don't actually step all the way through. They sort of drag the aperture with them.

She has contacted you and you her. The two of you are old friends, so there is a relationship beyond this new version.

When we had the image at the Roswell crash site and in the town during the festivities, why did it seem to have a more profound impact on small children and even infants and babies that were walking by?

Because, you know, it is an angel. They resonate to the angelic aspect of it. Youngsters are not permeated with adults' misconceptions, so they are more pure and more likely to have what I would call a natural reaction to anything.

27

Crop Circles

Zoosh through Robert Shapiro
July 29, 1997

D*o the aliens put a harmonic frequency into the Earth by imprinting crop circles?*

To some extent the crop circles are intended to put an energy into the crop itself in the hope that, ideally, it will work its way into the food chain. Of course, it doesn't harm the food, and anybody who eats even a single grain might expand his/her intelligence or capacity for self-healing (known beyond Earth as regeneration). Or he might even have his subtle sensing abilities expanded.

It's also intended to reach you on the subconscious level, because these symbols have specific meanings to different peoples. As you know, peoples on this Earth come from different points of origin, in terms of appearance (what you would call race). Different places such as Sirius, Andromeda, the Pleiades or Orion, for example, have different sacred symbols. Therefore when a member of a culture looked upon a crop circle, he/she would react to [it in a specific manner] just as people from your culture would to the Christian cross.

Yes, they're being put here to help you integrate aptitudes, capacities and abilities beyond what you now have, whether it is by eating the crop (which is desirable), by walking within the crop circle (desirable for those of you who can do that) or by seeing a picture of it (this is a distant third, but it is something). The ideal is eating the crop, the second is walking in the crop circle and the last is seeing the symbol itself—and that is useful.

We can't tell you "this is what this means," because to people in different cultures it will mean different things. Cultures can mean races, even a race within a race that has its own culture. So to different people, the crop circle might mean something entirely different. It might have a powerful meaning for one, but only a minor meaning to another. To a still different group it could have a variation of meanings. The important thing to remember about crop circles is that they are personal. If it were strictly a visual message, it could happen in skywriting—you'd see it, and that would be that. But this is multileveled.

Does it put a harmonic into the Earth that helps raise the Earth's frequency?

Maybe, maybe not. It depends where the crop circle is. If it's in England where they are commonly found, then probably. Very powerful grid lines run through there. But there are lots you don't hear about that aren't in England.

Is there a particular access point to the grid in England, or is it because it is the crown chakra of the planet?

Well, it has lots of different meanings, and I'm not going to put anybody's meaning down. I'll simply say that it's an access point, a particularly useful one. You know the old saying, "All roads lead to Rome." In this case it's more like all roads lead to Chicago. Lots of different rail lines come from all over the country into Chicago. This is also true in England, where different grid lines lead in and out. England is a place where vast amounts of energy can be quickly and easily disseminated.

How does this relate to the fact that the grid is now lifting up above the planet? Will there still be an energetic connection within the planet itself?

Even if the grid does lift above the planet for a time, there will ultimately have to be an equal grid *under* the planet just deep enough so that you cannot readily access it. If the grid exists for surface dwellers, that's the one that would be above the planet. The grid must now exist for the planet herself, especially when there's been mining and she's lost something. She needs that energy there; therefore she must have a grid line deep underneath her mantle that you can't easily penetrate so she can connect with someplace where she does have the needed material. She'll run a grid line from point A to point B to support the energy of the material that is no longer there but which performs a function for that area.

Are these injections of resonance meant more for the planet than for the people? And the symbols are for the people?

Sometimes the energy itself, the resonance, is meant for the people and sometimes it's meant for the planet. On rare occasions it's meant for the solar system. [This is] because the planet herself, not being from this solar system but basically parked in it, occasionally has to send out a resonance meant for this planet but might have something to do with Sirius, her home galaxy. Therefore her resonance, when felt by the other planets, would come from Sirius. It might be instigated by something on Sirius or by something on Earth. Then it is reflected through Sirius or through Sirian beings who create the resonance that goes into Earth, emanates from Earth as a planet and thence onto the other planets, so that the other planets will understand what and why through feelings. As you all know, the quickest way to understand something is through feelings, even though you don't often do that. You have experienced this feeling when you've had your *eureka*!s.

*Is the video we saw of two balls of light that buzzed around the field an accurate depiction of how the crop circles are made?**

No, I don't think that was really too accurate, but it was a nice special effect.

Put out by whom?

I think that's been revealed already, but it was put together by somebody. However, there have been times when actual probes (much smaller than the one in that video) would be there and produce that effect. I'm not pooh-poohing all those people who've seen probes, either through their subtle vision or actual physical vision, but that the video that shows the two balls whizzing around and then flying off—that's not real.

You know what you can do for fun? Tell people to put the finger(s) of their right or left hand (whichever they feel is more receptive) on each of the crop circle pictures and see which one feels best. Whichever feels best probably relates to the planetary system through which your soul is focused in this life.

Some people like to ask, "Where am I from?" Well, most of you are from beyond and before this universe, but my answer to that question to people in private sessions is always, "Well, you're focused through these planets at this time, having to do with those planets' lessons, jobs, priorities, principles, agendas and so on."

---

* This refers to the short videotape of balls of light that seemed to create the Snowflake formation at Barbury Castle near Devizes, Wiltshire, England on August 11, 1996 (shown on *Sightings* and perhaps elsewhere).

28

Human Earth School Not Possible without Dark Side

Zoosh through Robert Shapiro
July 29, 1997

What is the relationship of humans to their shadows? How do we work with it?

Give it something to do that it can do as itself and that you can appreciate, even if it is an imagination in which you are angry at someone or something, and, as in a fantasy, destroy the person or thing. Do you understand? There is such a thing as constructive violence, but the pleasant side of a person's personality is entirely incapable of it. Only the so-called shadow side is capable of constructive violence. Of course, it's also capable of destructive violence. So you want to do things whereby you can be violently constructive because it's violence that transforms some discomfort within your body and also allows you to let go of circumstances, situations, people (alive or passed over) that you are holding in a fixed position, thereby creating a block for yourselves.

Even if you have to make up a story and think it or say it out loud, you understand, it allows that side of yourself to *be itself* and perform a task that only it can provide you and be appreciated for. There will be times, as in any person's life, when you have to do something aggressive that helps you. That is the so-called dark side. It is not possible for the so-called light side of a person or their immortal personality—that part of you that lives on other planets in other lives—to even be aggressive if that level of aggression is more than assertive.

Let's say that you want to get into line before somebody else and so you step on the gas and zoom forward. That's aggressive. Assertive is one click down from that. That kind of aggression is available only from your so-called dark side. Learn to recognize it when it's helpful to you and say thank you. Saying it out loud is better because it puts it into the physical world. "Thanks for being available to support me that way," says you to your dark side.

Fascinating. But is there an eventual integration, then?

That is the integration. What people think now is that to integrate the dark side means, essentially, to transform the dark side into—what?

The light side.

But that's not integration. Now, if I take the right hand and the left hand and clasp them together, you could say that the two are integrated, yes? Yet the right hand is still the right hand. The right fingers, the thumb, are still of the right hand, but they are integrated and working together to perform a function that both hands might do. They are working together, they are even blended together when I interlace the fingers, yet they are uniquely themselves though they work together.

If an individual *could* transform it to the light side, that would not be integration. That is literally conversion by the sword, because it is transformation against the will of that which is transformed. It could conceivably be transformed (and has been in the past), but invariably that leads to a dead-end street. That street is labeled with a sign that says, "This is what you naturally are." So if you transform the dark side—and it's possible to do that and maintain it, but of course you have to be a monk the rest of your life and work constantly on maintaining that—then you are what you are elsewhere. You're not going to learn anything, because your dark side is what becomes morally angry or upset when you're up against a lesson. It brings to your attention that something is going on that is causing you to be angry, which only the dark side can be. It brings to your attention that something is going on. The more conscious person, at least after a while, says, "Ah, maybe there's a lesson here for me." Then the next best thing to say is, "Thank you, dark side."

A person with only a light side never comes up against anything, and if they are exposed to something that others are coming up against and it is uncomfortable for them, they will put distance between them and that because they cannot stand the energy. This is why most ETs can't be here, because their growth cycle is infinitesimal compared to your own. They are not capable as living beings to be exposed to major growth all the time.

The main thing to remember, then, is that we want to find a way that the dark side can work for you (which it does all the time), be appreciated, thanked and loved, not transformed. Here's the thing: If a child is regularly bratty, you could punish the child—that is the usual procedure. In some cases that will "work," meaning the child will stop the behavior. But what the parent does not know is that very often that sublimated (as psychologists would say) behavior comes out some other way either later in life or someplace where the parent is not in observation, such as school.

That is like working on symptoms instead of the cause of disease in the body

Exactly. So a parent might be able (and I'm not criticizing parents here) to love the child and transform the child's behavior. I'm not talking about violent, destructive behavior but about a behavior that is not good for the child, such as sticking its finger in electrical outlets, creating mischief and worry for the parent. If a parent is able to transform the child in some loving manner, maybe even transform the child's behavior through some humorous way, which works well, the child does not feel like there's anything wrong with itself. Then the child integrates that nurturing advice and support and does not feel bad about itself. I'm not giving a lesson in child psychology but saying that the so-called dark side is often blamed because it is usually recognized only for some act that is self-destructive or destructive to others (which I also call self-destructive). But every day for every one of you, *the dark side is there doing things for you, quite unappreciated.* So the real integration of the dark side is appreciating it.

The Link between Immortal Personality and Physical Self

Now, here's something you don't necessarily recognize. The dark side, as it's called, does not function the same way on higher planes. That is to say, when your body dies and your personality moves on, you move on with the light side, and if the dark side comes with you it is quickly screened out through the first few veils. The dark side stays behind. Why? Because it has the capacity to feel and interact physically, and the lightbody no longer needs to feel and interact physically because it's a lightbody and functions as light. Though you might see it there as your physical body, it is not the physical body you had here. This tells you that dark side functions as an appropriate and necessary means of protection or warning (or any other security device you can think of as an analogy) that works here on Earth to support you. When you see that group of people down the block that you'd just as soon avoid, it's what signals you to walk around the block to avoid them. If you had only your light side, you'd walk right on up to them.

So we're talking about intuition?

I want to put a common term on it so that it's easily understood. We're talking street smarts, which convert to physical-body smarts. The dark side—and this is more meaningful than you realize—is literally the go-between for the immortal personality (also known as the lightbody) and the physical self. Your dark side is that part of you which can communicate on an instantaneous basis between your physical self and your immortal personality whenever any emergency (otherwise known as threat to the physical self) arises.

You might say, "But Zoosh, there are exceptions." Let's say you're in an argument with somebody about an intellectual point over which there is no threat to your physical body. If you pay attention to where your physical body reacts in an argument, especially if it becomes heated about what is strictly an intellectual point, not something that has anything to do with your life, it begins to transform. It feels certain ways that are very much the same as the ways it would feel if you were physically threatened. That's when your dark side steps in and is essentially your soldier, that which protects and defends you in all circumstances.

It is usually recognized as anger. You become angry in the argument, and maybe the other person does, too. That is your dark side coming up, not to attack—*not* to attack—but to defend. Very often in the past, psychology has referred to this loosely as the ego. But I don't want to call it the ego because the psychological approach incorporates the personality as associated with the mind. And as you know from talking to me long enough, this approach is more complete. So you literally cannot exist in this Earth school without a dark side, short of (I'll make one exception) being a full-time monk or guru who is constantly working with benevolent energies for your followers or simply for yourself.

Arming the Dark Side with Love

Now, there certainly are plenty of circumstances in which your benevolent energies interact with the benevolent energies of your body, such as in the love exercise that is the foundation for the instinctual-body homework (the heat felt in the chest). Your dark side does not have to be present to do that, but it is, because these are the few moments when the dark side feels love. What we're really doing during this instinctual-body homework is relieving the dark side from its urgent need to protect you at all costs and giving it a tool by which it can stand aside—be with you but not have to make a decision based upon no facts.

When you're using the warmth in the body (which is, as you know, the physical evidence of love), you're giving the dark side or the survivor or soldier in you and your physical body an alternative connection to your mental body to understand how it functions through your physical. All of your physical features include your physical body, your feeling body, your spiritual body as it interacts with these bodies, and your dark side. Normally I do not mention the dark side separately, because when I say the physical body and your spiritual body, the dark side is between them in some sense. I'm calling it the dark side because people have come to the conclusion that they have to "transform the dark side"—but I don't recommend that these days. Rather, I recommend supporting it.

So with this heat you're giving it a tool by which it can work with your light side through your physical body and your spiritual body to perform functions that work for you so that the soldier has tools and does not have to become violent. It's like giving the soldier more than a gun to survive out in the field. It is giving the soldier a compass or some direction-finding equipment so he can find his way back to his lines. Do you understand? Or you give him training so he can read the stars and find his way back. You give him water, you give him first aid equipment. You give the soldier not just a gun, but lots of things so that he can survive out in the field.

When your dark side has only a gun, then you're a fighter, a warrior. It will come up all the time and tend to limit your interaction with the rest of your world, whether it be your immediate family or your entire world, your work, your family, your church, everything. It will tend to limit your interactions on the basis of survival, meaning protecting the rest of you at all costs. "At all costs," as we all know, can mean something self-destructive or destructive to others. To understand this is very important: For those of you who are attempting to embrace your dark side, recognize the things it does for you. If you can recognize it during the day, just whisper if there are people around. You want to say it out loud in some way because that's acknowledging a physical act in the physical world. If you only think it as thought, *it won't get to your dark side.* Why not? you might ask.

Recognizing the Dark Side in the Physical World

There's no connection to the mental?

That's right. There's no direct connection from the mental to the spiritual and the instinctual, meaning the combination of the spiritual, the feeling and the physical.

What's the connection in the body, the solar plexus?

The connection in the physical self that forms the instinctual from the feeling, the spiritual and the physical, is anywhere across the chest, including the solar plexus and even down to and including the abdomen—

basically the chest and the abdomen. It is not so much a physical connection as a place. The connection is your entire body, but that place is where you can find the connection through the heat and the gut feelings and all of that.

There is a need to thank your dark side, and say, "Thank you, dark side." Say it out loud so you're using the physical body, and yes, you're also incorporating the mental body into a consciousness beyond its capacity to rationalize. You see, the mind has a capacity to rationalize based upon its program. If you give the computer a single program, its basic program, it might not be able to do word processing because it needs another program for that. So the mind's capacity to rationalize is limited to its tools.

But if you say out loud, "Thank you, dark side," in a situation where the dark side has helped you to do something aggressive that supported you and did not harm anybody else, you fly in the face of the mind's logic. For instance, driving your car, you saw that the signal might change—it was the last of the green or was turning yellow and you looked both ways and made sure it was safe—and you went through the intersection on the yellow. You had to step on the gas a little bit, but it was safe. Then you said "Thank you, dark side." The light side would never have done that, *ever*.

The light side is fully realized, which means a couple of things. "Fully realized" means that under all circumstances it is absolutely patient and tends to wait for things to happen rather than go out and make them happen. To go out and make them happen requires the dark side. The connection beyond the rational, or beyond what the mental body knows, comes when you say—with your physical body, using your diaphragm, your lungs, the air, your mouth, teeth, lips, everything—out loud consciously, understanding why you're saying it out loud: "Thank you, dark side," and mean it. Don't just say it in passing; if it comes up only later and you think about it, then say, "Thank you, dark side" out loud.

When you do that, the mind will understand; or you can explain it to the mind in thought, showing it—in remembered pictures of going through the intersection safely but on the yellow light, in remembered pictures of the circumstance—that everything was safe and that it was okay. It's important for the mind to know that. The mind then begins to gradually over time, not immediately, grasp the idea that the so-called dark side is performing a vital task necessary on Earth and very few other places, only other places that might have some need for spiritual (otherwise known as immortal personality) growth on a vast scale.

The Dark Side's Accumulation Process

If we have many incarnations, does this part stay here and rejoin us when we come back? Or is it a fresh thing connected with this life, with the Earth?

With each life it forms up; it accumulates. A newborn baby might have two different experiences, for our example. In the first, during her pregnancy the mother carries the baby and she and the father and the other children are careful. The mother is nurtured, and the baby is perhaps born in a water birth, as is done in some places. It has had ideal circumstances and is welcomed into life in the best possible circumstances. Then gradually over time the baby becomes frustrated because it's unable to communicate in the telepathic language that is its actual means of communication—pictures with the occasional word. Real telepathic communication has nothing to do with printed language. It has to do more with pictures and feelings.

So the baby gradually accumulates that. But let's say the child is born in the more conventional way nowadays, where it comes out of the mother and the doctor holds the baby up and slaps it on the bottom. That's not because the doctor is punishing the baby, but because the doctor wants the baby to breathe on its own. After a slap on the bottom the baby takes a big breath and cries. When that happens it's a shock to the baby, and it immediately begins to accumulate its dark side. It is likely to accumulate it faster than in the ideal situation given in the first example. It accumulates its dark side from the energy around it.

You see, there is an energy floating about all the time here, since people are constantly frustrated by things they want to do, or at the very least delayed from doing things they want to do. This energy is here on Earth on this teaching planet, all right? It is usually referred to as polarity, but let's just say that it's this energy that's floating about and is available to function as what I would call motivating energy, certainly in the beginning for a baby.

Remember, the pure light side has almost no motivation at all. Its only motivation is to feel love and to emanate it and pass it on, period. If, however, it's in another culture on some other planet, some higher dimension, where they have their own cultural agenda, then it will also have that. But it won't have the motivation stimulated here by delay, frustration, urgency and so on. That's all available here because this is a learning planet and the learning curve is faster here. The baby must accumulate something that is its own.

I will tell you exactly where it will take it in initially. If you move your fingers down your sternum, the place where the ribs come together in the center, the point where you get to the bottom of the sternum, where it's softer and you can push in, that's where the baby takes in its necessary (needed for its own survival) dark side. When it gets slapped on the bottom and takes that first breath [he claps his hands and then follows with a sharp breath], the baby gasps and then cries. You understand? When it does that it takes in some available energy, which begins its dark side—its soldier and its survivor, its warrior—and it immediately yells in protest, and of course also breathes outside its mother.

It begins its dark side then and will rapidly assimilate it. Because the baby is born in such a fashion, which is more the convention now, it would immediately have to deal with things that it might not like. For an example, in hospitals they put a chemical (not a harmful one) into the eyes of babies because it prevents a lot of cases of blindness. It's a good thing, but it doesn't feel good when you're first born, so the baby will cry some more. That crying and kicking and the motion of the baby is to some extent its first ability to defend itself. The crying isn't just "I object." It's "How *dare* you!"—which is a form of defense.

The First Earth Humans and the Original Dark Side

Can you say this energy has been left here by other humans, or is it part of the Earth's emotional body?

It's not a part of the Earth's emotional body; it is an accumulation by humans. When the first Earth humans started here a long time ago, the first surface dwellers (not counting people who came with the planet inside it, but people living on the surface), they developed their culture on the surface. These people didn't have much of a dark side. As a matter of fact, the first few generations were very benign and benevolent. If you were to meet them during the first generation or so they would be so kind and so loving that you would not recognize them as Earth human beings. Oh, they would look like Earth human beings, but you would not recognize them as that. You would say, "You people must not be from around here."

The first Earth humans, surface dwellers, were in Africa. They didn't have that dark side. But gradually, as time went on, one person had some frustration about something. One person, a single human being, has a fantastic capacity for generating many different things. So let's say someone was walking along, not paying attention to where he was going, and stubbed his toe. "Ouch!" At first he got mad at the rock—it was frustration, all right? Then he got mad at himself. Then he felt foolish; maybe others giggled, although one or two others might have come over to say, "Here, can we help you?" A lot of things happened in that moment. Immediately exuding from the human being was the form of energy that has come to be known as the dark side.

The Creation of Our Individual Shadows

We each have our own shadows that we have drawn to us and created?

When you have inner conflicts, here you have your dark side, which protects you. Then you have inner conflicts with that dark side, or conflicts within the dark side itself. It's like driving wedges into it, so that it begins to battle amongst itself. These kind of wedges are not usually initiated by the dark side, but by conflicts in thought, things other people have told you, things you believe you're supposed to live up to and so on.

Let's say that you believe you're supposed to behave in a certain way, but you don't, and therefore you have an internal conflict. It becomes like a raw edge after a while. (If you rub your fingers together long enough, they're going to get raw.) It becomes an internal pain, which can become an anxiety. When you see your dark side as an enemy, a thing that tries to destroy you, it happens within the dark side because that is the only part of you that's capable of doing battle within you, even if you're not consciously aware of it.

The light side can't do it, it just can't. It's incapable of it. So that means it is happening in the dark side, but not initiated by the dark side. Dark sides do not initiate, meaning they don't start something. They react, always. The dark side is the counterpuncher, but it does not punch first. It doesn't start it; it reacts, even if it's reacting to something that happened a long time ago. Something else initiates the conflict, and that's generally something somebody else said or you read, or else (this is always a potential) the basic programming of the mind is in conflict with the actuality of life here. Because the mind is separated from the actual life here, it can establish, rationalize, maintain and enforce behavior within the physical self in terms of outward behavior based on an entirely false principle. The mind can do that, but that doesn't mean that the false principle is not recognized from within.

The dark side completely understands how Earth works; there is no confusion about that. The physical body also understands how Earth works, because it is made up of Earth. So there is complete and utter understanding between those two parts of yourself. But the linear mind is not a part of Earth and is, even as we speak, being gradually siphoned off toward Andromeda. When it imposes a belief that it has come to, not based upon actual Earth life (which is known and completely understood by the physical body and by the dark side because they have to deal with it), then the outer behavior becomes self-disciplined (disciplined by the mind).

But the inner behavior, meaning the physical body and the dark side, is struggling with this idea artificially imposed by the mental body's grasp of some belief that might have absolutely nothing to do with Earth life. Then there comes a struggle, which can take place only in the physical body, an internal struggle usually defined by pain and disease (eventually, if not immediately), or within the dark side itself, making a person perhaps edgy or easily angered. It comes to the surface because the dark side is trying to tell you something, not that it's angry at the person it's shouting at, but that it's agitated by something else. That's why people overreact to something. When you get more conscious and you realize you're overreacting to a situation, you can either look at what might be causing it by analyzing it through the mind, or just look at the simple fact that the dark side is overwhelmed and agitated in general. Maybe the way you're making your decisions is too mental and you have totally ignored your physical sensing device (which can tell you how things actually work on Earth) and your dark side, which acts as a connection between the physical and the rest of you.

And if there has been trauma, abuse and blocked and repressed memories, all these symptoms, they exacerbate it.

Yes, absolutely right. And there have been things that have been told you even by well-meaning people, which you hear from your parents, your grandparents, your uncles, your aunts, your schoolteachers, other children you grow up with, to say nothing of what you're told when you're an adult. You're going to get all of these bits and pieces of knowledge, some of which might actually be based in reality, though that reality might not in fact be functioning today during your now life; it might be in the past or be a philosophy based on the famous healer Louise Hay. She says, "What should be is not what is."

In order to fully grasp how valuable your dark side is, it's essential to go out (if you can, away from people who are telling you what is) into the countryside and just observe the animals, observe nature, notice how it functions, then do the same thing with yourself. You'll get to know yourself.

The Dark Side As Teacher

You know, when people try and get to know themselves, they do so through their thoughts, and that's okay. But you also need to get to know how your physical body functions. When it's feeling something uncomfortable, it's not "what does it mean?" mentally. You can extrapolate on what it might mean mentally, meaning build on what you can imagine, but if there's some pain in some part of your body, your body is trying to give you a message in the simplest possible terms, because it doesn't think the way your mind does.

It might be trying to give you a message that your mind can interpret. This has to be done through the dark side, because the dark side has the capacity to function with pain and disease. The light side simply cannot function there. That's why you as the Explorer Race cannot live on Earth without a dark side. You can't come to this school without a dark side, and you necessarily leave it behind you when you go on because you don't need it when you go past Earth. It stays behind, and that's why a lot of your accumulated lessons in linear comprehension, linear thought, go to Andromeda, though you have some access to them.

The body lessons stay behind. Your physical body stays behind. Your dark side stays behind because it's not your permanent dark side, just what you have accumulated out of necessity over your physical life-time. Then you go on with your lightbody. Your lightbody does not have the capacity to access your lessons toughly learned, and that's why everybody has teachers. When you go beyond at the end of your natural cycle, you see, or even at the deepest levels of sleep when you are just connected to your physical body and your dark side, your dark side stays with the physical body.

At the deepest levels of sleep—what you call dreaming, but the very deepest levels that you don't ever remember—when the soul or immortal personality goes out to communicate with others, not needing to sleep, you are tethered by a piece of light, a light cord. This means that the dark side cannot run up that light because the light cannot deal with the dark side. So it stays with the body when your physical body sleeps and your teachers talk to you. Your teachers can look at the dark side. They're evolved or shielded enough. They can look at your dark side and your physical body, they can look at your linear thoughts and work with you because they know. But because you're in your light side and in your lightbody and you're dreaming, you cannot know this. It would injure you, it would harm you, it would distort you.

At the deepest level of dreaming you don't know it when you get lessons from your teachers. And you don't know it when, at the end of your natural cycle, you go through the veils and go on with your life in your lightbody. That's why you have to have teachers there also. You go on with your life and there are guides and teachers who help you and teach you and tell as much as they can to your lightbody, but they can't tell you everything. They can't help you feel the pain so that you will learn that lesson. They can only tell you what will not harm your light-body.

That is why souls desperately want to come to Earth, because they can accumulate wisdom in huge amounts within the short time that you live life here. In a given life you can accumulate vast amounts of wisdom, especially if you are conscious, meaning aware, thinking about, yes, and feeling your feeling self, which also functions as an interpreter for your physical self, your dark side and your spiritual side.

If your mind can understand what the feelings mean in your physical body, which you all need to explore, feelings will communicate to the mind. Souls come here so they can get all of that. When they're beyond here and in their lightbodies all the time, they cannot feel pain and suffering. It would destroy them. So away from here they can get lessons only from their teachers. Put yourself in the teacher's position. You're a teacher and your own teacher tells you (talking to the teacher of a typical teacher of souls/lightbeings), "Now, you know you can't remind them in a way that they can *feel* the lesson. If you reminded them, yes, they'd get the lesson right away, but it would destroy their lightbody." The teacher is being reminded here.

"Right, right," says the teacher of the lightbeing, "I can't let them feel it."

"You've got to communicate to them in ways," says the teacher's teacher, "that will allow them to understand their lessons without feeling any discomfort." So of course the teacher of the lightbeing has a conundrum, because in order to understand the lesson quickly and thoroughly, the student—the lightbody, as it were—has to go to Earth and encapsulate itself within a physical body, and only then can it completely understand.

If there is a total and complete understanding that is accepted and appreciated by the lightbody, then in those moments the lightbody can understand, appreciate and embrace the lesson, feeling total patience with it, recognizing and loving the lesson. In that circumstance it can take the lesson with it. It does not leave it behind in its physical and dark-side body. That's why people reincarnate here on Earth in the Earth school. They'll reincarnate here, even though you might say to yourself afterward, "Oh, I never want to come back. This is too much suffering. What am I going to do?"

If you haven't lovingly embraced the lesson to the point where you have total patience with it and appreciate it consciously as well as on the feeling level, then you will come back sometime. If the teacher is at its wit's end, so to speak, and you as the lightbeing can't get it, then you will come back here for a reincarnation in the hope that you will be able to embrace the lesson lovingly. This doesn't mean embrace the circumstances of the lesson, but that once you get the lesson you can say, "Thank you, dark side."

When your mind and your body have complete communication, when your mind eventually says, "Thank you, dark side" enough, "Eureka!" says the mind. "*This* is what this is about! I love it!—I've now learned it!" Then you don't have to experience it anymore. You might experience it in some mild way, just to apply, "Oh well, I know what this means and that's fine," and then forget about it. Nothing happens, it's integrated, it's loved. That's what gets integrated, see? And in that way the teacher is freed up and you can go on to your next lesson.

I can see that if a child is born very open, with the wisdom of the physical body, and sees and feels things, it will respond to the feeling of the other person. But all the humans say, "You're lying. You don't know what you're talking about. You're wrong. I didn't say that." When that happens and they're slapped or beaten, they can build a really large dark side, then, can't they? I mean, that's the way it begins.

You can, and you also grow to mistrust your true telepathy. Then you have a hard time getting it back, coming to terms with it. But consciously thinking about such thoughts as you just had makes progress, because then as a person you can say, "Well, I unlearned this. But I came in with it, so I've still got it. I just have to go down through the layers to get there."

But that's what causes people not to trust their feelings, knowings and insights.

Exactly.

29

Angels Are Really Guides in Training

Zoosh through Robert Shapiro
August 7, 1997

Angels are special beings, it's true. I've always, however, gone out of my way to bring the human perception of angels into something familiar rather than reverential. That's why I have used terms like "Uncle Mike" when referring to Michael, because I see no advantage for human beings to become reverential about other beings, including myself. I have gone out of my way to keep from being deified and I'm still doing it. Perhaps I'm bending over backward a little too far, but I'm making an effort to give you the facts and (at least from my perception) at the same time I do not wish to become the all-powerful, omniscient being.

I feel strongly about that, because in the past when human beings deified someone, that's the time they usually went far off track, not because that being was necessarily telling them to go off track, but because of the mythology and the lore that developed—what that being might have said, what he/she could have said, and all the stories that go on around it so that eventually you're reading and hearing more about what human beings said to each other than what the beings or entities said.

Angels' primary job in their interaction with human beings is to be with you in the birth cycle when you are birthing—most often for the baby, sometimes for the mother—or in the death cycle, either when you are dying or if you are experiencing the death of someone else. You might see them at other times, but that would have to do with something secondary. Their primary job is to deal with birth and death.

In practical terms, angels are guides in training, period. That's why there are so many angels. Think about it. Guides are really interacting on a very subtle level with people. It requires a significant amount of spiritual advancement to be a guide, and it is also very helpful. With an occasional exception, 99.999% of the time it is required that you have at least one life as the type of being you are guiding, meaning that if it's a human being you have to have been a human being at least once, though it's preferable to be a human being many times so that you can speak with a sense of having been there and you can emanate your messages, such as they are, to the human you are guiding from an eye-to-eye position. Angels are training to become guides. That's why they don't have constant interaction with human beings. They tend to interact with human beings in times of trauma and/or emergency. Granted, there are other times, but the bulk of the interaction is birth and death and headings underneath that.

Near-Death and Emergencies

Yes, emergencies. You might ask, "Why don't the angels interact with us more?" It's because they don't have the experience and the training. Being an angel is training academy for being a guide. You don't just become a guide, bang! There's a lot of responsibility to being a guide. You become an angel first. And while it is a nice idea, a sweet idea, even a cute idea that angels have wings, they really don't. Angels having wings is a result of years and years of European theology. That was originally merely to point out the fact that angels can fly. At the time the idea was originally put out, the only physical being that could fly was a bird, so they put wings there to suggest to people that these beings are more than human. That was the original rationalization, although it was done in a spiritual way. But now it is time to let angels be more than simply a graphic (artistic) image superimposed by the reverential community of old Europe.

So that's the bulk of it. The main thing is that angels move through the golden light and the white light. They can move through any benevolent light. Interestingly enough, if angels have to go someplace that is polarized or where there is great pain or misery, they bring the golden light with them for the persons they are assisting, but also for themselves. Angels, as guides in training, cannot go someplace where beings are suffering without having golden light! So the golden light comes to aid the angel, and in the process it also aids the person the angel is helping. I'm not trying to make angels less-than in any way; what I am saying is that they are guides in training.

Archangels

Since I'm not shy about being controversial, I will go one step further and pose the question for myself: "If angels are guides in training, then what are archangels?" Archangels are like supervisors of these guides in training. They have achieved the ability to be guides and have usually done that. Because they have that experience, they work with the angelic world to teach them and support them in their training to become guides. They are not, however, wonderfully involved. They are in healing, but they are not what I would call master teachers.

They are usually spiritual masters, and because they've been guides they are usually material masters. Occasionally they will be well on their way to being teaching masters, period. They are not ever dimensional masters or quantum masters, no. Granted, it's because they don't need to be. To be an archangel means that you are probably (it's not an ironclad rule) working on becoming a teaching master. When you're doing this you're not working with only one type of being such as angels, but also with others such as humans. That's why Archangel Michael and other archangels communicate to different types of beings. It's not as if they're attempting to accomplish only a personal agenda; it is because they want to serve in a greater capacity than they have been serving. You can all identify with that. Those of you reading this, almost to the last person, feel exactly that way. You want to serve in some greater capacity. You want to make the world a better place for your having been here, which is a wonderful motivation. Archangels are the same. That is what archangels are.

Angels' Work Is Changing

Are there suddenly an awful lot of angels channeling through humans?

There are more these days than ever before, because angels have been put on notice. This is not a frightening notice from Creator, but it is a notice to say that the work they've been doing with the human race as they've been doing it is changing, because the human race is changing. The angels greatest opportunity to learn, especially to become guides and so on, has been by working with human beings, because you have been challenging to work with. It wasn't like being a guide to a being living a benevolent life on the Pleiades, where the angel can easily communicate directly in the language of a person because there is no great suffering or polarity. There is no distraction for the person they are helping. It is more challenging to be an angel to a human being on Earth. There are other places that might be challenging, but not as challenging as Earth.

Angels have been put on notice that they need to change the way they interact with you and, more important, that they won't be able to interact with you exclusively as in the past. As you move up the dimensional scale in this great experiment on Earth—or, as I like to say, the genetic experiment on Earth of which you are all the result—as you move up the dimensional scale you don't always need from them what you have needed in the past. Nowadays you tend to need more feeling guidance. It's true; going back even forty or fifty years, angels did the same thing as they do now—work with the birth and death cycle and visit people occasionally for moments to encourage them, the same thing they're doing now.

But they also had opportunities to spend brief moments . . . what's a brief moment to an angel? Oh, less than one-hundredth of a second, but less than one-hundredth of a second is significantly impactful on a being who does not experience linear time. They would have brief moments, fractions of a second, of suddenly being somewhere in your midst to experience a brief moment of polarity, but not cruelly in any way. It was brief enough that they did not get injured. They might leave behind some of the gold light that came with them to protect them, and as they left they might leave some behind to benefit the scene or those they observed briefly, so that there was an equal exchange.

But you see, those times are really drawing to a close. Now all angels need to begin doing more guiding unlike the past [when] they would gradually ease into being guides one at a time. For angels this is like on-the-job training. It's as if the entire class—everybody, including those who've had lots of training in the angelic world, those who've had just a little and those who've had lots of training—are helping the ones who have had only a little training. It's as if the entire class was suddenly sent out into the lab. There is not as much teaching; now it's the lab, and they have to work with you more constantly.

More Intimate Interaction

The issue is that there's more of an intimate connection between you and the angels, if not immediately, then coming up. For most reasonably enlightened people, there's more of a connection now with the angels. As a result, your personal guides are helping angels who have the most experience in becoming guides, and those angels are helping the angels with the least experience. The school has become more populated. Those of you who can see with subtle vision (more than physical reality) have probably noticed that there is a whole lot happening. A lot more lights are moving around. A lot more shapes are moving around.

This has to do with the much greater interaction spiritually between spiritual beings, which include angels and for the briefest moments of time, discarnate spirits. You're beginning to briefly see discarnate spirits moving [snaps fingers] quickly, and you might catch a "piece" of that person or animal, it is like a shadow. This is not an evil thing; you're briefly seeing a discarnate spirit moving toward the light. What I'm saying is that you as human beings are seeing more and the angels, as guides in training, are doing more.

Being a guide presupposes a human life, but I didn't know that angels had human lives.

This is an interesting point. Guides, you understand, have had human lives. So if angels are guides in training . . .

Are they the next Explorer Race?

Angels Aspiring to Be Guides Briefly Become Humans

Not quite, but that's a nice question. No. In the past when an angel has all the training it needed to become a guide and that was its intention, then and only then would it have a few human lives—one, two, three at least. Interesting. They take their immortal personalities as angels (just like you all have immortal personalities) and live two or three physical lives. After those physical lives they become guides. After the end of the last physical life, they go through the veils and all that, but they then return, having qualified to become guides who interact with people.

Are they going to become guides for the Sirians?

They might, but angels are universal. They are guides for the Pleiadians, Orions, Regulans, whatever. The main thing is that this is the process. I am not attempting to downgrade the value of angels, it's just that angels are beings who are pure in heart and pure in spirit—but what does that also tell you?

Not much wisdom or experience.

That's right. Not much wisdom or experience in Earth terms—or in the case of an angel becoming a guide for a Pleiadian, for example, not much wisdom and experience in Pleiadian life experience, which is infinitely easier. But that is the process. As an angel you can be totally compassionate, totally loving without being a guide. But you can't be a street-smart guide (and all guides are street-smart) and compassionate and loving *without knowing what it's like to be a human being!* Simply put (I don't want to make it too coarse), if anyone has an itch, he's gotta scratch it, okay? Now, angels don't know about that. It may sound very mundane, but it is true: A guide knows that if you get an itch, you gotta scratch it and all the other mundane things you all know about.

This tells you something. Is it possible that some of the human beings you have met running around on Earth are angels? Yes. It is possible that these beings are angels, and because they're veiled, they don't know they're angels. They know it at the deepest levels of their sleep, just like you know who you are at the deepest levels of your sleep, and all their guides and teachers know it, and between lives they know it. This is pretty interesting to note: You'll never really know whether you're an angel or whether you're meeting or interacting with angels. It is important to understand this, because if you see angels only as beings who are above you, you will not recognize your true value. When you do recognize your true value, you will appreciate that you are the Explorer Race and you will appreciate the loving source, which is not only directed to you but generated by you as well.

It's important to bring up these things from times to time because it is very easy, to want to be led and saved and otherwise supported by some "higher authority"who seems to know more than you do. It is even addictive to become involved in this, because it is so very simple to give away your power of choice. But you must know this: Guidance given by any being (certainly including myself) is always given with the intent that *it does not interfere with your freedom to choose.* If it is given in too grandiose a style—if the being speaking through someone or making a magical appearance as a gold-lightbeing showering particles of gold light, or looking godlike, it would only be natural to beings cut off by the veils from who they really are to give these beings their power. They might not necessarily bow down to them but because what they say is so grandiose and wonderful, it is easy to follow what they say and totally disregard everything you know to be true. You might discard your wisdom, which is the knowledge you put into practice in your life because it works. In these times what is being tested, what you are being eased into doing and in many cases herded into doing, is practicing your wisdom.

Expect the Unexpected

You will all experience the unexpected now. It is not intended by Creator to harm you or inflict anything on you, but that you learn your wisdom so well that you can benevolently and gracefully move through any unexpected thing as easily as possible, doing the best for yourself and hence the best for others. It is intended that you not know very much about the future. That's why I and other beings are often vague when we talk about the future, because if you knew what was coming, you would all get together and say, "Okay, we know what's coming; this is what we've gotta do." You'd all agree on it, whether as a group or loosely as individuals. Not knowing the other groups are doing it, you'd all say, "This is what we'll do then so we can be prepared." You would follow the dictum of knowledge rather than apply your own wisdom.

So you see, Creator has you in this school so you will learn your own wisdom and apply it. You're in the application time now, so you can see what actually works. If something doesn't work or has consequences that harm yourself or somebody else in a way that is destructive, then you're going to have to modify that wisdom. Perhaps your wisdom has been what you thought, what was your philosophy, what seemed to make sense or was based upon experiences you have had in the past. It seemed to work, but circumstances are changing now, and you'll find yourselves in different circumstances. I don't mean just some of you; I don't mean just the enlightened ones. I mean *everyone*. You will find yourself in changed circumstances. They might not be permanent changes, but they will be *unexpected changes*.

That is vitally important to know. Most of these unexpected changes will be minor, not something that is life-changing. I'm not talking about a comet blasting into Earth and all of you all going on to other lives. I'm talking about simple annoyances, unexpected changes. You get to work and the phones are all down, you have a huge office and suddenly because the phones are down you find yourself going back to the old ways where you're basically running messages from one person to another. This passes, the phones get fixed eventually, but in the process you discover good things about interacting on a personal level with your office mates. This is just an example, I'm not predicting it's going to happen to everyone, I'm just suggesting an example.

You know, it is intended that wisdom accumulate. Some is discarded because it is no longer applicable in your life, and new wisdom is acquired based on your new experiences. Ultimately that's why you're here—to apply your wisdom in ways that benevolently work for you, and therefore for others. When you move through this time of the unexpected, which is a time of testing, when you get through it you'll know. How will you know that you're through it? Is it a time measured by years? No.

I will tell you exactly how: You will know because the unexpected does not perturb, distract or disrupt your life in any way and because you are used to applying the unexpected in the same way you apply your wisdom to what is expected. That's how you will know. These kinds of tests are not tests for children or for benevolent beings living in benevolent worlds elsewhere who are not training to become creators. These are tests for creators, and you are all creators in training. As a result you are expected to pass the tests at a higher standard than simply mouthing back the answer. "Oh," says you, "here is a test of the unexpected. I am supposed to apply my wisdom. Am I right?" That's not enough. "Yes, you're right, now apply it."

When it gets to be natural and easy and it just flows—"Oh, do this. It works for me"—you flow it as gracefully and gently as possible, then it's over and you move on. When it gets to be like that, then the test will be over. That doesn't mean you won't continue to experience the unexpected. It means that it will no longer be a burden.

30% of Humans Are Angels

What is the percentage of humans who are angels at this moment?

Never any less than 30%. At this moment it's right around— 42.8637%, something like that. Is it not vitally shocking to you how many human beings on Earth now are really angels?

Yes! I thought about 2%.

Oh, no. And do you know that they are in all walks of life? Not only people who are ministers and physicians and counselors, but people . . .

Rock musicians, starving children, everybody?

Yes—criminals, everyone. There are no exceptions, no job descriptions. You might be a soldier, a police officer or a burglar serving time. You might be something more extreme. You might have been murdered or be a murderer, but not in your heart. It's surprising. I don't want to talk about this stuff too much, but even the most extreme murderers are not that in their hearts, though usually they do not discover this until after their deaths.

I'm not trying to say that you all have an excuse for being what you are, because you always have a choice. Sometimes the choice is very hard, other times the choice is easier. But you do have a choice, so just know that you never know until life is over or at the deepest levels of your sleep. It's an interesting thing: Most of you, at the deepest levels of your sleep, can know this if you want to, though the chances of remembering it when you wake up are almost nil—about 0.03%. So there's a chance of knowing.

How are these lives chosen? Is it because of their inexperience that they make agreements to play certain roles, or do they consciously, deliberately choose certain roles?

They usually deliberately choose those roles. It is done with a little consulting with beings who are their teachers and (dare I say?) guides. Perhaps I ought to just say teachers so we don't get confused in words. Usually they pick lives that are representative of the beings they will guide initially. Once you've guided three or four beings, you have it mastered a lot more, just like any skill. Once you've been a guide to someone throughout his life and then go on to be a guide for somebody else throughout that life for two, three or four times, at most, perhaps you've got it down pretty well. You can still learn more, but you can handle the job.

Often the lives angels live are similar to the lives of the people they will be guiding. It practically is never the actual being, meaning that they'll incarnate later and have a similar life. Perhaps you're going to be a guide for someone who's a building contractor. For instance, a person's a building contractor and is married and has children, but as a youngster maybe got into a little trouble with the law but nothing he couldn't get over. In the latter part of life he/or she is a grandfather or a grandmother many times over (just giving a general potential). You might be a guide for a being who is generally like that so you would try to get a general idea of what the person you will be guiding someday will be like or what he/she has to deal with. I'm just picking out a job at random.

40% of Humans Not Explorer Race!

There's something even more spectacular here. It means that, unless they deliberately choose to go on, they're not part of the Explorer Race. You have 40% of the human population who are not part of the Explorer Race.

Interestingly enough, though, they will usually opt fifty-fifty. Fifty percent will go with the Explorer Race in some capacity, maybe as guides, if they're qualified. There will be a guide wherever you go in the future as you leave Earth and so on, at least as you leave three-dimensional Earth. Fifty percent will simply go on with what they were doing, with whatever their agenda is. So some of them will go with you, and so while they are not actually the Explorer Race, they will become supporting beings of the Explorer Race.

But they will leave when the Creator leaves?

They will make that choice when it comes. You see, as a result of being supporting beings or supporting guides or what-have-you, as you move toward becoming your version of the Creator [see *The Explorer Race* books]; you will have the chance potentially as a guide, an angel, a human being, to take a progression and then guide. You will have that chance if you affiliate yourself with the Explorer Race as it goes on. You might have the chance when the Explorer Race ultimately re-merges and becomes its own creator to replace this Creator, who is going on. It's too soon to say in experiential time, but you might have the chance, as a being like this, as a guide, to join the Explorer Race and become a portion of the new creator. This doesn't mean you have to, but you will be given that choice. At this time it looks possible.

The Problem of Deification

So then many times angels are used as messengers—as in stories in history, in the Bible, in mythology, all the way up to Moroni, the angel of the Mormons. They're used as messengers, but then they become deified because of the golden light?

Yes, this has been a real problem—how to cause an angel to simply be an advisor, a giver of love and support, usually at times when it's vitally needed, without being deified. It is because they are surrounded by and seemingly emanating gold light. The gold light is sent to protect them and pass to those they are exposed to (a benevolent gift for all concerned), so it has been a real problem to keep angels from being deified. That's part of the reason I'm trying to say that wings were a nice idea, and if you want to keep doing it in little children's books, okay. But I think angels look so much better with gold light emanating from them. They will always take the form of the type of being they are working with. If they are on some other planet as an angelic with someone in a death or birth cycle, they will look like that type of being. If they're on Zeta Reticuli attending a death cycle or one of a few ceremonies that the people there have, they will look like Zetas, but they will be emanating gold light and white light, as they do here.

This is fascinating.

You know, it is my job as end-time historian to give you information you can use if you wish. Sometimes I will say the same thing in different ways because different people respond to what's said differently. But also it is my job to mete out this information when it is needed. Sometimes that moment will come before the actual moment it's needed— maybe ten, fifteen years before, as with some of this material in this book. That's my job, to let you know these things when you need to know them. Fortunately, I have help. Others will say things, others will hear things and others will spread these opinions around. When I say "opinion," I'm doing it on purpose because I don't want you to deify me. Don't, okay?

There are a lot of angels channeling through humans now and giving guidance, but they don't really have that much experience. So possibly humans should really look carefully at that channeled information from the angels?

Michael Is Sometimes a Go-Between

If the information from angels coming through human beings now is about the angelic world or the angelic world's interaction with human beings at this time, it will probably have a fairly benevolent overview of human beings and what you've done on Earth. If it's about that, I think it's fine. But to hear from angels (I guess I'm going to give away a little secret here, . . . okay, I can do it—consulting with my friends) if it's about personal information or information that the angel does not in its own right know, two things are possible. If the angel is reasonably evolved, such as Michael, that angel being channeled will go to other sources and let those sources (in this case Michael) inspire, and pass that information on after being screened through Michael's personality. This means that the information will pour into Michael if Michael does not know.

This is actually a responsible act on Michael's part. If Michael does not know, that information will pour in, and it will come out through whoever's channeling Michael), but through Michael within the context of Michael's personality. When that information pours into Michael, it is a very responsible act by Michael because Michael would be opening itself up (Michael is not really a "he," but I'll say" he" for your convenience,) because he needs more information to give you what you need based upon someone's question or a need. Michael and other archangels are being responsible when they are doing that, but all archangels have blank spots. Many other beings have blank spots, too (I don't want to sound omniscient). Then they open themselves up and get inspired from others.

The Possibility of Loving Mistakes

For example, when I need inspiration about something physical on Earth, I have often gone to Speaks of Many Truths and others. I'm putting that out there again to make darn sure you don't put a pedestal under me. A moment—there is one other circumstances that some angels have if they're not very evolved and haven't gone through the whole process—meaning they're not an archangel. *They might be very loving and might feel your need for the information stronger than their experience in understanding consequences.* (I want that underlined or emphasized in any way you wish.) This might take the form then as an angel feeling your need for that information so strongly that it might clutch at straws of knowledge it has and fill it in the best it can, because it doesn't understand consequences very well.

You get to learn about consequences by living a life on Earth. You don't experience a life on Earth *without* learning about consequences. I am not saying these angels are bad, but that they feel your needs and love you so much that they clutch at straws of information they have. They don't know that it's more responsible, because of consequences, to open up to others who can give them the facts of the moment (you often learn something in the moment and then it's built on later) that are desired or needed by the questioner. That is how some information comes through that is erroneous. I want it to be understood that by "erroneous" I do not mean a lie or something malevolently intended, but a loving mistake.

Information that could cause the person hearing it to be frightened, or else take the information and let it guide them in a way they wouldn't take if they didn't have that information?

Yes, those hearing the information might take actions that they otherwise would not have taken, which might or might not serve them and others. All of this would have been as a result of a loving mistake. Now, *you've all done that before.* I don't want you to get mad at the angels, because you've all done it. Many of you have made mistakes out of love for your fellow human beings, family, friends, loved ones. You've made a mistake and it turned out wrong. You felt bad about it, but it was meant from love. The angels are more like you than unlike you.

30

A Message for People Seventeen Years Old and Younger

Zoosh through Robert Shapiro
January 30, 1997

N ow is the time, the calling, of the new people. The new people are what you call children or teenagers or adolescents—generally speaking, those who are seventeen years old or less. "The calling" simply means this. Most of you have been born into a society that has really had no real influence from you unless you were here in a recent life, which very few of you were. Now is a time for you to begin acting more on your inspiration. Those of you who are seventeen or younger are beginning to get inspirations meant for people who are not already thoroughly colored by society. This means that you will have chances to have ideas, pictures—in short, inspirations—that I'd like you to consider writing down or drawing or sketching if possible.

Many of you will have the opportunity in the coming years to influence society in one way or another. If you can begin to make some notes now about what is popping into your head, you will have some idea within the next four years of what to say, when, where and to whom to say it or what to show, because some of you will have visuals.

I'd like you to begin making some notes. When I say "the calling," it truly means that there is an exact preordained moment when something would happen for the younger people in this country and all over the world. This would be a moment when your future selves, roughly from around the year 2600 (experiential time along the lines of your calendar) would reach back and give you ideas and inspirations based on how they live in their time and, from their perspective, how they believe you might get to what they are. Begin looking and feeling for these things; begin imagining (that's what your imagination is for) what it might be like to live in a benevolent, benign society in which fun (if I may make a small joke) is taken very seriously indeed as an integral and necessary part of life in no way along the lines of schoolwork. I'm not talking about fake fun; I'm talking about real fun and the fact that true education, which impacts you and stays with you, often has to do with something pleasurable.

I'd also like you to understand that you new people have been living for a long time now with something that is arbitrary and not particularly natural. Many who are beyond the "new-person" range can also understand this: Adolescence, as it is called, is a time of life that is quite thoroughly misunderstood by your modern society. Its primary purpose is not just a sense of argumentativeness by individuals or a time of biological changes, but a time truly meant to move you away from your birth family. This is not because they are not good for you or you are not good for them, but because when you go through that time of change it is intended that you be more independent.

In more ancient and sometimes sacred societies, these are the times when a young girl or boy is moved from his/her birth family, usually to someplace nearby where they are able to learn the traditions associated with being a man or a woman. In your society the time of "adolescence" is considered something more biological than a true change. If youngsters moved out of their house into more independent surroundings when they were twelve or thirteen years old (or whenever they go through that change), you would find that a great deal of struggle, strife and even crime would disappear. I'm not talking about moving into group homes, but there needs to be some encouragement to be more independent. That is, after all, what the organisms in the body are urging every individual to do.

In ancient societies when people were that age they would ofttimes get married and start their own families. I know that would be controversial now, but it's something I want you to think about. At this time the young people of the world need to understand that older generations might be unable to show you how to live your life in a benevolent way. They might be able to give you what they have, but that is not always so benevolent. I want you to consider the idea of forming networks with each other, as some of you have already done with computers. Those of you who don't have computers, write to other people your age and begin to discuss how you would create a society that is more benevolent and fair to all, that encourages life and nurtures all beings.

31

Manifestation Powers Peak: The Ultimate Creatorship Training

Zoosh through Robert Shapiro
September 18, 1997

It's put-up or shut-up time. For a long time you have heard about—and some of you have dreamt, certainly some of you remember in past lives at higher dimensions—times where you want something or something is needed by you and—*pouf!* it is there. Instant manifestation. You also know that for the past several thousand years you have been kept from that ability here on Earth because instant manifestation would have been mischievous at the very least and catastrophic at times because of things you might have been thinking or feeling that you didn't even have full consciousness of (to say nothing of those of you who would like to wreak havoc in a moment of emotion and regret it afterward).

Now you are coming to the time of the reintegration of your higher-dimensional abilities into what you have learned—otherwise known as applied wisdom on the physical plane. It is a time in which you have to be very, very aware of what you are thinking, because even a stray thought might almost instantly manifest. When I say "almost instantly," I am not using a euphemistic spiritual term meaning sometime within the next few years. I mean manifesting almost *instantly*—sometime within the next ten minutes.

You are now at that point where you are being trusted by Creator—let's just say you're being given final tests by Creator and trusted sufficiently to take responsibility for your manifestations, and you're not being allowed to play very much on the fantasy level anymore.

Under some circumstances you can still have fantasies, but to do that you'll need to differentiate them clearly from your thoughts. Let's say you have decided to have a fantasy, to image something pleasant for you. You must create a separate stage for it—literally. It could be a stage or a place inside a dome or something clearly separate that is for your private pictorial (or even pastoral) place where you create your fantasies. If you don't do that, *it's going to register in the area of potential manifestation.*

I want to make this really clear, because a lot of you have fantasies. Most of them are very innocent, but some of them are fleetingly associated with temporary discomforting feelings. Perhaps you might experience a storm such as happened here in Sedona this afternoon and have a temporary thought, for instance: "Lightning will come through the window and hit me because the weather people say not to sit near the window during a thunderstorm because it could be dangerous." For a brief moment you have the feeling that lightning could come through the window.

When you are cognizant of that (you'll probably get a picture of it, not a worded thought), begin erasing the picture, as it were, like using a pencil eraser, erasing that lightning coming through the window and taking the thought back to its point of origin.

For those of you who have had point-of-origin thought training, this will be easy. You notice what you are thinking at any given moment, then you trace that thought pattern as far as you can back to when it began. When you get good at it, you'll easily be able to trace a thought back to where it started. It's good training. For one thing, it helps you to understand why you're thinking or feeling something, but in this case it can become almost a matter of life and death.

Now, I am not saying that every stray thought you have of lightning striking you will cause lightning to hit you, but ten years ago a stray thought or feeling of being struck by lightning would have manifested once in 1500 times. The 1500-to-1 odds really is equal to the potential ten years ago. Now, let's say today you have that same thought. The chance of that happening—this is why I am telling you this now—is *one in ten!* This tells you how far along the trail you are in being trusted and tested about manifestation.

Uncreating the Not-So-Perfect Creation

So the moment you notice that negative thought, as it's called, don't just say, "Uncreate!" That's not good enough. You have to actually see yourself erasing it or erase it in the air if it's a picture, trace that thought back to the point of origin, continuing to erase it, then go on with what you were doing. Obviously, if you are driving, you would want to pull over to do it or else ask to be protected until you can. But don't just forget about it, because it will accumulate, and the accumulation will have an effect. The next time that thought should happen—which might be twenty-five years down the road (but it could also be five hours)—will make it even more likely to manifest.

I am talking about the dark side of manifestation. Since you are living in a polarized place, it's a reality you have to deal with. *It is important for you to pay attention to what you are thinking!* If you catch yourself worrying, try and trace that worry back to its point of origin and rub it out. It's different if you're planning what to do about your challenges or difficulties; planning is different from worrying. Worrying is just fretting, "What's going to happen if . . ." That's not so good. But if you are making a plan, that's different; I make an exception for that.

This tells you something important: If manifestation is that possible now, now is the time to begin really focusing on *manifesting what you want in a benevolent way.* Whatever it is you want to manifest, say, "this benevolent thing in a benevolent way" for you. If it's something you're wishing for all people, then ask for it "in a benevolent way for all people," all right?

The reason I make this stipulation is that a person might ask for money or something and say, "I need $50,000 right now," thinking that, Well, if I had $50,000 I could coast for a while. But if you don't stipulate "in a benevolent way for me," you might or might not get your $50,000 (you know, there are no guarantees), but it *might* happen because somebody drives over your foot. You don't need that. It would be better to have the $50,000 in some benevolent way. So make sure you include that. (This is old stuff to a lot of you, but I am underlining it for those for whom it is not old stuff.)

I can't put too much of an exclamation point on this because *it is really happening now.* It's been coming on stronger for the past three or four weeks. It will peak, in terms of its intensity, in about six to eight weeks, but *it will maintain that peak for quite a few years.* I cannot tell you how long at this time because that's up to Creator, but it will maintain that peak for as long as Creator thinks you need it to become absolutely cognizant of what you are thinking in terms of what you want to manifest. For some of you whose lives seem out of control, pay attention to what you are thinking or what you are worrying about. It won't be easy, but begin disciplining yourself to think things that are more benevolent for you.

That's wonderful! We should be able to use that if we can plan and visualize and focus our thoughts on what we want. Right?

Yes. Try to be clear. If you want something, try to say, "This is what I want," but also try to picture how it might look, even if it doesn't wind up looking exactly like that. Picturing it will give your manifesting ability another means of identifying the value of that thing or that experience for you. Put yourself into the experience of it (as the moviemakers say, "Put yourself into the frame"), walking around enjoying it. It's going to have to be benevolent for it to work for you. Putting yourself into it makes it more effective. Reading a long list of what you want isn't good enough. Say it, picture it, see if you can feel it, then move to the next thing. It will take longer, but it will also work better.

Response to September 11 Caller on Art Bell Show

What can you tell us about the man who recently called the Art Bell Show and was cut off? Everybody is talking about it. What was he trying to say and what happened to him?

Regarding this incident [see next page for excerpt from Art Bell show] on the radio show you ask about, I will say that for a long time, since the late forties, some governments (certainly not all governments, just a few, one of which is the United States) have been aware that certain disasters could happen. When I say "governments," understand that I am referring to a few people in the government, not necessarily the president, all right? That applies to some people in the government and certainly plenty of people in the sinister secret government—that goes without saying.

Commenting directly on that call on the radio station, I want to say that it *could* happen. But you have been getting all this training in manifestation, in applied wisdom, in responsibility and consequences and all that, so you can change these things—because you *can!*

For years you have heard (those of you who read UFO and contactee literature) about people who have read the Yellow Book, sometimes referred to as the Gold Book. Generally, you have heard from various sources that ETs ain't what they're cracked up to be. It depends on who says it and what their attitude about ETs is in the first place. You are experiencing a polarized world and, for people on a growth curve as strong as yours, in the long run you will consider it an opportunity to have dealt with some polarized ETs. But by and large most of the ETs who come,

Excerpt from the Art Bell Show

Two hours and seventeen minutes into his September 11/12 CBC broadcast, Art received a call on his designated "Area 51" call line, as follows.

Art: *On my Area 51 line, you're on the air, hello.*

Male caller: *Hello, Art?*

Art: *Yes.*

Caller [sounds frightened]: *I don't have a whole lot of time.*

Art: *Well, look, let's begin by finding out if you're using this line properly or not.*

Caller: *Okay, in Area 51?*

Art: *Yes. Are you an employee, or are you now?*

Caller: *I'm a former employee. I, I was let go on a medical discharge about a week ago and, and . . . [chokes] I kind of been running across the country. Damn, I don't know where to start. They're, they're gonna, they'll triangulate on this position really soon.*

Art: *So you can't spend a lot of time on the phone. So give us something quick.*

Caller [voice breaking up]: *Okay, uh, uh, okay, what we're thinking of as aliens, Art, they're extradimensional beings that an earlier precursor of the space program made contact with.*

They are not what they claim to be. They've infiltrated a lot of aspects of, of, of the military establishment, particularly the Area 51.

The disasters that are coming, they, the military — I'm sorry, the government — knows about them. And there's a lot of safe areas in this world that they could begin moving the population to now, Art.

Art: *So they're not doing, not doing anything.*

Caller: *They are not. They want those major population centers wiped out so that the few that are left will be more easily controllable . . ."*

Art: *. . . discharged . . .*

Caller [sobbing]: *I say we g . . .*

Bell's radio engineer reported that the network's communication satellite lost 50 channels, including Art's feed. It took awhile to figure out what happened. Although Art's signal was okay, the network was not, yet while the network was working, Art's signal alone dropped out. Different channels on the satellite dropped out at different times.

To get the entire story, see www.artbell.com/satoutage.html.

have ever come, or will ever come here are benevolent. They don't hang around too long because the polarization is hard for them to take.

In the late forties certain ETs (I won't go through this because it's in *The Explorer Race*) came to share their technology with some governments. They went to England, France, Russia and the U.S., sharing a little with this one, a little with that one; they went to various places. Since the forties they've been to Canada, Chile (I will name a few), Switzerland, a few more places. They've talked about things, shared some of their philosophy and in some cases their technology. All this was designed to help you alter your future.

Mother Earth's Survival Mechanisms

Understand that you can poison, damage and hurt Mother Earth only so long before she has to fight for her life. (Speaks of Many Truths has talked extensively about this.) You know it's natural—what do they say a rat does? You don't think of a rat as violent unless you've seen one when it's frightened for its life or when it's hungry, and it can be pretty formidable in either of those circumstances. I am not comparing Mother Earth to a rat, but a rat is one of Earth's creatures.

We all know that people might tend to fight for their life in a pinch —all people, beings, animals, everything. That's not because spirit causes you to fight for your life. Spirit absolutely knows, whether you are a rat, a mouse, a caterpillar, a human being, an apple tree or whatever form, that you are going to go on, so it would never—and I mean *never* —encourage you to fight for your life. It sees life as continuous.

What encourages you to fight for your life is Mother Earth. That urge is natural to Earth beings. And while it might be demonstrated by other beings, it is always and only demonstrated because of the material that makes up the being, but *not* because of your immortal personality, otherwise known as your spirit or your soul. You have to understand that absolutely or you will miss the point here.

ET Intervention

This tells you something. Given this natural phenomenon on Earth, when the ETs came in the late forties and talked to various governments and said, "This is what's going to happen," the people on Earth asked, "How do you know?" The ETs replied, "We have gone ahead in time and we've seen what's going to happen. We want to help prevent that. In order to do that . . . " And that is what the sticking point is, why you haven't heard about ETs in a big way from governments (in a small way but not in a big way). The ETs said, "You've got to change spiritually." They didn't mean they wanted to sell you a religion they've got, but that you've got to change individually, each and every one of you, in your spiritual outreach in life, in your spiritual approach—meaning *how you act.*

Recognize that everything is alive, including the beings we have been talking to recently.* If everything and everyone is alive, you must treat them accordingly. (There is no "if," but I use it as a conceptual structure.) That was the sticking point. When the ETs said that you must act differently, all the human beings took a step back, saying, or thinking at least to themselves, "I'm not giving up *my* religion" or "I'm not giving up *my* nationality" or "I'm not giving up citizenship in *my* country." But you have to move beyond that, you see. You don't have to give up being an American or a German or a Brazilian, but you do have to expand sufficiently so that you can become an Earth person. If someone lives in Germany or Argentina or Norway or Thailand, they are your brothers and sisters—not just conceptually; it's a heart connection.

In other words, you have to take spiritual steps forward, not as a mental spirituality but as an applied, felt and feeling heart-centered spirituality. The ETs say if you can do this, then *you can avoid all this,* because you will then be connected to all your fellow beings; you will know when fellow beings are suffering and you will want to help them.

Mother Teresa, an Embodiment of Heart-Centered Spirituality

An example of someone in your own conceptual awareness who knew what other people were feeling and did something about it is obviously Mother Teresa. Now you are going to make a saint out of her, but she was a human being. I will tell you something: She didn't *want* to become a saint, but go ahead and make her a saint if you want to. But if you make her a saint, that means she is more than human. Mother Teresa would much rather have had you identify with her as a human being and say, "If Mother Teresa did that, I can do it, too." That's the whole point.

The idea is that if you can feel other beings, then you know what they want and you can help them. *That's* how you change the future from being a dramatic, unpleasant one to being a pleasant, benevolent one.

What this individual [caller on Art Bell show] was referring to was that these documents—I am loath to call them predictions, because that word has been bandied about so much—these spoken words based

---

* This refers to the Creator's consultants, friends and forebears, particles of entities here and beyond our ken and intelligences far beyond our past imagination, all of whom have been giving information and answering questions since July 1996. Available now are *Explorer Race: Origins and the Next 50 Years, Explorer Race: Creators and Friends—Mechanics of Creation* and *Explorer Race: Particle Personalities.* To be released in spring 1998 is *Explorer Race and Beyond,* with further volumes forthcoming..

246 • SHINING THE LIGHT: Humanity Is Going To Make It!

upon eyewitness accounts of people who traveled in time, were considered very valuable. Obviously, if someone tells you the future, they say, "So-and-so is going to be president and such-and-such will be the main trends of the economy." If you know all that stuff and keep it to an esoteric group, your group is obviously going to be rich, powerful and influential.

That's the way it was heard, not because everybody in all those governments was greedy, but because external forces were applied upon those people to keep that information to a select few. In some cases they wanted to keep it secret, but in other cases they didn't. They wanted to go public and say, "Hey, we can change the future into something more benevolent." But someone said, "That's nice; we'll think about it and take it under advisement. Maybe it will happen that way, but for now don't tell anybody about this or you'll be sorry." That's basically what happened."

Averting Man-Made Disasters with Clear Intent

The reason for this issue to be up for you now is that if these catastrophes are going to happen, most of them will be *man-made!* I said *most.* Let's say there will be ten catastrophes, for the sake of example. (There might not be that many, there might be more, but ten is a number that makes it easy to do percentages.) Among the ten catastrophes, about six or seven would be man-made, and *all* the people who bring those catastrophes about are people who have been in pain about something or other for a long time. They have wanted those grievances redressed in some way. They wanted somebody to help them, to do something or at least try. Now, I am not trying to justify terrorism, because there is no excuse for it even though it seems like the last resort for many people. You could easily say that the United States was founded by terrorist acts —that's exactly how England saw it, and it certainly was the way native Americans saw it. Whether you identify something as terrorism depends on your position.

Without positioning myself one way or another, I would say this: If 60 to 70% of these catastrophes will be man-made, don't you understand that *if you link to all your fellow beings and feel their pain, then do what you can about it, you have the chance to change all the catastrophes caused by human beings?* That takes out 60 to 70% of the catastrophes right there. Then you *do* have the capability to deal with the Earth-change catastrophes. Even if they are earthquakes, volcanoes, typhoons or hurricanes, you can deal with this because you've dealt with all of these catastrophes before and you know what to do. It is the man-caused things you might not have experience with.

You see, *that* is where I want you to put your focus. And, I might add (as an aside), that is why most of the more influential governments of the world have a big staff of people doing psychic stuff to feel into what terrorists are going to do. Although I completely understand, and would even go so far as to say that I sympathize with that effort, ultimately what will change these acts is doing something to resolve the grievances people have. I freely admit that sometimes there's little you can do about it because the grievances are sometimes so polarized, but you can always do something—not just make promises, but an actual effort. I can leave that up to you.

I won't comment on the drama of the call or the individual who called. I will say that the points brought up [government's response to the ET warning of future catastrophes and urging for change] were valid and important. I am *not* going to say that ETs are monsters who are taking over your governments with some vague intention of taking over your world, because most truly negatively polarized ETs cannot tolerate surface living. They could tolerate only subsurface living where the environment is very closely controlled. But we all know that Earth is a living being; things are moving all the time, and closely controlling things is not so easy.

So don't hit the panic button about ETs taking over your planet. I think you'll find that the ET influence on your planet is for the most part (you want a figure?)—93%—is benevolent. The 7% that isn't benevolent is not directly caused by the ETs, but by the people they influence. If 93% of it is benevolent and encouraging people to do benevolent things, I think ET contact is good.

If you don't mind my joke, for years and years I have been hearing, "Zoosh, when are the ETs going to land? When are we going to be able to be with the ETs?" Now that the ETs are getting closer and more of an influence with you, don't hit me with that bit about, "Oh dear, the *aliens* are coming!" I am not going to listen to that: I won't have an ear for it.

I don't think you have much to worry about in terms of real ETs. As a matter of fact, I think you have almost everything to gain. I think you have only one real challenge of ETs that are not benevolent, and that will play out in the theater of politics. I want to tell you a lot about it, but I feel that I could change it, so I would rather say this: *Watch out for those who drape themselves in the flag or with religion and accuse others of being evil for simply being who they are.* That kind of despotism has been what you as a planetary human society have been very susceptible to before. *That* will be the challenge you will face from not-so-benevolent ETs.

I am not saying that every politician who is patriotic or religious is a negative ET or influenced by them, but watch out for it, because that kind of extremism ultimately and frequently leads to terrible harm to innocent people. That's my comment.

Yellow Book Predictions Not Set in Stone

We haven't talked about the Yellow Book for years. What's the time frame that the catastrophes peak at? Around now?

Right around now, yes—'97 to '99. It stretches potentially out to 2005, but a lot depends on spiritual changes on Earth. You are being tested with your manifestation ability. These things are built in; it's going to happen, so what are you going to manifest? I know you all want to manifest something benevolent for yourself.

And for the planet.

The Umbrella Effect of Benevolent Manifestation

Yes, for the planet and for all the people. Here's an example. (This is not going to happen, but I will use it as an arbitrary example.) Let's say, as a *fictional* example, that the city in which you live will be hit by a runaway atomic bomb. The rocket has gone off and nobody can stop it. It's coming toward your city—this is right out of a movie plot, okay? But *you've* decided and are absolutely manifesting a benevolent experience for yourself. You are either going to feel a sudden urge to leave town, or (ten times more likely) you will stay right where you are and that bomb will not hit because *it wouldn't be benevolent for you!*

That's how powerful benevolent manifestation is. If even *one* person is doing this and it's working, *it's not going to happen!* Think how powerful it would be if ten people are doing this, or a thousand or ten thousand. It pyramids. It works well for you and it tends to have a protective effect on others as well—not because you radiate it to them, but if you're in an elevator when elevators all around you are falling because the cables aren't working and you are manifesting benevolent things for you, then you *and everybody else in that elevator* will be safe as long as you are on it. Do you understand? So this works for you *and* others. It has a sort of umbrella effect.

For the readers could you say in one sentence or two who the beings were who gave the information that's in the Yellow Book?

They're the little people with the big eyes and the big heads. These people are sometimes called Grays. They hate that name. Don't call them that—it's an awful name. Those of you who are white people (although you are obviously not white like a piece of paper) don't like being called white people. You like being called who you are—by your given name or at least by your nationality, if you are Irish or German or whatever. Being called white makes you feel like a thing. It is the same thing for those people whose skin is not really gray but because it has a slight tinge of grey they get called that. It's the worst possible approach.

But there's a way to begin. You know they are from Zeta Reticuli, so if you have to call them anything, call them Zetas or Zeta Reticulans. That's where they're from. These are beings who were inclined (at least from the mid to late forties, the fifties and as late as 1960-61) to show this material to some people. Toward the end it was with individual contactees. After 1961 they didn't show the book much. They kind of gave up.

In the beginning they tried it with governments; that's what you would do if you were coming from another planet. You would say, "Well, let's try the governments first." Of course, in the late forties they didn't really have a viable United Nations, but thanks to Mr. Turner [who today announced a donation of $1 billion to the U.N.], the United Nations might become more viable in the future

You alluded to the human-caused 60% of the possible ten incidents.

Sixty to seventy percent, give or take—and ten was an arbitrary figure.

The Influence of Humanity's Intent

I understand. So what we are basically looking at, focusing our benevolent energy on, are people from countries who have grievances, who might support terrorist activities, whether it's with bombs or plagues or whatever?

Yes, and if you *are* these people—these people are not just psychos, to use a term out of the movies. Granted, it's psychological, but it's become larger than life with the moving pictures. They're not that. If you talk to them or are one of them, they feel the rightness of their position with a great passion, and bombing and terrorist acts are not the first thing they have done. This is a desperate last act of someone who's saying, "Well, we are going to get their attention if it kills them."

Or us.

Yes, "It will get their attention if it kills us *or* them." That is usually the last resort. If that's the last resort, there was a first resort at some point. It might have been a simple conversation between two people on the street. If someone tells you that you are an awful person, you don't have to accept the abuse of that person. On the other hand, if that person is saying that a government (for which you might feel some benevolent feelings, not necessarily your own government) has taken certain positions and it's been terrible for your people and your family has directly suffered, you can be sympathetic.

You might say, "I wonder if there is something I can do to help, perhaps write a letter to my congressman in the United States or petition somebody," actually do something. Be willing to take a position where you actually *do* something. You are not going to be able to save this person; if they're destined to do something, they're going to do it. But begin to help people who are hurting, even just by putting them in your prayers, saying, "I hope" and asking God to help them to change them, but to help them get what they want in a benevolent way.

You know, that word is so good—"benevolent." It means that they get what they want and it doesn't hurt anybody else. If everybody puts them into their prayers like that, even if you can't go to the other side of the world to help them, it helps. *It really does help!* I have said this before and I will say it again: Much of the reason World War II ended the way it did is that *a lot of people prayed.* You would be surprised how much an influence it was.

32

SSG Downs Military Planes

Zoosh through Robert Shapiro
September 25, 1997

F rom September 13 to 19 several U.S. military planes went down in different places, four in the U.S. What really happened?

You are curious why so many military craft would crash within a week. Understand that to some extent the rationale that the President made is true. It is a dangerous profession, and a certain amount of crashes will take place. On the other hand, I will say that some of the crashes were aggravated by conditions.

Now, I've said for a while that the sinister secret government [SSG] is attempting to perfect weapons that are basically undetectable by conventional means. They might be detectable from satellites only because satellites can be focused to see the whole picture (the whole Earth and its immediate atmosphere). As a result, it is more likely to pick up an energy anomaly when looking at the whole Earth from, say, several different satellites. Because of so many radiated energies (not the least of which are power lines) picking up an energy anomaly from the Earth's surface is much more difficult.

I will pick out a specific crash—that of the Stealth fighter [Air Force F-117 fighter at the September 14 Maryland air show] where the pilot made a heroic effort to avoid casualties. I compliment the pilot on that. The part of the plane that fell off was not due to a breakdown in the metal (metal fatigue). The plane does not use only metal in its framework, so it wasn't caused by that. It was caused by the SSG testing of an underground weapon partly based in ultrasound, where the sonic waves are used as an agitator. By this I mean that the sonic waves do not

Sept. 14, 1997: Air Force F-117 Stealth, Maryland air show; pilot lived.

actually come up through the ground, but activate another weapon, which when focused at a given object causes it to be struck. The beam is not necessarily round; it could be flat and 8 to 10 feet wide—at least that's the aperture through which they were firing it at that time. When it's aimed at a specific part of the plane, it causes a vibration whereby the object it's aimed at moves very slightly but intensely.

If you were to put your hand on the wing of the plane, you would not feel the vibration because the motion is so slight, but it is very intense. The test was also done against a naval ship at one point. The superstructure essentially disintegrates anything it is aimed at. As far as I know, you do not at this time have a metal that can stand up to this weapon; you might be able to manufacture one, but it would require the use of rare earths and might require significant mining on the Moon to get enough.

That is what caused that plane to fall apart in midair. When you consider the piece that fell off, it's quite impressive that the pilot was able to deflect the plane from crashing into the homes of people. He did a good job. It could have been much worse.

Usually, when the SSG tests such an exotic weapons technology, they aim at something local. This test at the air show was intended to be a visible threat. There's not much point in military circles of having a threatening weapon unless the other side knows you have it.

To be able to negotiate or win your point of view in an argument, the other side needs to be afraid of you or at least respect your power. So the SSG very slyly (as always, through a third party) established a threat, through one of their terrorist front groups, against the Air Force—and also more broadly against the military forces of the U.S.—to demonstrate an unstoppable weapon that could be used against a single target. If you read such a threat, you might consider a single target to be a city; it wouldn't occur to you that a single target might be a single plane.

You are saying that someone sent them a letter through . . .

The terrorist front group communicated with one of the foreign embassies of the United States that a weapon would be used on a single target of the U.S. military to demonstrate their power—and that would have been put in grandiose terms, because terrorist groups are known to speak this way even though they do not always do so.

Considering how many threats the embassy and their chain of command receive all the time, it wasn't disregarded, but because it was so vague and there wasn't a specific thing stated, the investigating agencies did what they could. But of course, how are you going to protect every possible target?

SSG Targets National Guard

This plane was therefore a demonstration of the weapon. Previous crashes of National Guard and more localized military targets were initially brought down this way. Normally such weapons technology are initially tested against National Guard units. This is because even though many pilots in National Guard units might have years of experience, the public and even the chain of command within the National Guard might perceive that the crews are not as finely tuned or as well-trained as an Air Force crew on constant duty.

The beam does not have to be flat and wide. It can be as tight as a small pinhole or a precise laser. Anything hit by it would come apart and it would look exactly like metal fatigue. In the case of other types of materials, it would simply look like a flaw in the original material. It would be otherwise undetectable. So the weapon, when it was originally tested and caused damage and people died . . .

How long ago was that?

I will just say within the past six months. It was not detected; it was assumed that either the crew was not experienced enough or that there was some problem with the machine itself. One of the targets in the past six months was a naval ship, but it didn't cause great harm. It was simply an attempt to see whether a long-range target could be struck precisely to do minimal damage but could conceivably be expanded on.

Think about it. Let's say you had a naval ship with a conventional hull. You could fire something at that ship without causing an explosion, and anything like that would appear to be an accident. Thus this weapon would be extremely secret and you might be able to destroy vast amounts of hardware, yet be undetectable to the people servicing that hardware. In the process you might be able to break down the trust that is necessarily established between the government, the military and the industry that supplies the military's needs. If you can get the military to distrust industry, you can, by such manipulation, cause the military to use your own industrial front. Then when you provide them with weapons graded to military specifications, you can throw in a few extra goodies that you can then activate to eavesdrop or whatever you wish. You would be surprised at the sophistication of such things these days!

So the first goal was to do the damage, then see what happened. The second goal, which was just as important, was to manipulate military contracting as to the cause of the accidents, breaking down the trust that

Sept. 13, 1997: Air Force C-141, off Namibia; nine crew killed.

must exist between military contractors and the military served by them. Now, I am not saying that everybody is starry-eyed and blindly trusting, but there has to be a degree of faith. If you can break that down, you then might easily manipulate the contracts to go to the industry *you* are backing (from the SSG's point of view).

Of these six incidents—the National Guard had two planes—you said one crash was caused by the SSG—were any of the other five? For instance, on September 13 an Air Force C-141 off Namibia crashed; nine crew members were killed.

Yes, the one that collided with the German plane was also a test, but it was a different weapon. The SSG is working on undetectable sonic weapons more than ever these days. Sonic weapons have been tested at length by the conventional militaries of many different countries, but they have seen only limited usage because they have in the past exhibited undesirable side effects. If you were firing one of these weapons, your own crew could be injured by being nearby and it has also been almost impossible to disguise the source. The moment you pull the trigger, so to speak, if the other side has the means to detect it, they will know it instantaneously and knock out that target. That's why most sonic weapons have not been pursued to any great degree by the conventional military, with the possible exception of some satellite military technology.

SSG's Electronic Field Technology

Now, the SSG has been working for some time to perfect sonic weapons to make them undetectable and have a wide range of application. They have also attempted for quite a while to establish what I would call an electronic field effect that would create a radionic pattern that the computers would read as normal and acceptable. The computers on a plane (either military or civilian) do not inform the pilots if something is detected that is considered normal.

They have wanted to create an electronic field, a blanket of energy that would cause the computers of two planes flying on a collision course to read out everything as normal, especially in circumstances where you might not see the other plane until it was too late. There would be no warning of an impending collision, including no ground warning. Now, in the case of less sophisticated airports and terminals, you might not have equipment that would broadcast a warning on the ground, but this weapon has been perfected to such a degree now that even if the planes were to take off from the most sophisticated military airport or an average civilian airport, no ground equipment would detect an impending collision—which they normally would.

This is highly sophisticated electronic warfare and, once informed of this, I believe it will be possible for your military to establish a fairly quick solution. But instead of the usual electronic detection you will have to use some other means, most likely utilizing satellites, which I think you will be able to very quickly use to map all aircraft. Although this is largely done now with global positioning satellites and so on, it is not foolproof. So I think there will need to be other means. This particular wave of energy that can be established between two encroaching objects in midair flight is so apparently innocent that even a global-positioning satellite might be fooled.

Trying not to be too technical, I will just say that this deserves a significant amount of action and reaction from those who are in the field of electronic warfare to establish a defense against this. Should the SSG decide to establish another country or even a terrorist group's minimum air force as a powerful dominant force in the world by utilizing such electronic weapons, this could cause the air forces of other countries to become inefficient to the point of useless.

All right, that's two of the events. What about the others?

The others were genuinely what they seemed. Two out of the six were not accidents, but the other four are.

And the B-1 bomber near the Montana-Wyoming border, four crew members killed?

Yes, the B-1 bomber—that was a malfunction aboard the plane, which I think is traceable.

Would you like to say more about that, since that might help some people?

I think that it had to do with the plane's thrust mechanism, meaning the engines. Unfortunately, since the plane was almost entirely obliterated, it would be very difficult to trace it, but I would look in the area of the air intakes for such planes. I would also look in the detection equipment. As you know, with such modern planes almost every system has sensors in it, but I think there are not enough sensors there to detect difficulties in the air intake.

Okay, they do something underground that's ultrasonic and that triggers something else. What is triggered? Is this something on a satellite? Is it HAARP? Is it something moving around? Where is the other part of this weapon?

I am loath to describe it, and I will tell you why. Understand that right now at least half of the conventional military forces around the world have done enough background research on ultrasonic weapons that if I were to tell you how the rest of the weapon worked, they would be able to perfect that weapon for themselves in less than two weeks.

This tells you that the rest of the weapon is not particularly exotic.

For those who are looking for how it works, is there no way for anyone to see where it is? Does it move around?

It can be moved around, but it usually doesn't because it is basically undetectable by conventional means. If you can use satellites at a distance (the farthest distance in their orbit around Earth), you might be able to detect it, because the point of detection is underneath the Earth. You can't detect the energy field being broadcast once it clears the surface. The system to detect the initial sonic energy is not in existence now.

HAARP's Mapping Assignment

Is HAARP functional? Have they got the bugs worked out? Is it being used? Is it beamed at us?

It is being used. It is not particularly being used against human beings at this time. Its primary military use is for mapping. Although it is said to check things about the atmosphere, ultimately one of the main rationales for its use is that it can send a broad signal, not just a pinpoint signal, that remains relatively intact for quite a distance. Its reflection, not unlike radar or sonar, can be used to map nearby objects such as the Moon or passing asteroids and also to detect the shape and to some extent even the details of flying objects. Of interest to you would obviously be flying objects from other planets. This is the actual intended purpose, I would say. They have managed to get a pretty clear picture of some of the really large so-called motherships. They have been able to get surface details not ordinarily detected by laser techniques.

I would say that it's serving its function pretty well. At this time it's not being utilized intentionally against human beings, though that could be done at any time. I might add that this is part of the reason that some of these bigger motherships have pulled back to a greater distance. To be struck by such an energy wave would be unhealthy to the beings onboard the ships. Using their methods of deflecting such energy waves (this is the sneaky part about this detection system) tends to make the ship itself more easily definable. If you were directing this energy wave at something, you would get a pretty fair picture of it. But once the mothership began to use its own energy waves to deflect it, you would get a much better picture.

Thus the systems used to sustain life aboard the ship actually make the ship more vulnerable to detection. That's why they have pulled back at a distance. Not because the people onboard the ship were being seriously injured, but the cumulative effect would have harmed them.

Pulled back to what type of an orbit?

Comparing the distance from the Earth to the Moon, generally three times that distance. Once they get out about 1 times the distance of the Earth to the Moon, a ray does not at this time injure the people. Needless to say, enlarging the array is certainly in the plans if the project proves itself valuable—and it *has* proven itself to be valuable in a clandestine way, such as mapping techniques.

What ships have they mapped? From what planet, what star systems?

Most of the ships are from the future, so it might not make a difference, but one of the ships is from the Pleiades and one of the other ships is from a star system that doesn't exist in your now time.

The Birth of a Future Sun

Why are they here from the future?

They are curious to visit the point of origin of their sun. In the *far distant* future (and I do mean distant) your now Sun and its five closest planets will merge and become a sun of its own. That will be the sun source for the galaxy [solar system] that will bloom from this. But understand that I am talking about something in such a far distant future that I cannot measure it in years.

You mean a galactic or cosmic cycle.

Yes, so they are curious. I might add that if you went back far enough and were able to travel in time with your own sun, you would see that it too originally was a planet. Not all suns are like this, but suns around this area—which is basically dedicated as point of study (that is why the Explorer Race is here) for other races for other potentials, other solutions—normally come from planets. It is not an anomaly here.

Did the planet that became our Sun have life on it, and what was its sun?

Yes, it was a planet with life on it—again, in the far-flung past—orbiting around a sun that is no longer present. As a result of the sun gradually dying (this is a point of study), the populations of that planet were lifted off, with their acquiescence, to other places. That planet was converted to a sun and moved so that planets could orbit around it. There are technologies that exists—in other realms, let's say—where a planet can be converted to a sun. Obviously, that technology does not exist here; it would be used, to put it mildly, mischievously.

SSG Loses a Member

So the secret government is continuing all of its endeavors. The inner circle is still going strong and they haven't lost anybody by revolt or defection?

They have, in fact, lost somebody.

Just one?

Yes, they lost somebody who actually transformed. Since we originally began talking about this there have been a lot of individuals and groups of individuals beaming lots of transformative, loving light energy toward the SSG to try and transform [its members]. They are able to deflect most of it, of course, but some of it, as with any vast amount of loving energy, gets through. The youngest member was transformed and left. By being transformed, he was *able* to leave, so they are one down.

Is he out in the general population or ascended, or what?

If he ascended, he would have to be dead.

So he's sort of anonymously out there someplace?

Yes, he's out there and is just like everybody else, as it were. He's living a normal life.

That's wonderful!

They probably will not replace him.

What about the alternative negative-future's ongoing attempt to influence the SSG? Is that still strong?

It's not as strong; I'd say it's one-tenth of a percent less strong than it was, but that helps.

SSG's Current Project: Fueling Racial Conflict

All right. Last time we asked (I think you couldn't say) they'd moved out of the underground bases and were under Las Vegas or something. You can't really say where they are?

No, I can't say where they are. The reasons I haven't been commenting on them is that things are in such a stage of being now that what *you* are all doing on the surface is quite significant, and what *they* are doing under the surface (the SSG) has not been as significant. To the greater degree of your own evolution spiritually on the surface, they're more likely (the SSG) to be quiet. They usually strike only when you are down. As any bully knows, that's when you are weakest. You've been up lately. Now, I am not saying you haven't been having some hard, tough times and getting hurt now and then, but by and large you've been up, and as a result they are quiet.

The weapons testing—I do not consider that a major influence. Of course, their ongoing project is ever-present: the attempt to keep the races fighting amongst each other. The whole racism project has probably been their biggest "success," because they have managed to fuel the fires quite well. So they keep that going. I am not saying that peoples do not have their own prejudices, but racist organizations that operate as a profit-making business usually have an unknown silent partner.

What about the Middle East? Are they fueling some of that terrorism—the suicide bombs and so on?

If you look at the Middle East situation in the cold light of reality and step out of strong feelings one way or the other, most of the terrorism in the Middle East is desperate action by people whose causes are just and are simply not being heard, as I've mentioned before. They are not really fueling much of that. What they are fueling in the Middle East, as in other places such as Africa, is intertribal warfare amongst the Arab peoples (using that biblical term for the sake of clarity, speaking to the Western world). They are also doing what they can to fuel the concept and practical application of racism there. They want the Israelis to hate all Arabs and all Arabs to hate all Israelis, and they will fuel *any* cause that will further that means. But are they directly responsible for Middle Eastern so-called terrorism? No.

You said there is quiescence. There are no plans at the moment to go off to another solar system or go forward in time?

No, they are waiting. They have also been informed that there are certain bacteria on Earth, most of which are not on the surface (you have benevolent bacteria in your digestive system that are not on your surface, either), and if they do this push or that pull on Mother Earth (mining or detonation as examples), some of these bacteria would come to the surface and cause widespread damage to Mother Earth and to the surface populations. Of course, ultimately they don't want to destroy you—they want to manipulate you and be the boss and make the money.

Who informed them of that?

They are informed through their own satanic techniques. They are now able to detect what might be or could be the more malevolent potentials.

El Niño: Mother Earth's Reaction to Atomic Testing

What about El Niño? What they are doing with the energies,? Does that have anything to do with this weather?

They are not actually stimulating El Niño. That is really a reaction by Earth to things being done to her by people who are mining and, most important, by people who have in recent years set off underground or undersea atomic blasts, what they call tests. El Niño is a reaction to all underground, aboveground and undersea atomic tests and other atomic explosions that have taken place since 1951.

The problem with atomic blasts, aside from the damage they do, is that the devices use uranium, and uranium is Mother Earth's brain. It's part of her mental powers. I've said many times before that Mother Earth does not think as you do, but she does think as *she* does—meaning immediate or now thought, not positioned in the past or future as in linear thought.

So if you take some of her brain structure and detonate it (dig it up out of her body, out of her brain), transform it into the modern devices and then detonate it, like taking your brain and installing it in your hip, it doesn't work well. It's scattering her brain energy all over. This tends to activate her self-defense forces, which are inclined to put things back together again. Those forces will include water in some context. For the past fifteen or so years when people have asked about Earth changes, I've always said that the number-one Earth change will have to do with water, and to a secondary degree, Earth motion such as earthquakes (or even creep, a slow, gradual motion) and to some extent vulcanism. Vulcanism has increased in recent years compared to 150 years ago.

This has all been activated: If somebody is invading you, your body's defense systems will go to work, and your bodies are built on the same frame of reference as Mother Earth's body. It is automatic. El Niño is part of her defense system.

Status of Fresh Water

This is sort of off the subject, but we are so desperate for fresh water. I read just recently that 80 to 90% of all the fresh water is at the north and south poles. Is that being saved for the next era or something?

Saved by whom?

It's not available to us. We are desperate for safe drinking water, but most of the fresh water is poisoned.

Yes, that's true, but the poles will and are intended to very gradually melt. When Mother Earth has a cycle of surface population, she condenses her ice at the poles. This is something she is doing rather than something that is being saved for future generations.

When she doesn't have a cycle of population (as in past ice ages when there wasn't much population) and she needs to rest and restore herself, then she will allow an ice age to take place. Underneath the ice she can rest, but she will not generally do that when there is a cycle of population.

There is no way for us to get that water to drink. There are so many people on the planet and the water is polluted . . .

Well, not a practical way. Believe me, people have thought about it. There isn't a practical way now. Of course, if people really wanted to do it, it might be possible to bottle it, but you would have to sell it, and I hardly consider that getting the water to the people.

Passing of Princess Diana and Mother Teresa
Sparks Wave of Compassion

You on the surface are now experiencing a greater benevolent energy coming *not* from someplace else, but largely from your own actions and reactions, most recently as in response to the death of Princess Diana, who was loved more than most people really understood in a mental sense. And of course also Mother Teresa. Sometimes the simple passage of such people gives the rest of the people permission to be expressive in ways they do not usually express.

Many people (those reading this know it's true) did not feel particularly attached or even interested in the Princess's life. A lot of you liked and respected her at a distance, but no more than you would like or respect anyone else at a distance doing things of value. Your reaction to her death ran, in many cases (over half) deeper than the loss of a family member. It was not only because she was a particularly beautiful being, but it was the timing. When such a being leaves you, usually it is when he or she is doing something really worthwhile (not the least of which was the Princess's project of removing all land mines and banning them in the future, which I heartily support) and when you feel you need her the most. At that time he or she might pass on unexpectedly, such as in the passing of other loved teachers.

This is always and only to activate the same powers and abilities within you. She had the power of absolute compassion, which completely engages forgiveness, love and allowance. That's what absolute compassion is. She had that power. She was born with it. It was natural to her.

When she passed over, it was as if all of you had that button pushed in you, at least for a time, of absolute compassion. You were able to identify that compassion with her, but more important, with yourselves. A great deal of compassionate feeling toward your fellow beings, regardless of race, religion or nationality, was very evident during that time and even today as a result of her passage.

I am not saying that she was a god—no more or less than any of you. I am saying that because of that natural ability she had, which has been latent in all of you (some have that ability to the great degree she did her passing has activated that ability in you. It was followed in a one-two punch with Mother Teresa's passing, a person who all people, I believe, recognized for the saintly behavior she demonstrated, though her intention was to demonstrate what all people could do. Both of those people had absolute compassion, and their passage left you a legacy of absolute compassion in yourselves.

33

Space-Age Questions

Zoosh through Robert Shapiro
October 22, 1997

T *he Wednesday, October 8 edition of The New York Times has a picture of a* *star 10 million times as bright as our sun at the center of the galaxy. Will you tell* *us what it is?*

The Brightest-Ever Star and Galaxies in the News

If it's at the absolute center of the galaxy, what they're perceiving as a star is really the place where material emerges, physical material. It is more of a portal than what I would call a star. And it's fairly obvious from the form of this particular galaxy you're in, the Milky Way galaxy, that it flows outward from the center. It is simply a point of emergence of energy that forms suns, planets and so on. It would be perceived to be a sun because its light signature is very similar to such a body, but it is not one. It is more of the thumbprint of the Creator, which you would find in other galaxies.

So there's one of these in the center of *every galaxy?*

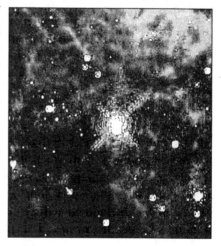

The brightest star ever seen, hidden by dust at this galaxy's center, was revealed in an infrared image from the Hubble Space Telescope.

From *The New York Times*, Oct. 8, 1997

Well, not necessarily in the center. It depends on where the stars are flowing from in any galaxy. It doesn't have to be the center. If you were to stand back at a distance, you would see it isn't the exact center of this galaxy either. But it's where things flow from—the stem as it were, the petals flowing outward.

You mean stars come out from this?

Yes, stars and also planets, when called for. But planets are in the form of seeds, because in order to come through this particular portal they have to accumulate their mass later. They don't grow exactly the way a seed grows, the way a mighty acorn becomes an oak, but they will sometimes come out in compressed form. Yes, this is an opening.

If you had the capacity to pass through that opening, the voyage through the opening itself would be quite fantastical. For one thing, it is a one-way portal, but let's just say you could pass through as an observer. You would see everything flowing outward. You would have the

As the two galaxies—known as the Antennae—merged, the
Hubble Space Telescope captured these images resembling a
heart (below) and a human fetus (next page).

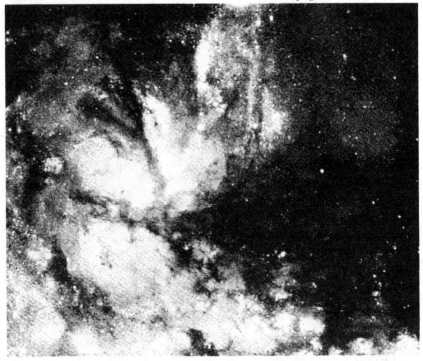

Reprinted from the cover of *Newsweek*, Nov. 3, 1997

impression of a sun, but it is actually brighter than a sun. One of the reasons scientists are somewhat confused by it is because its signature is similar to that of a sun, but it is brighter. That would be expected.

The light from Creator Itself is this bright, so it is rather like a window unto the eye of God.

So if you could go to the other side of it, it connects to . . . What?

It's not like a door; it's not like walking from one room to another where both rooms have describable furniture. If you went to the other side, you wouldn't see that much. What flows out from the Creator might be energetic and would be felt more strongly on one side, before it goes through the portal, whereas on the other side it has more mass.

Since you're talking about telescopes, there has been a joining of galaxies recently to send messages, though I'm afraid the scientific community did not interpret the message. But I'll comment on it since it has been in the news recently. I can't put a date on it, but these two galaxies that merged briefly not too long ago . . . seemed to collide but really merged to form a rather perfect heart shape in the sky—clearly a message of symbolic nature. Another galaxy in the exact shape of a human baby inside its mother was also shown recently through a telescopic device.

Reprinted from *The New York Times*,
Oct. 22, 1997

When these things are seen (I remind the scientific community here), please do not overlook the obvious. One of the most critical factors on Earth in the time of the intellect in which you are living is overlooking the obvious—symbols, shapes, forms. Please don't overlook this, those of you who are involved in studies beyond the purely scientific: As science finds its heart, it will remember symbols, shapes and forms in a new way for science.

Scalar-Wave Experiments

In this month's Kryon channeling he says that in Pine Gap, Australia, in 1987 they experimented with scalar waves, using two towers, which caused earthquakes on the other side of the Earth. Can you comment?

You have to recognize that any form of energy experiments, especially the kind that are involved in ranging energy through the planet, regardless of what waveforms they are, are usually done to see what is under the surface, part of the ever and ongoing attempt to penetrate Earth's crust to get the "goodies," otherwise known as "follow the money."

This is not the first time that such waveform research has caused disturbances on the other side of the planet. But did it directly cause the earthquakes? I cannot say that in and of itself it directly caused them. But I will support Kryon and say that it exacerbated an already dangerous situation where fault zones are precarious to begin with. It doesn't take too much of an effort to accidentally (and it *was* accidental) trip the mechanism that will cause an earthquake.

Let's just say that, allowing for where the earthquake took place, if that particular country felt for one split second that there had been a purposeful attempt to stimulate an earthquake in that locality (allowing for highly sensitive documents, to say nothing of loss of life—and some loss of life did take place), you would have had a serious battle on your hands.

The material you refer to inferred that this was stimulated by some international or even sinister secret government. I would be doubting that somewhat. This is why: One of the things the sinister secret government is most interested in is what is where, and how can we find it and control it? They would be interested in what is inside the Earth, but I think they already know that. So I think we can take them out of the picture in terms of being behind this. The deflection into the Northern Hemisphere was not intended. The outfit that was involved in this experiment literally folded their tents and scurried away into the night after this happened, because this deflection was unexpected, needless to say. Can you imagine the wrath of the United States to such a circumstance? I'll just say that those involved in the experiment beat a hasty retreat.

Was this research a prelude to HAARP?

I'm not going to say that because it assumes an actual progression, which I can't really say. You have to recognize that basic research sees what is at hand to see what might develop. If you have waveforms that scientists can access, if they're financed reasonably well or even sometimes on a shoestring, they're going to try it and see what works. Recognize also that for a long time several reasonably politically influential countries (to say nothing of countries that can afford it) have been working overtime to create a planetary defense. Even recently, your government in the United States tested a laser system to fire at an old satellite to see if it worked. The test was reasonably successful.

A lot of testing of waveforms in those days was an attempt to find out what worked and what didn't and what the repercussions would be. The primary purpose of this particular test (which, I might add, has been done on a smaller scale in other places) was to see what the effects would be if we arrange an array here and shoot these waves out into space. On the one hand you want to see for defensive reasons. Does it do any good? Does it protect us? And what happens if it's bounced back at us? If you were firing a bullet, you'd want to know where it's going to ricochet, and if it does, what happens?

This test was done primarily for defensive purposes. You *could* say offensive, but let's just say for defense purposes. That's why I say the effect was wholly unintended.

And unexpected.

They did not expect such a thing, and it was certainly not intended. It is not something that will be repeated. These waves have proven to be useful in certain ways. There was some attempt for a while to use them in weather forecasting or for electronic cloud-seeding. Largely, the side effects are so precarious that they are not used much. The unknowns are the problem. Even though the current trend is to use these waves in a broad-beam array, if this is to have any offensive (or defensive) capabilities, to say nothing of other useful capabilities, the beam would have to be highly condensed and probably a few other elements would have to be added (I will not say which ones).

I'm not pooh-poohing it; I'm just giving you the details.

Did you tell me that as a result of HAARP, some of the motherships had to move farther away from the planet?

I think I might have mentioned it. Others have said it, too. Yes, that's part of the reason they had to move away. I don't think it was intentional, but it certainly was noted in government circles where such things are acknowledged. In the long run cooler heads will prevail.

You are really in a very interesting time on your planet where even though you get the impression when you watch the news that everything is going to heck in a hand basket (to a G-rated audience here), a lot of things are changing and good things are happening. You are moving through the time of the corporate model of the world order. What will follow inevitably will be a more benevolent "order." I'm putting "order" in quotes, but I'm using that term because it will be an orderly and more benevolent society. It's not going to stifle spontaneity or creativity but it will certainly be less violent. The roots of violence will be acknowledged and addressed, and certain things that society tolerates now, such as the abuse of anyone, will have a zero tolerance.

Mining the Moon and Mars

Daniel Dzegar, the editor of Amaluz, *the Brazilian* Sedona Journal of Emergence *in Portuguese, called me today and said a fellow named David Adair was in Brazil. They say he's a genius. He went underground at Area 51 and saw objects and propulsion systems not of this Earth. He told them he testified before Congress in April. He also talked about helium 3 on the Moon, super energies that would be worth billions if we could get it here. Can you discuss this?*

I'll skip over the Area 51 stuff, since that has been discussed in various metaphysical and other journals ad nauseam. But in terms of elements desired on the Moon and other asteroids, there has been a pell-mell race to exploit (hopefully for geological but certainly for financial purposes) minerals on the Moon. I might add that the current furious race is to explore, navigate and hopefully (from the position of investors), reap some benefits on Mars.

Now, I don't want to suggest that scientists are purely interested in Mars for cash reasons. Most of them are certainly not, but their money comes from somewhere. It's not just your own tax dollars, because those who are sending up space probes and so on are not all from the United States.

So yes, there are certainly elements as well as ores available on the Moon and secondarily on Mars. The means to get to these places is no longer impossible. Certainly a lot of the work done on the Mir space station has proved the feasibility not only of long-distance travel, but perhaps more important, how people survive in space for long periods. This research has been invaluable.

Certainly there has been a desire to mine the Moon and Mars.

But is anybody going to admit that the secret government is already mining the Moon? How long before the American people will know that the Moon is being mined now?

That is a small sector of beings. It does not benefit one country more than another, and they're not bringing vast amounts of material here anymore. They brought a little bit when they thought they could create a fantastic weapon.

You can't sell something that doesn't exist on Earth and have it remain a secret very long. They thought they could make a fantastic weapon, but it turned out to literally blow up in their faces. It was very easy to cover this up. For one thing, most of the action is happening on the dark side of the Moon, which is discreet. I don't think that anyone's ever going to admit this. I'm not going to say it will be swept under the rug, but I'll say that at some point—the point when it is possible to speak of these things—people will be less interested to hear about them

You're talking 25 years away?

Anywhere from 35 to 55 years from now, at which time people will be less interested and perhaps uncomfortable to hear of things that are based in greed or corruption.

34

Education and Medicine

Zoosh through Robert Shapiro
October 22, 1997

Future Education

In the not-too-distant future a different educational system will be slowly demonstrated through governments and world bodies (at this time most obviously the United Nations, but something else might supersede it someday). Right now in schools all over the world people tend to learn nationalistic things and also international things— mathematics and so on. While that's all well and good, most of the things you really need to know, you don't learn in school. And I'm not just talking about balancing a checkbook.

Future education will be how to raise a child, how to treat yourself, how to show love in ways that others can gently and benevolently receive it—things like that, things you really need to know, because raising children hit-and-miss isn't working. Most of the roots of violence come from children being raised in ways that are not so wonderful and also from being exposed outside the home to violence and things that are not so wonderful.

The new educational system will address that directly. That's what people will learn in schools. It will take a generation or so, and then things will smooth out. It's one of those things where people will say, "If I'd known this before, I would have done it differently," you know?

These are obviously the essentials. Leading-edge educators have been crying out for this for years, and they will soon be heard. It will be applied simply because the world will no longer be able to turn a deaf ear to atrocities and violence. People will begin to feel literally the pain of others on the other side of the world.

The Disappearance of Psychosomatic Disease

And far-reaching doctors—not just spiritual doctors, but physicians of all forms of practice—will begin to correlate the presence of pain from unspecified and undiscovered diseases (what has in the past been called psychosomatic disease) to other people's pain all over the world. To the extent that their pain is decreased, psychosomatic illness will cease to exist. Physicians as well as other people of medical inclination will begin to write about these results and say, "Look, see—it makes a difference. We can't afford to let other people suffer. It is literally causing us to hurt, and has been for some time." This will become more well-known.

It is something that will have to go beyond nationalism, and it will. A lot of religions have suggested this in the past. I might add that some of the world's most well-known religions talked about such things when they began, but these tenets of the religion did not stick.

One religion that proclaimed this loudly during its first 80 to 100 years was what you now call Christianity. In the very beginning Islam was very much in the forefront of these things. I believe that Islam has made some effort to preserve these tenets, but they are hard to apply in this modern world. There are certainly other religions that have been involved in these things, but I mention these two religions since they are perhaps most in the news these days.

35

HAARP Revealed in New Film

Lee Carroll

W hen I finished the United Nations channeling in 1995, I had no idea about the high-energy experiments going on that Kryon spoke of. Even as I write this, things are being revealed that are changing what I thought Kryon meant back then. Here is what I know: There are two major experiments being run by the United States government, one in Alaska and one in Australia, both of which use tremendous new technology originally developed by Nikola Tesla (inventor of the radio and alternating current).

When I found out about the High-Frequency Active Auroral Research Program (HAARP) a month after the 1995 United Nations channel, I absolutely knew that this was what (one of the two high-energy experiments) Kryon was speaking of. Scientists in Alaska at a hush-hush project site were planning to build an atmospheric heating station using Tesla technology. It promised potentially astounding solutions to very basic defense problems in our country—perhaps the Holy Grail for all branches of the military and a cheap solution to heretofore very expensive weapons systems. For less than the cost of one nuclear sub, this experiment is thought to be scientists' finest hour since the Los Alamos project brought us the ability to split the atom. It's that important.

HAARP represents a plan to pump more than a gigawatt (that's one billion watts, folks) of energy, directed through the use of scalar waves (a Tesla term), into the ionosphere in an experimental way that will begin by blowing a 30-mile-wide hole. I wrote an article early this year for this magazine that dramatized and explained in layman's terms what HAARP was about. Now there is a very exciting update on this potentially frightening project.

The Miracle of Synchronicity

It was Christmas 1996, one month after the last Kryon channeling at United Nations, when we had a Kryon event in Laguna Hills, California. In the crowd one woman who heard about HAARP had a profound reaction. Paula Randol Smith, a Los Angeles resident, was startled by the information, which "rang" within her.

Paula was in the right place at the right time and recognized that this HAARP subject was somehow related to her contract. She could not ignore the calling that she felt. What could one woman do to make the planet more aware of this dangerous experiment? Was this political outrage or spiritual appropriateness?

Within a few weeks of the channeling, Paula had sorted it all out. She was not a show-business personality, nor was she wealthy. Paula was a single woman who was starting to vibrate with why she was here. She realized that her job was indeed to make the planet aware. How? What could she do?

Exemplified in Kryon's parable of the missing bridge, Paula did not "think like a human." She sat in the presence of Spirit and gave *intent* to follow her passion, that of somehow changing the consciousness of our country by informing an entire population about HAARP. How could she do something that the TV show *20/20* had refused to do? How could one woman with no background in science carry such a load? Was it dangerous? Where would she start? Paula started at the beginning.

"Paula, don't think like a human!" I could hear Kryon saying. On her own she located an award-winning documentary film producer/director named Wendy Robbins. After hearing Paula's concerns and doing some study, Wendy agreed to participate in a big way, sacrificing normal remuneration protocol. She became a committed partner in the production, eventually traveling all over the country with Paula, toting cameras, tapes and gear.

There was no time for a funding program, and besides, how does one organize such a project immediately and by oneself? So Paula sold her land and business. With her regular income and assets now gone, Paula was heading toward the missing bridge in the Kryon parable.

"Keep going, Paula. You are loved, and there are gifts for you along the way," I continued to hear Kryon saying.

To hear Paula tell it, there was synchronicity everywhere. Doors that were opened in her quest to interview and photograph were closed almost the instant she was finished, never being granted to another. She met with and filmed Dr. Nick Begich, cowriter of *Angels Don't Play This HAARP,* and then she was granted permission to film and interview John Heckscher, director of the HAARP project. Many scientists and authors who represent both sides of the discussion were also included before she and Wendy were finished. She discovered things she didn't want to know—enough for another documentary.

She was followed by black cars, had her phone tapped, was under surveillance by folks she will probably never meet, and yet she continued. All through this, integrity and fairness were paramount in her quest to present something that would tell its own story without her having to generate sensationalism through clever editing or scriptwriting.

Almost one year later, the results of Paula's work are in her hand. In Breckenridge, Colorado, during the summer of 1996 I stood proudly among a group of enlightened humans who were there to view and celebrate a rough-cut presentation of the new documentary, *Holes in Heaven,* the first-class one-hour documentary film on HAARP. It will be syndicated nationally in 1998. At this writing she is still trusting Spirit for the balance of the funding to complete the project. I know that it will happen. Perhaps there is even someone reading this who can help.

It was a very moving time for me. Emotions welled up in me when I thought about what she had been through, what the results of her efforts would contribute to the planet. Make no mistake, this was not a fairy tale. This took work, conquering fear, lots of cocreation between Paula, Wendy and others (many in the Kryon seminars) who worked and helped fund the project after the initial monies were gone. But while racing toward the chasm of the missing bridge, Paula found all the pieces and parts of the new bridge, and at this writing she is moving over the precipice (metaphorically) with a professional production that will inform literally millions of people on this continent about HAARP.

Holes in Heaven is a fair presentation, with scientific argument and discussion, about the basic issue of HAARP. It is not fear-based or sensational. It is factual and unbiased, but potent in its revelation about what the project is and its potential results. If you are interested in contacting Paula, obtaining the tape or perhaps helping with the next project, here is the address: Holes in Heaven Project, P.O. Box 91655, Pasadena, CA 91101-1655. One year ago there was nothing. Does this show you what contract is all about? Thank you, Paula.

Now, there is one more thing to do, and perhaps there is still more synchronicity for us to see. When in Portland, Oregon, a couple of months before the 1997 Kryon tour of Australia, Kryon started channeling about the other high-energy experiment he had mentioned in 1995.

Pine Gap is the name of still another dangerous experiment using (what else?) more attributes of new-age Tesla technology. The facility is deep within the Australian continent. With the use of scalar technology, energy is somehow being transmitted through the ground. According to Kryon, it has already caused earthquakes, and he advises us to expose this work as well. There is already an organization in Australia publicizing it; perhaps this is a good starting point toward reaching the mainstream here.

Does Kryon want to stop HAARP and Pine Gap? Are we supposed to get militant and march on these facilities?

No. In both United Nations channelings, Kryon advised that we (1) get informed and (2) slow down. We as human beings can't "uninvent" any technology. We can, however, be responsible for how we develop anything that is so new that it might shake the very foundation or ceiling of our "house" if we are not careful. "Go slowly, be responsible," are the words of Kryon.

Meditate with Intent

As meditators with great *intent,* you readers can do something even on this very day: Visualize these things and meditate on them. The year-long effort on the Internet, with meditations led by Steve Rother (contact RotherEnt@aol.com) of San Diego, involved many people all over the country who gathered around their computers to read Steve's words and give energy and intent to somehow bring HAARP into public consciousness. Their efforts, under Steve's tireless direction and those of meditators like you, have paid off—a woman scheduled to be sitting in a chair in Laguna Beach at a Kryon seminar in December 1996 arrived on schedule and felt the tug of love that she came for. It changed her life, and it will change the awareness of millions.

Do you start to understand how family makes a difference here? Do you ever feel that you can't make a difference? As Kryon says, "Your *intent* is everything." Start using your collective power and watch things happen. I have seen this up close and personally. It still astonishes me to watch the reality of it.

36

We're Feeling Mother Earth's Energy

Zoosh through Robert Shapiro
November 10, 1997
(Excerpt from a private session by permission)

W*hat is happening within my body now? I feel different energies, some-thing like a kundalini energy I have had experience with. Could you shed some in-sight on what is happening and what I need to do?*

These days many individuals are experiencing something different from the previous normal cycle. I have not spoken of this before to any-one, but I will choose you to begin. Until very recently a soul would come here and manifest, setting out a program of either lessons or goals, sometimes both, in which it would manifest certain opportunities during a lifetime in order to accomplish them—a normal life.

But now the planet and its occupants are moving up in dimension and going through veils that one normally goes through between lives or at the end of one's natural cycle. The changes need to take place in a way that will provide opportunities to fulfill the soul's goals and lessons, whether you have the physical experiences or not.

While karma as you know it has come to an end, there still needs to be a resolution of things the soul does not understand. Thus the acquisi-tion of knowledge and wisdom from the Earth is taking place.

Until recently the Earth was letting go of the excess negative energy she had absorbed from human beings over the years. This was done in a way that allowed you—all human beings—to serve her, and for a while there was a feeling of discomfort or strange dreams and odd feelings, some people feeling depressed and agitated for no apparent reason. This has really been your processing within a thought, action and deed something that Mother Earth had heretofore been processing for you.

Mother Earth does not see a separation between herself and you. She understands that you have your immortal personalities and occupy a life form that suits you, but your form is made up of her cells, her body. For you to serve her in this way seems natural and fitting within the evolutionary cycle of why you, the Explorer Race, are here. These sudden spurts of energy passing through you are not exactly a reward, but since you all have passed the test, Mother Earth knew you were ready to process her excess discomfort.

She has now begun to give you the energies that she herself uses to resolve her own personal discomforts. In this way you are being assisted. Not all of you are feeling it at once, but as with everything else, some begin to feel it first, then eventually others do, too. This will occur in its initial stages sometimes as a feeling of nervous energy, where you feel that if you up and run around the block a few times, you'll be fine. Others will feel it like an actual wave of energy passing through them, either back to front or upward.

Some people will get feelings in their hands and feet and so on. It won't generally go front to back; I mention that because others you know might have these experiences.

The reason I'm giving you this elaborate explanation is that it is good for you and others to understand this now. Understand that this experience will allow you to resolve certain things that have become unresolvable. There are things that your souls came here to do now that are no longer resolvable because of the motion up, through and between the dimensions and because of the change in human activity. This means that certain things people were able to do before are no longer really possible for a long enough time, so the soul needs to have its resolution energetically.

Mother Earth is a repository not unlike a bank or treasure trove; she has a wider range of feelings in the body and emotions, interpreted by the mind (there is a slight difference), than you do. But she is now beginning to train you to feel feelings that you have not personally stimulated but that she feels when physically transforming.

Even a casual study of science shows that all things on Earth transform. The leaves are now changing; they fall, yet new buds form next year. A man or woman gets older and becomes different for themselves and others. These are reminders that cycles of transformation are not only necessary but useful for the re-creation of life. Since all souls came here and went through the veil that says, "You must forget," you have been shown that re-creating—learning new things that can powerfully affect you in your life beyond here—is a natural function.

So what is occurring for you personally as well as for others right now is the felt physical experience of the re-creation of your entire soul dynamic. This means that what you are physically feeling is allowing all your past and future lives to come into a greater concordance, or balance. This won't relieve you of all of your lessons, just the ones that can no longer be resolved now because people are more focused on their own individuality—the last of this experience as you have known it here.

This gift and training is given by Mother Earth to allow you to know and feel what it is like to consciously create. When Mother Earth consciously creates things such as rain, snow—*things,* you understand—she experiences energy running through her body exactly the way you do.

You all came here with spiritual mastery from previous lives and accomplishments and from future intentions. You and everyone who comes here *must* have done it before. What you personally arrived with was the experience of material mastery (in terms of apprenticeship), which no more than 7% in your generation has when they come here. It doesn't mean you're a material master but that you have trained to become one, and this was the best place to finish that training.

But Mother Earth is more. Mother Earth is also a spiritual master, a material master and a teaching master. She is a dimensional master and she is working toward completion of quantum mastery, which is the mastery of consequences.

What you are now feeling in your body is lessons associated with quantum mastery. This allows you to experience lessons, feelings, goals and (most important) attributes associated with quantum mastery, which is the internal resolution of external motivation, because the soul is your immortal personality—that which you know yourself to be, what you arrive with and what you leave with, with no break in continuity. And the soul is having its goals fulfilled.

I don't want you to worry about it. If you need to be a little more physically active sometimes, go ahead. If on the other hand you suddenly feel like you must sleep in the middle of the day, go ahead if you can, or at least rest, relax deeply or meditate. These feelings are associated with the seasons of change, which are obvious cycles; you're surrounded with the evidence of that. You as a physical person are becoming an apprentice to Mother Earth for the moment, which means that you will do what she does.

Sometimes she will assign jobs to you, as an apprentice might sweep up the shop even though Mother Earth might not need it. The apprentice cleans up, does things that Mother Earth usually does, but she allows you to do it so you can feel you are participating. As an apprentice you will begin to feel more of the feelings that she feels.

Now, I have given this long, elaborate explanation that I have not given before. I have given some aspects to the general public, but I feel that at some point you might pass this on to others in some way generally or individually that will serve you and them. It might not be an announcement on a street corner, but an easy way to do it. You don't have to do it now, but you might have the opportunity.

This is an opportunity by which all people, especially people who are sensitive and spiritually integrated, can have the pleasure from time to time doing things for Mother Earth and, as a good apprentice, sharing in the feelings of the master teacher. One has the opportunity to feel not only what one can lovingly give but what is lovingly given in exactly the way an apprentice feels. Apprentices often don't know whether their master teacher is just talking to them, kidding around or actually teaching them. You can identify with that.

This is that occasion where you don't know whether Mother Earth is kidding around with you or whether she's teaching. I will reassure you that she is teaching, but doing it lovingly and in such a way as to be certain to get your attention.

37

Surfacing Memories

Isis through Robert Shapiro
November 11, 1997

Tere is some interference tonight, so the connection is difficult. The interference is not intentional. I will tell you what it is so you're not concerned. Your planet in this specific time right now is being radiated with a type of particle that will allow the memories you have accumulated as the result of all your experience here as the Explorer Race to be retained, but not on this planet. Many of these memories are causing some stress to Mother Earth in her regeneration process. But these memories are important to the accumulated wisdom of the Explorer Race.

Right now the entire planet is being radiated with these small capsulelike particles that will accumulate the raw material of the memories and take it to a place of storage where the rest of the Explorer Race is waiting. In that way the movement by you all between dimensions will be made easier since you will not have to retain the memories of your experiences, either personal or collective, some of which are difficult.

So in the coming weeks and months—I should think at least for the next four and a half months—you will experience memory loss. There will be times when it will be difficult to read things that are conceptual, or if you do read, it will be polarized—you will be able either to absorb tremendous amounts or read slowly and have to stop and think about what you've read. Then the pole will switch and others will have these experiences. Right now that energy is interfering slightly.

Those particles are coming from the Earth, or from someplace else to the Earth?

They are coming from where most of the rest of the Explorer Race is waiting. They are coming to serve you by removing the more burdensome elements of memory that cause and tend to recycle conflicts, both internal and external, yet when taken in a total and complete experience, including all the members, will serve the cause of wisdom well.

This will go on now for weeks?

This will go on perhaps for the next three to four weeks up to four and a half months. It will reach its zenith in about three and a half weeks, then in about two and a half more weeks quickly decrease quite a bit and gradually taper off in the next few months. Some people cannot release their memories right now but they will within this time period. It's been going on now for a few weeks—about six weeks. Altogether, the whole experience runs not quite six months.

People who understand through reading will be able to read well. People who understand through pictures will need to understand through pictures, and too much reading will give them difficulty. People who understand through sound, such as musicians or even parents with little children, will have that experience in contrast to people who understand by smell, such as animals. When I say "collective memory," I'm referring to not only the Explorer Race as human beings, but to some extent some of your consultants—plants, animals, parts of the planet herself, which, when taken together with the personal experience of individuals, lend physical sensations to the memories.

Memories make little sense if solely mental, but they make a great deal of sense when one can utilize the whole range of senses to understand why and how.

So how does our project fit into this, because we're trying to bring back the memory of who we are?

It will be unhampered because you have to understand that most of the memory being taken away are memories of difficulties or traumas, hard-fought for wisdom. It will clear and make it easier.

38

Art Bell Interview with David Adair: An Adventure at Area 51

This is an edited excerpt from the Art Bell radio talk-show interview on August 19, 1997, with David Adair. All questions were asked by Art Bell except, where indicated, by a caller.

My guest is David Adair and he is a rocket scientist. His new book, America's Fall from Space, tells the story of the U.S. space program through the eyes of a child prodigy turned rocket scientist. He is an internationally recognized leader and expert in space technology consulting with the world's corporations. He crossed swords with NASA as he learned of the corruption and technical problems faced by the Challenger shuttle prior to launch.

David will share the testimony he gave under oath on April 9, 1997, to the U.S. Congress on extraterrestrial intelligence, recovered extraterrestrial hardware and reverse engineering of downed ET spacecraft. He has firsthand experience of top-secret underground Air Force bases like Area 51. He claims that reverse engineering—the investigation into what makes downed UFOs work—has been responsible for inventions such as fax machines, modems, cellular telephones and laptop computers. David says, "You're not going to believe what's going to happen in the next ten years."

David, you were a child prodigy?

I was fortunate as a child. I had a big machine shop I could work with. My dad had retired from an injury. He worked for a man named Lee Petty, who has a son named Richard Petty. In some parts of the world, like in the southeastern United States where we are, those guys are known pretty well. They're famous race car drivers and my dad was an engine builder for them.

So I'd worked in the shop. A shop of that nature is extremely closely related to a shop that builds rockets. By the time I was twelve I could overhaul a 426 Chrysler Hemi by myself in about three and a half hours. So I started putting rockets together. The first one I built was a liquid-fuel drive. I used liquid hydrogen and kerosene, which is similar to the Saturn V fuels. The rocket left the back yard at about 3500 miles an hour. I'd built a calorimetry device where I could measure altitude. By being 500 feet away from the pad, [using] the cosine of tangent one on the trigonometry table, I could multiply for the altitude . . .

I got about 80,000 feet on the first flight. It came back within a half-mile radius of where I'd launched it. The first place I launched was at the very end of the yard, which was toward a cow pasture. I incinerated [an area of] about a quarter the size of a football field. It was burned to a crisp to the roots of the grass. I turned around to my friends and they were gone. . . . We had enough foresight to call Columbus [airport]—we were in Ohio at the time—for flight times, and I knew by the FAA charts where the airlines were, so I could time it. We had parachute recovery.

That started the whole thing. I just kept building them, and they were getting bigger and bigger. Eventually my parents moved me away from the house. I was able to strike a deal with four farmers in the area.

Right now I make a living as a TTC, which is a technology-transfer consultant. I take space technology that is designed and used in space, redesign it and put it into commercial applications that really have nothing to do with space. I can give you an example. In the Apollo days the astronauts went out to the moon and back. Some people don't believe that, but they did.

Well, I'm certain we did, because when Neil Armstrong was walking on the moon, I was leaning against Viola Armstrong's knees (that's his mother) in her living room. We watched Neil walk on the moon—and all the original seven astronauts were on the floor with me. When the astronauts went to the moon in the Apollo program, they were eating solid food. [They were] about three days out, three days back, two days on the moon, so you would normally have about an eight-day mission. Well, after about three days eating solid food, something's got to give, plus it's weightless up there. There's no bathrooms on Apollo capsules, so they used diapers. Diapers—that's all they had. Yeah, you're in a broom closet, [everything's] weightless, [and] you don't want anything floating with you. So they made a really interesting material that could absorb nastiness away from you and still kind of keep you dry. So in technology transfer, we called Johnson & Johnson—and you got the disposable diaper. That's where it came from.

Another little transfer that happened—this started way back in the '60s with the Mercury astronauts. You know, you had an astronaut out there in orbit and the doctors want to know, "I hope he's doing okay up there," so they decided to do something about that. They hooked sensors to their bodies, then the sensors would pick up blood pressure, pulse rate and respiratory function—all the vital signs—and relay it back to the ground by telemetry. Well, in technology transfer we'd walk in and look at that and say, "Hey, you know what we can do? You've had a head-on collision in your local town and your neighbors or family members are dying. The paramedics come rushing up and they open up this little suitcase. They hook these leads to the person and the information is sent to a local hospital. A doctor looks at the blood pressure, pulse rate, respiratory function and all the vital signs and tells the paramedic how to stabilize that person and get him to a trauma center." That's where that suitcase came from.

There have been to date over 75,000 transfers from the space technology program into commercial applications. I can take you through a house, and it would take an hour to show you all the stuff. I think Corso [see Col. Philip Corso's new book, *The Day After Roswell*] is right on the money [about technology transfers from retrieved ET technology].

I spent about four days with the man in Roswell at the fiftieth anniversary, plus I flew back on the plane with him, and I met him again here just recently. So we've had a lot of time to talk. What is interesting, in a way, [is that] what he was doing created an industry that I've made a living [from] for the last nineteen years, off the transfers, yeah.

There's a lot of strange stuff in the area [of] the way the technology has made such quantum leaps. Backtracking certain things in the computer areas, when we went from the vacuum tube to the transistor, then we jumped from the transistor to the microcircuitry board, that was such a quantum leap! What's interesting is, [if] you try to backtrack some of this technology—like run through the bibliography of abstracts of NASA's files—you'll run into the original source, and it will be stamped "Unknown." "What do you mean, 'unknown'?" You know, "Here is the stuff in the field—don't worry about it, use it!" I'm going, "Well, wait a minute, guys."

A lot of things just developed and dropped right out of the sky, literally, and we've then used it in our technology. Have you ever looked at the technological rate at which we're moving? It's in an exponential-level climb.

Well, there's a reason for it. The reason it's doing that is that we get this technology—let's say it's from a really advanced design of something

—and we have to reverse the engineering on it. Fine, [but] you've got all this fantastic technology and no infrastructure to support it. An example would be, "I'll give you a Ferrari, but I'll put you in 1865." Well, if you don't have any fuel and there are no gas stations, what good is that car to you? Well, you could tie a horse to it and have it pull it around.

We've had the same structure. This incredible technology drops in, [but] there's no infrastructure to support it. What has happened is we've just gotten to the point through the space program where we had an infrastructure [in which] we could dump this superior technology. That builds another base. Then we build up another infrastructure layer, like a wedding cake, and dump another load of technology. We quantum-leap, the infrastructure is built, and [we] keep going. But we're [climbing at] an exponential rate and nobody ever slowed down long enough [to ask], "Where did this come from?" So it's real interesting.

I knew for the last nineteen years I've worked in it, and I'm [saying], "Man, the quantum leaps we're making are incredible!" If you think we've got something pretty hot right now, give yourself another ten, fifteen years. You're not going to believe what you're going to be staring at.

We're not far from AIs (artificial intelligence). Once we get the AIs online with computers, they'll become self-aware. Once they become self-aware, then the cycle starts again. The first thing they'll probably build is the voice transponder, where they can talk to us. The next thing they'll [AIs] want to do is start building themselves, which they can do faster and better than we can. We fall out of the loop at that point.

It's going to happen as sure as you're breathing air. It's inevitable, and you will not stop it. It's already on a cannonball roll. . . . It's going to originate out of the big academic labs like Georgia Tech, where I live, where they're working on the computers for the Star Wars systems. They have to have AI in order to pull the Star Wars system together to get all the target acquisitions and things done. It will come out of someplace like that. It will be a remarkable thing when it does, because once [computers] become self-aware, they'll build themselves, and you'll see computers jumping to 30 to 40 gigahertz speed.

Eventually they'll [AIs] want the bipedal anthropoid package so they [can] move around in a three-dimensional world that we have built for ourselves—in other words, they'll have to have the android-type body so they can interface with us on a more interpersonal level. I believe what's going to happen [is that AIs will] become a subclass, where we have Japanese, Chinese, Blacks, Hispanics and AIs. They'll become grouped right in there with the rest of us. I think they'll have more of a tendency to try to figure out what's going on and [solve] the problem. They probably could ask some really potent questions that would be very difficult to answer. For instance, why do we spend 75% of our resources on military systems designed to blow ourselves into oblivion? That's not very logical, is it?. . .

When NASA was launching Challenger, how did you get involved in that?

I was there on the pad when Challenger was being launched. I was in the area because I was busy working on some programs of my own called GAS (getaway specials). That's produced now by the technology-transfer division of NASA, where you can rent this thing that looks like a 55-gallon drum for three, seven or ten thousand dollars if you take the whole drum. You can have it bolted on the inside wall of the cargo bays of the shuttle and run microgravity experiments. It's available to anybody—private citizens, academia, corporations, whoever. They've already flown 1500 GAS canisters already.

Let me show you a good example of technology transfer. I went to a very large chicken manufacturer that was a client. First I asked them, "How long does it take a fertilized embryo to [become] a chick?" They said, "About twenty-seven days." I said, "Let's rack up a bunch of fertilized eggs and put them in a GAS canister and send them up in orbit and let it run for the full duration. We can alter DNA while it's being formed up there in the weightless environment. When the RNA-factor links are welded together by the enzymes, you can start changing coding." Why would you want to do that? Well, chickens are killed by certain chicken diseases here on Earth that cost the poultry industry billions of dollars annually. . . . They signed before we could get out the door. Unfortunately, that project was on Challenger. That's why I was there. . . .

How did you cross swords with NASA before the launch?

It goes back, at least the part I was aware of. They knew about the O-rings failing at least nine months before. They had brought the SRBs (solid rocket boosters) in and they had lateral burn marks down their sides; they were already burning through. They just kept pushing the roulette wheel, and they came up with a black number.

It was just insanity. The first thing NASA told Morton-Thiokol to do was reduce the weight of the SRBs. How do you do that? Machine the walls down to half their original thickness, take out the reinforcement struts and put in a higher-performance propellant. That's so they could get more lift and charge less dollars per pound of payload and be a lot more competitive. Well, you don't need to be a rocket scientist to figure this one out—that is a prescription for pure disaster. But they went ahead and did all that.

One of the main factors why Morton-Thiokol was not sued was because they were following NASA's instructions. The reason NASA did it was because they were under tremendous political pressure. There's too much politics in that program. There's still way too much. NASA opened its fat mouth and said, "The space shuttle's now operational." That was a lie, an outright lie. That thing will never be an operational vehicle; it will always be an experimental vehicle. We have a model A going here, and until you get to a Ford or a Plymouth, you're not going to have an operational vehicle. You've got to go to second- or third-design generations. That thing's twenty years old.

But they got out on a limb when they said they could compete. We in the private sector and the commercial side of the space program were saying, "You're crazy. You can't possibly do this." The bloated bureaucracy [of NASA] drives the cost up too much. They're constantly cutting back because of budget restraints and they don't have the infrastructure to compete on the commercial market. But nevertheless they said they could.

So they started selling the cargo bay [as] commercial space. Here's a scenario of how it works. Let's say you're Ted Turner and you just called me as the director of space programs. You're upset because we're already almost a year behind in our flight schedule. You just paid for a $500 million satellite sitting in a hangar going nowhere. That's bad enough for you, but it's worse—you're losing tens of millions of dollars a week due to lost subscriptions, lost pay-for-view channels and commercials. You're furious, and you tell them, "Get that thing up in the air!"

So the pressure is building. Now you jump to the senators. The poor workers have the bureaucratic cesspool on top of them that's going nuts. Underneath them is a technological nightmare called a space shuttle. That O-ring is what we call a critical item. And when an A-1 critical item fails, you lose ship and crew. Do you know how many critical items are on it? Two hundred fifty. If any one of them fails, you'll lose ship and crew. How do you like playing Russian roulette in this game with 250 loaded cylinders? Welcome to space 1997. . . .

As I told you, nine months earlier I took photos of the SRBs being pulled by tugs into Port Canaveral, and they've got splits on their sides. I knew right then we were in serious trouble. On the morning of the launch, January 28, 1986, it was outrageous. It was 28°; you've got ice hanging on this thing fifteen stories high. It looked like Dr. Zhivago's ice palace. . . .

You can't bail out of the shuttle. They took out all of the ejection seats for budget cuts—did you know that? It's not funny. I lost two friends on that thing, friends I'd known since I was seventeen years old. I was the national spokesperson for the Rob McNair Challenger Foundation in Atlanta, Georgia, so I take this personally. [Challenger] was just yesterday for me, so it just doesn't end. We never even got our say out to people about what really happened in the Challenger incident. . . . Then NASA had the gall to come out with a film not too long ago of all the right things they did with Challenger. They murdered seven people and got away with it. . . .

By the way, I live in Pahrump, Nevada. It's over the hill from Area 51. It's an area they say doesn't exist, of course. Up the street from me not very far we've got a VFW, and every morning at about 4:30 or 5:00 they've got about five or six buses sitting there. Plastered all over the side of each of them is "Area 51." It says it right there "Area 51." A lot of people who live here in Pahrump work at Area 51. One day I'm going to go up there with a camera and take a picture of it. But I don't really need to, because we've got photographs of Area 51. I just got the most remarkable photograph of Area 51.

Do they show the three hangars? Are the three hangars still there? It's the center hangar where I had my little ride. It's a long story. You remember I was building all these rockets? Well, the rockets were progressive. They kept getting bigger and bigger and faster and faster. Finally the mass and stuff I was using starting changing one day with me, and I started to design a different type of engine. I hadn't really pushed all I could in the liquid-fuel area, and solid propellant is less practical than the liquid fuels in performance, so it was time to take a look at another engine. At that time there were several other alternative engines, but NASA would never even look at them, I don't know why. I guess because von Braun was such a good salesman, he sold the government on liquid-fuel engines.

This engine I built for my rocket is an electromagnetic fusion-containment engine. The best way to describe it is like a chunk of the sun inside a magnetic bottle. At one end you can punch a hole through it with a type of plasma beam that can open up the orsus [sic] field. When you do that you have the power of the sun available at SI, which we call specific impulse. It's a fusion reaction. With the particle accelerators you can collide deuterium and tritium atoms.

So you get a fusion reaction and you hold it all in a containment field with electromagnets?

Right. Let's back up to the beginning of all this. I started working on this design. I was about fifteen years old when I came to the end of my math capabilities. I just could not extend the algorithms of this thing, which would map out the containment field. You've got to understand this was 1969. There's no laptop, no CD, no hard disks, no CD-ROM drives, no cellular phones, no faxes, no beepers. All I've got is a chalkboard, pen and paper and a slide rule. Hand-held calculators didn't come out until eight or nine years later. . . . So in the quantum physics area, where I was working in math, I just came to the end of my rope.

My high school science teacher had a deal with me. He looked at my math work and took it over to some colleagues at Ohio State University. They mailed it over to Cambridge, England, to a little guy named Stephen Hawking. Hawking takes a look at it and finds it interesting, and three weeks later I'm taken to Ohio State during my summer vacation to see some people. We get there, go into a room and the first thing I see is all my math scattered all over the drawing boards. I get a little bit upset about that: "Who's messing with my work?" I hear this voice, "Your work indeed?" I go, "Yeah." . . . This little guy stands up with a cane and he goes, "Indeed, show me." I said, "Sure, watch this. This is how you can validate this theorem." So I write this down. He goes, "How do you validate it [physically]?" I said, "Rocket engines." He says, "Holy smokes! Have a seat." That was Stephen Hawking.

He had come to Ohio State for a couple of reasons. He worked for a place called Battelle Memorial. It's a big think tank up there. This was the summer of '69. We sat there and talked for a while. So for about two days while he was doing some work for Battelle I spent time with him. He was a big help in the math area. This was thirty years ago. Hawking was in his early twenties, still a young guy. We hit it off pretty well. He's a real nice guy. He was frail even then. He was stuck in the same area I was. We'd both come to the end of our rope in the algorithms because we needed very powerful, fast computers and nothing was available at the time. So we could sustain the field maybe for only five seconds—but let me tell you, five seconds is a lifetime in a rocket engine. . . .

So with Hawking's help, I got somewhat of a field stabilization for five seconds. Let me explain what a fusion-containment engine can do, why I wanted to go that route. Hawking was working on a black-hole theorem, so his math and mine were parallel—like going down a road where there were two separate planes headed in the same direction—but we had different functions. He was trying to get all the theorems necessary to regulate singularities in the event horizon of a black hole. He was trying to prove how black holes function. I just wanted to replicate a black-hole-type field, because a black hole is the only thing we know that could swallow the sun and we'd never see it again.

So therefore if you want a field that can contain a hydrogen-fusion detonation, what is it going to be? A black hole. I was trying to get a shell containment for this thing. I did it through a toroidal compressor-type cone shape in the mass waveform, and that gave me exactly what I was looking for in a containment field. His math really helped me establish the waveform guides necessary for that field's establishment. That was done and I started ordering parts. It wasn't long before I had tapped out my resources for pulling in all the necessary materials.

A local congressman of the area was a man named John Ashbrook. I want you to remember the name. He even ran for president in 1972. He was a pretty solid Republican congressman in the area and was pretty influential in Congress. It was a strange relationship we had, somewhat stressed at times. But he really came across with major funding, a huge amount of money even in those days. He called some other people, they looked at what I was doing and said, "Fund this."

At this time I was sixteen. I was building this design and all this stuff. I think Hawking had a lot to do with it; he was sold on the idea that this thing could work. So funding came through. In addition to funding, also authorization at the congressional level came through because I needed some fuel pellets from Oak Ridge, Tennessee.

After that happened another person showed up. This guy was a retired general named Curtis LeMay. His parents lived in Mt. Vernon, Ohio, where I lived. . . . My mother was a LPN and was caregiver to LeMay's parents. It's a small world, isn't it? The congressman asked LeMay to come in and work on this thing. LeMay hated retirement. . . . He came in on this project and looked at it. Apparently he'd been asked by the congressman to walk it through. When I met LeMay he scared me to death. . . . Anyhow, once everything was completed and the rocket engine was done . . .

Where did you build this thing?

The big machine shop I had when my dad retired from all the racing enterprises. When he was injured he retired and we left the Charlotte (North Carolina) Motor Speedway and moved to Ohio with our big machine shop. So there's the facility. The technical expertise was pouring through my little head and the machine expertise was coming through Dad and some other friends. The funding came from the congressman and the authorization clearance came from the congressman and LeMay and the Air Force, which really did get involved in this pretty heavily. We ended up going to Wright-Patterson Air Force Base in Dayton, Ohio, loaded the rocket and me on a C-141 Starlift and off we went to White Sands, New Mexico.

Another person who was a significant player in all this was Werner von Braun. He was helpful because he filled out the technical data. With the funding I got, I could buy off-the-shelf stuff that was really nice, the state of the art at the time. For instance, I could get the altimeters, generators, thrust vanes and on and on, all the stuff that goes inside a rocket. The difference in this thing was the cyclotron detonator area, which was the heart of this engine.

David, how was all this funding managed? Did it just dump into a bank account for you?

No, as an educational grant; it would come through and the congressman's office would handle disbursements. . . . So we ended up at White Sands. We landed there. Von Braun told me to be careful of some people I might run into and gave me some warnings about some things. Even LeMay, who stayed at Wright-Patterson, told me to be careful. He said, "Boy, you're getting into some very touchy areas, and you could be in trail wash." "What did I do wrong?" He said, "Actually, you did nothing wrong, but it's what you're building that could be a real problem."

I could sense something was not right, so I had told my dad previously, "If anything goes bad and I call you and tell you, I want you to burn everything in the shop and the lab—everything. Tear up the models, the prototypes—just crush them so there's nothing left." He understood that part. So we end up at White Sands. It's now June 20, 1971, and I'm seventeen years old. We prep the thing for launching and a colonel told me that there may be a plane coming in. He said, "If it's a black plane, we may have interesting people."

Sure enough, this black DC-9 comes in, and out steps all these people in suits with mirror sunglasses. And the colonel's going, "Oh god, DOD [Department of Defense]!" One guy stepped out, an older guy with silver-white hair and blue eyes, wearing a little khaki outfit. I recognized who he was because von Braun had showed me pictures of this guy before. His name was Dr. Arthur Rudolph. He's the senior design chief, chief architect of the Saturn V engines of the Apollo program—and he shows up! I thought that was interesting. So he comes over and I said, "Hi, what's your name?" He gives me a name like Henry Wilkerson. This snow-white-haired, blue-eyed guy with a German accent, and his name is Henry? I may be seventeen at the time, but I'm thinking, There's something wrong with this picture. But I knew who he was anyhow and already knew he wasn't telling me the truth.

I asked him, "What do you do?" He says, "I just go around looking at things for friends of mine now and then." I thought, Ah, god. I'm picking up all these adult innuendos that they're passing in front of me to one another, so I thought, Okay, I'll just be dumb. So when he asked, "Can I see the inside of the rocket?" I said, "Sure." When he's looking down at the engine wings I lean over and right in his ear I say, "In proportional size it has 10,000 times the power of your F-1 Saturn V engines, Dr. Rudolph." Man, he straightens up real fast and he looks white. Then he gets real angry and he asks who I am. I said, "I'm just a kid that builds rockets in Ohio. I launch them in a cow field, you know."

We started prepping the thing for launch. . . . When the engine took off, it was a little more than I was expecting. It left so fast, we didn't see it. . . . The blast out of that thing was a concussion wave that made it all the way to the bunker where we were. Right at the second of ignition the flames went to the light of an arc welder and I knew what had happened. The detonation took place, the containment fills up and the desert floor is now stirring up, the engine [is as hot as] the surface of the sun and it took off. These engines run hot, at about 180°C. . . . It was so bright that you couldn't even see the containment exhaust. It was like the sun. . . .

You extend the field outside the system. You can do that with a toroidal system. They use that same system on a fusion magnetic-containment compressor for a nuclear reactor. That toroidal-system compressor works inside the Soviet Union's Tokamak reactor, a breeder reactor. . . . I can extend the field in a certain direction in a cone shape so it goes right out through the specific impulse area.

When I finally caught up with my rocket, the fins, the very outer part, were just gone. They had vaporized in the heat. . . . But before it left [White Sands], Rudolph insisted that I change the trajectory coordinates on this thing so it would come down 656 miles northwest of us, about 120 miles north of Las Vegas in an area called Groom Lake. That's the only name I ever heard. I never heard of anything in Area 51—they always called it Groom Lake back then.

One thing I thought was kind of strange. I told them, "Look. I've launched out of cow fields for the last five years. I can bring this thing right down on our little heads. We don't have to walk more than 1000 yards to pick this thing up. Why are you guys shooting this thing so far out?" They said, "Just do it." They got a little bit upset. And I went, "Fine." So I did what they wanted.

When it was confirmed it [had] landed there, they said, "Get on the DC-9." I'm getting on the plane and I go, "You know, this may be stupid on my part, but let me point something out. You've got struts and rubber tires under this wing. Do you see them setting there? We're going to land in a dry lake bed. This thing's going to bury up to its belly." They told me, "Don't worry about it, kid. Get onboard." So we get onboard and an hour and forty minutes later we're there. Sure enough, don't worry about it—twin 10,000-foot runways with interconnecting taxiways. A 42,000-acre Air Force base is there, and it's not on any of my maps!

I'm going, "Why is this?" They wouldn't answer; everybody's quiet. And I'm thinking, Oh god, here we go! So we land at the very south end of the areas down there, below the end of the runways. Out a little further I could see the parachutes of my rocket, and it [had made] a nice soft impact. They were sitting there and I thought, Let's go look at my rocket. I can't wait to see it. This is exciting. So I started to walk toward the rocket, and these guys with these cute little hats and scarves that they wear grabbed me and threw me in this golf-cart-looking thing. We take off riding, but we head toward these really weird-looking hangars. They're low, lower than most hangars, but they're big, really deep and wide. It's got these weird-looking lights on top. There's a real strange-looking lighting system on that thing. It's kind of a rectangular-type light with like louvers in it. They're across the roof line of all the hangars so they can flood that whole apron area.

We went for the center hangar. It's a little bit bigger. When we get inside it's about the size of four football fields in a square. We're sitting there and it's just an empty hangar, and I thought, Well this is cool. This is nice. They're showing me a nice, empty hangar! We're sitting there and nobody's saying anything. Then these lights come on. They look like the old police lights called party hats, and they start flashing. Then out of the floor come all of these little chains that make like a guard rail. They come across the door areas, even the small . . . have you ever seen, on a carrier when an elevator goes down on a hangar deck, these little chains come up out of the floor? That's what this thing had; all these things came up. I'd never seen that before and I thought, Wow, that's neat. I wonder what that's for? Just then the whole floor of this giant thing drops out from under us. It's an elevator and we're going down.

It's a huge . . . oh my god, it's the biggest platform I'd ever seen. The first thing I thought was, Man, what in the world is the use in taking this thing down, because you can't use cables or chains, you know, like an elevator. Sure enough, I looked over in there and there's huge worm screws—a worm screw is the thing that turns a lipstick.

This is getting wild. This is an incredible story! But you know, David Adair testified under oath in front of Congress on April 9, 1997, about what I guess you're about to hear.

Yes, and I was going to mention this before we got started. You're absolutely right. This [is] a story that I've told Congress. I'm under oath; I'm facing a twenty-year federal prison [sentence] for perjury if I lie. They assigned a little task force of their own to do paper trails, and I'm off the hook.

Who called you to testify in front of Congress?

Dr. Steven Greer. Yeah, Steve really put some bait out there. I went for it because it was just possible that we might get a disclosure on the information. That's why for twenty-seven and a half years I did not tell a single human being about this story.

Let's continue with the story. So the floor is dropping in this hangar?

Right. It went down, and I was looking at the worm screws. They're huge. They've got to be the size of a semi in diameter. They're giant and there's twelve of them. They're lowering this floor down and we're going down rather quickly. The floor must weigh hundreds of tons. Worm screws can carry tremendous loads. So whatever they roll out on this thing is pretty heavy.

So we go down, I guess it must be about 200 feet. We get down, and boy, the floor flushes out and there sits this hangar bay down there. It is so huge. It's like a rainbow roof design, but the wall's kind of . . . they don't really curve, they taper at an oblique angle. All the labs and the shops and the work bays were built into this mountain underneath so that the center bays are open and not obstructed by anything.

This sounds just like Independence Day. *Remember when they took the president and so forth and everybody went into Area 51?*

Right. Whoever did that movie got somebody to come out and talk, because some of the stuff was correct, right down to the door handles, the way it looked. But they missed the lighting. The lighting was really neat. It was an iridescent indirect lighting. I really couldn't see where the light sources were, except that it was just like panels throughout the entire roof system.

We went down into this huge bay. It looked like it stretched forever. You could park three, four or a half-dozen 747s down there and not be in the way of anything. I mean, this thing's just huge. We were in the golf cart, and once we got flush with the floor, we took off and went down through a hangar area. All the workshop bay doors were closed when I was going through there, so I really didn't see anything other than a couple of interesting aircraft. I did see an SR-71 sitting there. The XB-70 was there. (There were two of them built. One crashed and the other one is now in the museum in Wright-Patterson.) One of them was sitting there. There were a couple other experimental aircraft I just didn't recognize. They looked like a teardrop; the front, blunt part of the teardrop would be the forward section that would be moving forward through the air. I've never really seen anything quite like that.

We went on down through there, and when we got to this one big set of doors—it looked like a work-bay area—they got out, turned a dial and the thing unlocked and the door slid open. I thought, Well, this is going to be interesting. I guess whatever they want to show me is in here.

So we got in, and as soon as the door opened the lights came on automatically. It was the way the room was lit that was really interesting.

The lights were the entire length of the room and they went into a rainbow-type arc. The best way to describe it is something you can relate to—a paint booth you paint cars in. There are no shadows cast, you see, in a paint booth. If you're painting a car and you've got a shadow, you could get a run in the paint and not see it.

This room was lit the same way. There were no shadows anywhere on the floor. I thought, Boy, that's interesting. So there was this big thing, whatever it was, sitting on a huge platform-type table that looked to be about the size (under the tarps) of a school bus or a Greyhound. My engine is about the size of a football in my rocket. When they pulled these tarps back, here sits a thing that's a twin of my engine, but it's the size of a school bus. It's an engine.

I'm going, "Holy cow! Man!" I was definitely impressed and kind of disappointed. I thought I had an edge on this engine, but obviously I didn't. Then they pulled it all back and they're asking me to take a look at it. I went, "God, this is fantastic. Look at the size of this thing!"

They said, "We've got some problems with it, and we want to know if you could give us some clues on some things." I started thinking [and said], "Well, is this your engine?" They go, "Oh, yeah. Our people have been working on it. But the people working on it are somewhere else right now. We'd just like to have your input." And I'm going, Something's wrong with this picture, fellas.

So I asked them, "You know, we're getting ready to launch Apollo 14 at this time. This is June 20, 1971. Why is the Cape getting a liquid-fuel engine when you guys have this thing?" They said, "Well, we've still got some problems with it. You do want to help your country, don't you, son?" And I said, "Yes, sir, I do." I just played along, you know, "Yes, sir, I'd be glad to help my country." So they said, "Fine. Why don't you take a look at this thing?" I walked away, you know, [thinking,] Yeah, you lying, no good . . . [laughs].

I get to the engine and the first thing I notice that's really strange is that there is a shadow on the engine. There's no shadows on the floors anywhere, so how can we get a shadow on the engine? It's a silhouette of me, so I back away from it and it dissipates. I get up closer and it gets very defined. I thought, That's interesting, and I reach out. I told the guy, "I need to crawl up on this thing and take a look at it." And he said, "Fine, but be careful."

Anyway, I put my hands on this thing and there's these outer panels, which I guess are like cooling baffles—the power flows were completely different [between Adair's engine and this one] the way they routed the plasma drives. So when I put my hands on these panels, which were almost translucent, the minute my hands went against the metal (you could see through these panels somewhat), you could see these real neat energy swirls coming off wherever my skin was touching it and going out through the metal.

So I pull my hands back and it stops. I put my hands back on it and you can see the swirls again. I thought, Wow, heat-recognition alloy! Gosh! I didn't know we even had that. Well, I don't think we did. I already knew before I even got up to it [that] this thing is just not ours. It's not theirs either, meaning the Soviets. It's something else. And they're not telling me the whole story on any of this.

And you were there because you had built something similar?

It was almost like a baby twin of it.

A baby twin. So I now understand why you were at Area 51.

Now you know why they routed my rocket there. Because now they have my rocket and me on that base. And it's not good for this camper right now because I'm up on top of this thing and I see what the problem is. Once I get up on top of the engine and start walking down it, I mean, it's a rush. You build something that's almost like it, but it's only the size of a football. Now you're walking on the same design. You just had to be there to appreciate this. But right in the center you see [that] the power flows run like an infinity circle. We build the power flows in an infinity design. That's how I can get a gravitron field to stabilize and then hold the containment field. Right where the figure eight crosses in the center, a good description . . . somebody once said, "It's like the eye of the hurricane." And it is. That's where the main core drives are, and this thing had a core breach. It dropped its field and the alloy of this engine is now exposed to a 100 million degrees centigrade. It vaporizes everything. The blast is going outward. But the fail-safe system of this design is [that] when the field goes down, it shuts its own power off in a nanosecond, in a billionth of a second. So imagine the explosion starting, but it implodes on itself to snuff itself out.

So it's like a pulse?

Exactly. That's real good, Art. So it takes its pulse and it stops. It just shuts itself off. So the blast only went out about four feet in diameter, vaporizing everything in its path as it's blowing outward, but it stops. So there's this four-foot diameter hole in the center of this engine.

I yelled down to them, "Hey, this thing has a core breach. The containment seals went down." They ask, "Well, what kind of containment seal was it?" I said, "Well, it's a gravitron field of electromagnetic generators." They're looking at me and I'm thinking, This is *not* their engine."

I looked at it a little bit closer and told them, "The firing controls, there's no circuitry on this thing." And they go, "Yeah, you want to

298 • SHINING THE LIGHT: Humanity Is Going To Make It!

explain that to us?" And that's when I looked at the thing for a minute. There is *no wiring* on this engine! I had almost five miles of wiring on my football-sized engine because there's so much I had to contain in the control circuitry. This thing doesn't have any. The reason it doesn't have any? There's something strange that's all over it—there's these little tubes like fiber tubes, but they've got a liquid in them. They're cascading all over this thing, and right at the very top of it is a big center trunk. I'm thinking, This looks real familiar. I know this pattern—it's a brain stem and the cascading nerve fibers [are] [nerves coming off of it. All the tubing looks like a big brain-wave pattern. It's the circuitry!

I started to turn around and tell them something. They started asking basic fundamental questions. Finally I just had enough and I said, "We have an expression back where I come from in the South. This thing ain't from around the neighborhood, is it, boys?" They're looking at each other and I went, "Let's do some assumptions. This is an engine. It came out of a craft. Where's the craft? If it's got a craft, where are the occupants? God, I'd like to deal with *those* folks!" So they got angry. The two guys that have been pulling [me] around like a puppet are heading up there to pull me off. I said, "No, I'm getting down." I get down and right where I'm getting off—I'm really angry at this time and my hands are on those translucent panels—it's not the nice little swirls anymore. I'm really angry with the situation. I'm just realizing a lot of things. Here is a technology that's so advanced, and it's being kept secret. Nobody has that right to lock this kind of knowledge up from everybody. I mean, my god!

If it's sitting there broken, it's still an amazing thing to look at—I mean, it validates we're not alone. And here they're lying. I'm really disappointed, you know. It really was [true that] I love the country and the people. But I'm not happy with the government at this moment.

Getting down off the engine, I'm really upset, and when I put my hands back in the same area where the nice little swirls were, now they looked like a hurricane or a tornado ripping through the alloy. It hit me right then: God, it's not heat-sensitive alloy! It's picking up something else: It's picking up mental waves. This engine is a *symbiotic engine!*

It's responding to what you were thinking.

I realized, Oh, god, this thing is a symbiotic engine! I knew right then this is not ours.

What is the firing order on that? [Here's] the way it works: When a pilot straps into this thing, or a crew member, it could be a sentient entity of its own. A pilot or crew would strap in and their mental waves would blend with this engine. *That* is the firing circuit. That's why they couldn't find any firing circuits on the thing. The crew walking around fire the circuits. They're like the spark-plug wires of an engine. My god, the pilot and crew merge with the ship! In aerodynamic engineering that's our wet dream. It would be unreal to be able to achieve that technology!

Actually, even back in the conventional world they're working on that now, aren't they?

Yeah, that's what I told Congress. I said, "It's hard to believe? Well, let me enlighten you boys about something. Let me bring you up to current events. Princeton University—you ever heard of them? They've got a department there being built with a guy named Dr. Bob John, and he's got a contract from McDonnell-Douglas. You ever heard of *those* people? Well, guess what they're doing? They're building a symbiotic screening system to do the opposite—to keep the pilot's thoughts *out* of the F-22 fighters, which are the most advanced fighters on the line right now.

Let me explain what all that means. A pilot comes home, catches his wife in bed with somebody else—he's having a really bad day, okay? He's got to get up in the morning and go fly this fighter. He gets in the fighter and he straps in. This thing is so sensitive with state-of-the art firing-acquisition controls and navigation and black boxes, it can actually sense what he's feeling.

You're now engaged with an enemy before you; there's something coming at you. You go into a 1600-mph dogfight. If you hesitate on locking controls, one-half second will determine whether you live or die. And he's having a bad day; he's thinking about what he saw when he came home. The controls sense that, and they stutter for a second—and he dies.

They are building a system to prevent that. I wonder where they got the idea. So symbiotic systems are the way we want to go in flight aerodynamics and technology, because it's the ultimate system. It would be for anything—computers, your car. It could be applied to so many things. But here I am on June 20, 1971, looking at this thing, thinking, God, this is a symbiotic engine.

So they drove me in the golf cart and we leave. They locked up the doors and we're going up the elevators. Things go from bad to worse at this moment because I hear them talking. They're all upset. They say, "Well, he's not helping us right now. It sounds like he's not a player." They think I'm not listening. I'm thinking about what I just saw, but I hear them say a term—it was the first time I ever heard it. Years later the public heard it: "We need first strike."

You know what was happening at that moment with America? We'd just bombed the daylights out of Cambodia. They're not even warring with us. We're up to our eyeballs in war with Vietnam. General Westmoreland's just asked for surgical nuclear strikes because he's getting his butt kicked all over the battlefield. The Soviet Union has been supplying weapons to Cambodia and we just bombed it. That's got them upset. They said if Westmoreland fires one nuclear weapon, they'll go [into a] full, global counter-thermonuclear war on the planet. Believe me, the Kremlin at that moment was not bluffing and neither were our people in the Pentagon. The only reason they didn't go at each other is because of the MAD—Mutual Assured Destruction—program.

Well, the only way to win MAD is to get first strike. You take this rocket engine of mine, load warheads on it, put it in a submarine, park it off Siberia, and the only thing the Soviets will see is white flashes, not even a blip on the screen. They can't retaliate. They're gone. So you take out the key military bases and population centers—and you've killed about a half a billion people in one day. You'd also have to go over and kill somebody else the same day—China.

So I'm sitting there thinking, About two billion would die in this conflict if they go first strike. I can't do this, so I have to destroy my engine. And that's exactly what I did. We went upstairs. We got to the hangar bay and when we pulled out, the golf-cart thing and Rudolph were there, Dr. Rudolph. I just started clobbering him and boo-hooing him. I'm really upset. I said, "I want to see my rocket. Are you guys going to take my rocket away from me? I haven't even gotten to see it. I worked so hard." I'm crying and crying. So Rudolph tells the two sergeants, "Take him down to see that rocket" just to get me out of the way.

I'm leaning against the hangar door and I reached down and put my palm on the wheel of the hangar door. Do you know what's on that wheel? Graphite grease. I put some graphite grease in the palm of my hand and they take me down to see my rocket. I get down there and I slide open the door and tell the guys, "Let me check this thing for a fuel leak." So I was checking it, but what I actually did, I reached in with my hand, smeared it across the particle-accelerator chambers, closed the door and set the particle accelerators into engagement.

If there are any physicists [out there], what happens when deuterium meets graphite? A horrendous chain-reaction implosion will take place. I've got sixty seconds before engagement of the accelerators, and I just run it through the guards, "This thing's got a fuel leak! It's going to explode. We've got to run for it!" We get in the golf cart and we're taking off. They ask, "How far do we need to get away?" I say, "I don't know." [Laughs.] And I really didn't.

Well, we get about a quarter mile away and it goes off and it blows a hole about the size of a football field. There's nothing left. It was gone. That was so frustrating because this engine has a lot more art than just being a rocket engine. Let me explain what these things do. It's not designed to be launched from Earth to space. It's designed to be launched from Earth's orbit into space. It's the principle that we use in Newtonian laws—for every action there's an opposite, equal reaction in space.

So the matter of a fusion reaction is coming out this thing's specific impulse, its orifice. It's how fast the matter moves in a hydrogen reaction: 186,756.54 miles per second, called the speed of light. In just a couple of minutes that shift will equal the velocity of the exiting thrust, which means we have light-speed capability June 20, 1971. So Piflin's gone. We get back up to the hangar. Rudolph asks, "What happened?" The guard said, "Well, he said there was a fuel leak." Well, Rudolph (I just want to show you how sharp he is) walks over and looks at me. He was looking at me real close, and grabs my hand and looks at it and sees the grease. He knows. I thought, Uh-oh. Rudolph looks me right in the eyes with those cold blue eyes and says, "You will be here for the rest of your natural life! Lock him up!" And they did.

They locked you up?

They locked me up.

In jail at Area 51.

That's right. Let me tell you something about little Mr. Rudolph. Check your history on this guy. On May 24, 1985, he was deported back to Munich, Germany, although he carried the Distinguished Service Medal from NASA—the highest award given. The Mossad put him away where he rotted and died. That man [had] killed 100,000 Czechoslovakian Jews while they were building the V-2s in Magdeborg. He was a Gestapo officer. That's what happened to Mr. Rudolph.

So they threw you in jail. A real jail, or what was it like?

Well, just a room with no windows and just a door. I was there for hours. Then finally there's a big commotion in the hallway. I don't know how long I was there—I guess six or seven hours, maybe eight. Finally this hallway door opens up and [there] is a big silhouette of a guy with a stogy in his mouth—Curtis LeMay. LeMay came from Wright-Patterson Air Force Base. When he lost track of me in White Sands, he then figured it out. He pressed some people to find out where the rocket was downloaded at. So he shows up, and if it wasn't for LeMay I would probably be in an *Independence Day* movie with Brent Spiner. . . .

LeMay took me home. You've got to understand where LeMay's at. He's the former head of SAC—Strategic Air Command. Wright-

Patterson has jurisdiction over Groom Lake, and he put everybody in their positions before he left. He may be a civilian at that moment, but he's still a four-star general who's really pissed off. So he comes in there ranting and raving, and he's pushing colonels physically out of the way. He puts me on his jet and we go home. Once we get back to Wright-Patterson, he drives me with his driver all the way back to my home in Mt. Vernon, Ohio, where his parents and my parents are.

He told me, "Boy, if you want to have any normal life, you have got to *not* build another rocket." And I haven't.

No, but you went in front of Congress and told this story.

Absolutely.

David, I'm curious. What kind of reaction did you get when you told this story?

Well, one of the senators came up to me and said, "In the name of God, which one of these things do we tackle first? You're standing on top of an alien engine inside an Air Force base that doesn't exist with a twin engine you built that matches the alien aircraft engine." I went, "Yeah, there's three different ones. Which one you want to pick and work on first, pal?"

You know, I personally don't care whether people believe me or not. I lived it, I know it. And the paper trail satisfied Congress, so here I am.

Well, the only thing I know for sure is they're lying their butts off about Area 51. There's a photograph. I've got it. There's no question. Everybody agrees and knows they're lying. But this tale you have just told, this story that you gave in sworn testimony in front of Congress, is the wildest thing I've ever heard.

It was a calculated risk on my part, because they had me hanging in the wind. They could easily say [that] we can't prove any of this, or if they didn't want to or didn't check it out thoroughly enough, you know—they could come have up with a dozen reasons why—and I would be indicted now. [But] I haven't had one threat. I'm not being observed, not being tracked. I've never bought into this paranoia crap anyhow—gloom and doom and all this despair and conspiracy and stuff. I don't think it's happening.

I was born in West Virginia. I'm a hillbilly, for god's sake. But, I'm no hero or anything. It's just common human nature. We always are so quick to assume that there's evil and they plot and conspire. You know, they're human beings; they make mistakes. They're trying to deal with a very difficult problem and a PR nightmare, and they're trying to figure a way to get out of this thing. And the walls are still closing in. I asked one congressman, "You know, I've never seen congressmen and senators so anxious about this. You're squirming like worms out there while I'm telling you this story. I've got a feeling somebody's coming to dinner and it's not Sidney Poitier, right? Are you guys looking for a Welcome Wagon hostess?" You know, I think there's something happening. They're being pressed by something, and they've got bigger fish to fry than me. . . .

I've never seen an alien. I've never seen a Gray. I have never seen a UFO—you know, one flying around. I've never seen a spacecraft. I never worked in Area 51. This is a one-day event in my life that happened twenty-seven and a half years ago.

Have you heard the name Bob Lazar?

Yeah, and I tell you what. That guy, Art, he's the best articulator of physics I have ever heard.

You buy his story?

I would really cut him some slack because of his ability to understand physics and articulate it. He really knows his stuff. I haven't got all of his story, but I've heard some really interesting stuff, cute little things—like he called [one craft] a sports model, that kind of thing.

A sport model of saucer, yeah, in the same place you were in.

Right. I am not going to be throwing any rocks at anybody. If you live in a glass house, you don't throw rocks. From what I've seen, the man is probably telling you the truth. But I do know he's no dummy. He really knows his physics. The only crime I think he's committed is, he's not a physics teacher somewhere, because boy he can really do a good job on that. I wish he'd become a teacher; he is a good one. But I would believe everything that Bob is saying at this moment.

So you think there is an entirely second-level space program, all black?

You know, that's really difficult for me to buy, but then I look back at what I stumbled across. I don't know what to think anymore. In order for them to do that, they can't use any conventional engines. They can't be using liquid-fuel solids. Two states away you can see a plume of these rockets taking off out of the Cape. So if they are coming and going, they've got to have an entirely different type of technology. It's very possible they've back-engineered this thing. I've looked at it long enough. You've got to understand they've had twenty-seven years to work on it. They could very well have developed engines like that. And boy, that really hurts. It's like I'm working with sticks and stones out here and you've got a big state-of-the-art machine shop. That's the way it would be happening. The rest of us are fumbling around with liquid-fuel engines and here they've got engines capable of light speed. I mean, that's really not right.

What a story! And you've got to remember, it passed Steven Greer's test. Steven Greer had this man testify in front of Congress. Let me read you a couple of faxes from Hawaii: "Symbiotic engines? That's exactly what Colonel Corso described.

This is also being verified as different sources begin to fill in the gaps."

From Perth, Australia: "Listening to David Adair right now, Art, I'm aware . . . of at least one public patent covering the Mobius-strip plasma-core-containment concept. It also utilizes a mirror field generated by induction from the spinning plasma in the core. Also, David, the lighting was probably a high-frequency one much like the plasma globes sold in stores. The Tesla radiated field can induce nitrogen to ionized levels, which would give light from all angles. Ergo, no shadows until you get too close to an object. That's why your hand made patterns on the engine's surface. It was an hf [high-frequency] field, I am sure, even if it was a symbiotic field . . ."

David, it's a split mix on the faxes I'm getting. Some people think you're totally flipped out. Other people think you're absolutely genuine . . .

Well, like I said, I really didn't testify for the public on this. I went for the Senate and Congress, and I'll let them make their decision. The only people out there who are willing to stand up and put their hand on a Bible and testify with twenty years of federal prison staring at them—if you think I'm lying, consider those odds I'm playing. I don't really know anybody else in the UFO community who's done that. And I am not a ufologist or researcher or whatever that is, because I haven't even seen one of those things. I work in the hard-science world. That's where I've been for the last twenty years. The only thing I've observed about the UFO community—why do they do so much infighting? [It's] totally illogical.

David, how is your life at this very moment?

Actually, it's pretty successful in the 3D world. I have worked as a technology-transfer consultant for the last twenty years. And I own a couple homes—I've done well. And I've never ever had an incident with the military or the government or anything after that. Sometimes it's like a dream. You just store it away and forget about it. I remember [that] the Air Force in 1971 gave me [an award for] the most outstanding in the field of engineering sciences. I went to the national and international science-fair arena with that rocket.

What brought you to tell your story at this time, and where are you going in this direction?

Steven Greer had a lot to do with it.

How did he find you?

People heard. I was real quiet about it, but about nine months ago I talked to a few friends (that was the first mistake) about something that happened with me. I really didn't give a lot of particulars with it, but it's definitely UFO technology. I've really very rarely talked about it. I've mostly talked about space-industrial applications, how we can do that type of manufacturing in space. But it came up and I answered some questions about it. These people got a feeling, "There's a lot more than he's saying." So they called Greer and then Greer called me.

How did Greer vet you? In other words, how did he dig into your story?

Oh man, I felt like I went through a sieve with the guy. He had hundreds of questions, and we talked for about two solid months before the testimony. He would ask things, then come back and ask more things. I would send him paperwork, then he'd ask this and I'd send paper trails. He must have a file about nine feet thick on me by now.

I bet he did, because to take this story to Congress, Greer had his butt on the line big-time. And Greer is one serious guy.

He's very serious, not to be taken lightly. One of the things that pulled me toward him was because I have nine medical doctors in my family, and he's an ER doctor. So I know how they think and feel and how they operate, and I could deal with that. I mean that in a kind way. He finally started collating everything together and said, "There's too much cohesion here. Everything is starting to stick together and you're checking out." He finally said, "You've got to testify."

I dragged my feet up until four days before the testifying was to take place. I finally said, "Okay, I'll go." They sent me a plane ticket and off I went. But the thing that really got me, to answer your question why I did it now, is because Greer wasn't sure, but he really had this feeling they might do a major disclosure at this meeting. I was sitting there and, knowing what I went through, I thought, God, if I don't go and I miss a full disclosure and I had a chance to hear it—I just couldn't resist it. So I decided to take the oath, take the risk and see if they were going to make a full disclosure. Maybe I would hear more about what I saw a long time ago. That's really what pulled me into it. Curiosity killed the cat.

Caller: Why was Congress investigating and bringing you in to testify? Do you think there was a hidden agenda there?

Yeah, but I couldn't figure out what it was. They looked as nervous as a long-tailed cat in a room full of rocking chairs.

Caller: They were afraid of what they might hear?

Yeah, and this is strange: Why are these people stepping out of line doing this? They don't have to do this. That's the thing that really struck me. The Congress and Senate *does not have to do this*, but they went ahead and set up an official hearing on this subject, the first time I ever knew of.

Caller: I've never heard anything of this.

Not of this magnitude. And I'm going, What kind of party is this? It's wild. I'll pay my dues, I'll take the risk. I've *got* to see what's going on.

But I don't know what their agenda was—just to see how much we knew or whatever. Or to see how far some of us would be willing to testify.

Caller: Do you ever think you'll do any kind of this research in the future?

Yeah, this thing's never left my soul. It's kind of like Jimmy Conners had played tennis up to about age seventeen and never played again. But there isn't a day he wouldn't think about it.

Caller: You want to build another engine? That's what I was thinking.

That's probably the ultimate question for all critics. I'm going to build it again. It's a matter of time. I'm just trying to get all my ducks in a row in the corporate arena, because it's going to be a different game this time.

Caller: You have no fear at all of the Men in Black knocking on your door in the middle of the night?

If they do, they come and get me and cart me off, then I'm gone. If they shoot me, I'm dead, I'm out of here. I go back to God. So what? That's a big deal? It doesn't matter. All the time you're here on this planet you're on loan anyhow, so don't worry about it.

Caller: Dr. Adair . . .

Not yet. Got my B.A. and I'm on my way to a master's—but I will be.

Caller: David, have you written a book?

Yes, I have. It's not published yet. It's called *America's Fall from Space*. It's about 456 pages.

Caller: Can you briefly describe what led to your creation of this motor, what inspired you? What was your education or interests at that time that led you to design . . .

That's an excellent question. Oh boy, where do I start? Space sciences that I work with—it started ever since memory started. I had the ability . . . even when I was seven, eight years old, I was working with some interesting math. I had a flair for numbers, I guess. A lot of people said I was gifted. I don't know about that. All I know is that I could do a lot of math problems and all that I worked with came to me in dreams, of all things. I had an artist pad I'd sleep with even when I was a child. I'd wake up sometimes [at] three [or] four in the morning and write this stuff down. I kept a journal of it.

When I started building rockets, the dreams became more frequent and regular, so I could get help. As strange as that may sound, while I was sleeping I actually got my best . . . thoughts came through to me. Maybe things were quieter in my head or something, but I was able to write this stuff down. I didn't want to tell anybody that until Hawking told me once that almost all of his math comes to him through dreams.

In other words, this knowledge may have come from elsewhere.

Well, I can't prove you right or wrong, that's for sure. I don't know. All I know is that it came to me on a regular basis when I was building the thing. Interestingly, some of my business partners are psychologists. I work in areas of business fields with them. Two of these guys specialize in sleep disorders and other problems. They asked a lot of personal questions at that time about what I was doing. I told them I was consumed by this thing, like eighteen hours a day seven days a week. I didn't kiss a girl until I was almost eighteen years old. I never dated. I don't know if you would have even liked me back then.

It was like some kind of obsession or, I think, a mental disorder. But it would not leave me alone even when I would want to do things like everybody else—go play football or something like that. I just couldn't stop long enough to go do that. I'd be on the field and I'd have to stop because I had to go back to the lab. It just would not leave me alone.

So the psychologist told me that that was not normal. Sometimes you get gifted early on in life and it consumes you like a fire. You're so hot at that moment it's like an athlete who trains. They're at their peak and they're capable of great things, and then when they're older and go back to try to do it, they never quite reach that peak again.

So I'm sitting there thinking, Oh god, you *know!* I hate to think I went through this and I can't do it again.

Obviously, you could go that far again.

I think I could, [but] you know, I don't know. Maybe I can. I do know that it's not like riding a bicycle. You can do that again. It's a little more complicated than that. Also, it's going to change my personality and I really don't know. I have a wife and family now, and I don't know if I want to go into that mode again. It may tear my private life up. I've been able to compartmentalize this thing for twenty-seven years and never think about it.

When was the first moment you told it publicly? Where?

Only about nine months ago. It was in Asheville, North Carolina. A friend of mine who is a professional videographer was setting cameras and lights up for something called Eckankar, which is some kind of metaphysical thing. I told the guy, "Don't tell them anything about me. I'll just put a baseball cap on and have raggedy clothes. I'll set your lights up. Just tell them I'm a roadie."

So we were okay until some guy sitting there—he's a kind of leader —turned to me and said, "Who is your channel or channeler?" or "Do you channel?"—something like that.

And I went, "HBO, Cinemax," you know?

They asked, "Who's your guide?" And I went, "Tonto?" I had no idea what they were talking about. But they asked me what I did. I told them that I'm a technology-transfer consultant and we do research in space where we can grow super electronic crystals and alloys in medical research. Well, the crystal thing got them all fired up. So much for the Eckankar meeting.

My friend looked over at them and he was holding his face in his hands like he's dreading this. Something just struck me. I thought, Well, this crowd is kind of remote from my life. I'll just throw this on them and see what happens.

And that's how it got out?

That's exactly how it got out, because of some of these people in that crowd. Steven Greer lives in Asheville, North Carolina, and some of these were his neighbors and they went over and told him.

Caller: Let's say that you had gone ahead and just gone with the program back there in Area 51. Where do you think you would have gone with this? Would your technology have grown? Your mind was young . . . and you're really sharp.

I tell you what: It's like a delayed-action stress syndrome for a Vietnam veteran. There's not a day that goes by I don't think about "what if?" They would have offered me everything. I would have had labs. I would have had whatever I wanted. But my God, I don't know what kind of world we would have had.

Caller: Considering the size of this rocket and the kind of craft it would have to be, how far could it go and where could it be coming from?

Golly, I don't know. I can only speculate. For a craft to move like that, it's capable of light speed or even better. I never got a chance to finish my work, but there was a secondary thing to this engine I would have liked to have done. I believe that the magnetic fields of this thing could be extended in a contained pattern outside the ship. If that could be done, since that field has the intensity of a black hole, you could create an artificial black hole around the craft. If that's so, then you can warp space by wrapping it around you like a burrito. The shortest point between two points like A and B is not a line, but rather [you] pull the space, wrap it around you and then it's just the thickness of those two points connecting, which on a linear plane is nothing.

So it's kind of like a riddle, how that could be solved. How can you go a thousand times faster than the speed of light without breaking [the law of] the speed of light? You could do that with a gravitron well, like a black hole. We know that's the only thing in space that can bend light. . . . So you can bend time and space. . . .

To answer your question, this craft [in the movie *Event Horizon*] could come from billions of light-years in a fairly reasonable time, [one] that we could stand ourselves. Or they could have been traveling for millions of years. I don't know what kind of timetable they have or whatever, but that craft would be capable of distances we can only dream about right now.

David, let me take you off for a second. I'm certain you're aware, but a lot of the audience may not be, that Steven Greer of CSETI and his assistant have both come down with very deadly forms of cancer. Steven Greer has been diagnosed with metastatic malignant melanoma. That's bad stuff. And Shari [Adamiak, co-leader] has been diagnosed with cancer of the right breast, which has metastasized to the lymph nodes. These are both really, really serious cancers. I don't believe every conspiracy theory that comes along and I'm not saying this is one, but I'm saying the odds are against that. I thought the audience ought to know.

I'm not aware of that. I heard a couple of rumors, and when I get home I was going to give him a call and ask him.

Caller: The hydrogen bomb uses a fusion reaction to detonate. Did this rocket engine use a self-contained fusion reaction and focus it to power itself?

Yes.

Caller: How did this start the reaction?

With a small particle accelerator. . . . The working of the small particle accelerator is like two intertwined octopuses having sex. The round parts on each end—draw a figure eight between them. The faster it runs, the more power. The energy can never overtake the field; it's a perpetual loop. That's how containment was achieved. Predetonation started the reaction. [The device] looked like a soccer ball.

Give us an address to get on the mailing list when your book is published.

David Adair, 108 Park Place, Stockbridge, GA 30281 (suburban Atlanta). And I've made some videotapes on all the work I've done.

I take it that you would like to hear from anybody who has had similar experiences or can confirm your experiences?

Boy, I'd really like to hear from somebody who was in Area 51 in 1971 if they're out there and could contact me.

Oh, they're out there.

I'd like for them [to] if they'd remember the incident that I just described. There were several people there—at least I saw a dozen in the periphery, so there are some who saw this stuff.

Caller: David, were you at any time debriefed by the officials at Area 51?

I guess it never came to that because LeMay interjected, and he was in a bad mood at that moment. He took me and he just pulled me out of there and took me home.

Caller: David, where is the vehicle that this engine propelled?

Excellent question. I don't know. I'm assuming that it was in that area, maybe in a different bay. The thing I was curious about is, I could only extrapolate in proportional dimensional size. My engine's the size of a football. It took about a ten- to twelve-foot rocket in a housing for all the peripherals for it. So if this thing was the size of a school bus, I couldn't imagine how big the craft could be. It could be the size of a football field or an aircraft carrier. It would have to be a pretty large craft, because this engine would be capable of tremendous power. So it would be a sizable craft. What was interesting, though, is that this thing wasn't torn—it was *cut* out of the craft. It was the fittings on the side.

Caller: So everything had been cut?

Yeah, there were some rips and tears where I guess the initial impact occurred when it went down, but mostly they were clean severs. But I don't know what they cut it with. It's really interesting that they could cut it like that. The most noteworthy thing was the fittings. We have B-nut fittings and quick-disconnect couplings. This thing's fittings (I don't know how to say this on radio) gave a whole new definition to male and female fittings. The female fittings fit in, and when they did, two of the couplings were still fastened. They looked like they were one solid piece, like fused. There was something else interesting about the entire—do you remember seeing artwork by a man named H.R. Geiger? H.R. Geiger is the man who designed—it's called organic technology—all the creatures in [the movie] *Alien*. This thing had the same kind of overall technological manufacturing look; it was like an organic technology. I swear this one looked like it could have grown itself.

Caller: I have a question for him. It's regarding the electromagnetic fields around the ship. He was talking about Hawking's theories of being at the event horizon of a black hole. Could you possibly freeze time, and could that be a way of time travel?

Absolutely. I'm still stuck in the theory stage. I never got a chance to have any working models of this thing or had time with it. Stephen Hawking agrees with that theorem that [with] the black-hole capability, you would be able to pass through different dimensions and time-travel. Exactly how you set all this up—motion and navigation, communication, all that stuff—I have got more questions than I've got answers. But the theorem he has, if you read his book *Of Space and Time,* addresses that issue. If you're going to do time travel in a natural way, the way to do it would be [with] the force of a black hole.

Caller: Are there any other books you could recommend to us?

Yeah, there's a book that NASA (ironically) puts out. It's called *Shuttles That Work.* I think you'll find a lot of interesting stuff in the microgravity-processing arena where the commercial sectors are working. That's an excellent book. There's another old book printed by the American Association for the Advancement of Science, the cornerstone of our science world, called *The Future of Energy,* published in 1973. A third way through that book—guess what, Art—they've got a diagram of my engine! It shows you the toroidal compressor. And in the very beginning of the chapter it says, "Electromagnetic Fusion Containment Engines."

Caller: I've seen the STS-80 video that you have as well, Art.

Bell: Yes, I have, too. It's a mind-blower.

Caller: David, there's no question about it: STS-80, the video that I have, shows things going on . . .

Right. Steve Greer showed it to me. And I'm telling you, I couldn't believe it. I called some friends at NASA and said, "Ice particles? Come on, guys, you've got to come up with a better lie than that. That one is so bad, it's not working out here." It's not ice particles. It doesn't look anything near it. I've never seen ice particles go around 90-degree corners.

Caller: On the engine you saw at Area 51, did you notice if there were any fiber-optic particles or strands?

Excellent question. Do you remember my talking about the circuits, the little tubing? The tubing looked just like fiberoptics except it looked like it had a liquid in it, but it had the same texture and look of a fiberoptic casing system.

Were there any markings on the engine?

Boy, we about forgot that. This thing was *covered* with it! It looked like a cross [between] hieroglyphics and the alphanumeric system. But some of the stuff, a lot of the emblems, had the look of a deck of playing cards. You ever seen the clubs and hearts? There were emblems like that. But, boy, I tell you, those markings saved my bacon in Washington! I forgot to tell you that. The other witnesses were testifying and I thought, Boy, if nobody else has had hardware contact—man, I know what a turkey feels like at Thanksgiving, because I was the only one who had had hardware contact at that time.

What happened was, a lawyer got up to testify who was an encryption officer in 1960. His commanding officer had given him three pieces of metal and said [it] was from a downed UFO. This guy's an attorney under oath—think about this. Anyway, I wrote them down and handed them to the guy and he goes, "Holy smokes!" I matched the emblems that he remembered! Incredible!

For a copy of the program on audio cassettes, call (800) 917-4278.

39

A Deeper Look at Adair's Testimony

Zoosh through Robert Shapiro
November 18, 1997

Let me start off by saying that this story by Adair is true. The Adair story is (as they say about truth) all the more interesting because it is true. I will also say that it was a good thing for him to wait and say nothing until recently, not just for his own personal safety but in the larger sense because people weren't ready to hear him and be comfortable with what they heard.

Cynicism and the Recognition of Truth

Now you are in a time when people want to know. They're at that critical point of cynicism, where the cynic within oneself wishes to be rescued by the truth and does not want to go down into the dungeon of cynicism, where in order to protect one's innermost feelings, one believes in nothing.

You could see a picture of the citizens of the world (in this sense, the citizens of the United States) teetering on a precipice, with fire and brimstone underneath, almost falling in but occasionally catching themselves. The fire and brimstone, for the sake of our illustration, is entrenched cynicism. And the ability to balance is provided by the desire to be rescued by the truth, no matter how wonderful or terrible it might be.

This is actually the moment of accepted responsibility. It has been awaited for many years and people have to be at a certain point before they can hear real truth. On one hand, it is a dangerous game to wait until that point. On the other hand, if you *don't* wait until that point, it is very easy to give people truth before they're ready to hear it and they can turn it into a fiction. If they do turn it into a fiction, by the time they hear it again they will feel as if it is a story and that it might or might not be true. And that causes a delay.

I will put my stamp of approval on this and say yes, it is true.

Can you tell me about the engine just like his that he saw in that hangar at Area 51?

The "Engine": A Navigational Force

The most important thing about it is less the engine and more the organic quality of what surrounded the engine. His word for it is "symbiotic," but I'd say that it was a feeling body not unlike your own.

The best vehicles are created by beings on a temporary basis, meaning if a vehicle is needed, reasonably advanced beings can sit down in a circle (or float, depending upon their consistency) and ask that material to volunteer to form a vehicle around them. Then they go places in that vehicle.

The so-called engine is less of a motivating force than a navigational force. The more advanced so-called engines don't propel at all; they release and attract. Let's say you have arrived in a vehicle and are ready for your next place. The so-called motivating force releases the vehicle from its current point of attraction and the vehicle will float upward or simply leave the spot it's in, not unlike when you release your hands from the arm of a chair to get up. Then the navigating factor in that little object (that's why it's so small) will attach itself by instructions from the crew (if I can call them that, though they don't actually man the vehicle; they are more like passengers).

The ship itself is an outgrowth of their feelings and the rhythm of their life, not unlike your own circulatory system. When it attaches itself to the next point where the vehicle is to go, it will then, using the feminine energy, attract itself to that place. You as individuals can do this yourselves without a vehicle by using what I like to call benevolent magic. One way is by essentially running an imaginary hook out to a place you want go to and pulling from your solar plexus, but it's faster to have the destination point pull you. I'm just going to say that and not elaborate further.

So the so-called engine does not push. It isn't even an engine at all. To some extent, the fact that it was assumed to be an engine was an advantage. It is natural for a people who would be using the masculine type of engine that pushes or propels to identify as an engine something that seems to be the only motivating factor of a vehicle. But the skin of the vehicle itself (if I can call it that)—the rest of the vehicle—is just as much the engine as its navigational center is.

Can you tell me the details of the craft that the artifact came from? What planet? Their system? What connection to Earth?

From the Seventh Dimension

Dimensionally speaking, the only reason it could be felt more than seen (I'll put it that way) is that it had traveled to this place (Earth), but it was not actually of this dimension in its point of origin. But because it could access this dimension it could be *kind of* felt and experienced.

Its point of origin was right around the seventh dimension. The place of origin? It's a little vague because . . . for the sake of spatial reference, which doesn't really apply to such a vehicle or its original occupants, the place it's from is simply not in your universe.

If you were to fly to the place, traveling at the speed of light to the twelfth power for about six to eight hours, you could get there. But it but it would be easier to get there by traveling in time, because the spatial reference is just not coordinated to where you are. It requires what your old friend used to call the "inside-out" travel. Let's just say it's from a higher dimension rather than here.

The people who assembled the device are more what I would call lightbeings than tangible, physical beings. These lightbeings still exist. I'm being a little circumspect because since these lightbeings still exist and because it is in their nature to harm no one under any circumstances (which would, of course, include themselves), saying where they are on Earth strains their capacity to harm no one, including themselves. But I will say that they are currently in a residence that is not of their choosing.

Can you tell us how our government got that artifact? How did it get into that hangar?

This and Other Artifacts Captured by a Renegade Group

I'm a little shy to say that it was your government—because it's not the government you voted for or the people who are civil servants, but elements associated with the government that have created a government within the government—not the sinister secret government per se, but sort of a renegade inner group. This was largely a post-WWII connection with scientists associated with the Nazis who had been working on advanced systems (which we've discussed before) involved with antiquated time-travel technology, meaning technology that did not concern itself too much with the safety of the pilot.

Read Montauk Project.

Yes, thank you. As such, these devices were essentially captured. But to say *captured,* you have to understand that if you've got beings who are breaking into the *routes* by which other beings are traveling interdimensionally, you can easily disrupt these routes (although not actually intending to do so) and unintentionally bring back bits and pieces of other cultures. This is largely what occurred. Larger versions of these devices were experimented with to acquire such artifacts that are currently in the United States.

Time travel must be done safely through beings who are loving and benevolent. If it is done by other beings, the chances of serious harm are, well, very likely. So at great loss to many people, such artifacts have been "captured."

There was writing all over the outside of the engine. Can you say what that was or what it meant? Would it help us to decipher it?

I'm going to call it symbols. The symbols had to do with the point of origin of the vehicle but also to some extent with the capacity of the vehicle to get from wherever it was to wherever it was going. But it wasn't instructions. That is not at all unusual. Remember that technology like this is by its very nature benignly spiritual. Think of all the other benignly spiritual objects on the Earth. To find writing on them is not at all unusual, but the writing is not instructions on how to use. Therefore it's not associated with operating instructions.

When you say "beyond this universe" you mean beyond this creation?

Yes.

So these beings were just going somewhere when they were intercepted.

Yes, exactly. Well said.

In his dreams as a young child, where did David Adair get the information to build an exact duplicate of this navigational equipment?

Others Received Portions of the Machine

When he was a young man he was not alone in such dreams and visions. He and about twelve others in this country and several others around the world (I won't say how many) were linked, and each was given a portion of a vehicle. They were shown how to create different parts of something. A dream is a good term for it, but it was what I'd call a living dream. Not only was there consciousness on the mental level, but feeling and to some extent the physical levels were involved so that the memory of the vision would be imprinted. The imprinting process created a motivation to reproduce the vision no matter what.

Because it almost obsesses you.

Yes, exactly. It's an obsession; it cannot be denied. Right around the same time (these people were all right around the same age) all over the U.S. there were people rushing out into their garages or wherever, putting bits and pieces together, having really little understanding of what they were building and for the most part being very frustrated in the process of this creation. While they were building it most of them were thinking, What is it?, What's it for? and, most important, Where's the rest?

If you were to ask him personally, the whole idea of "where's the rest?" would have been a familiar theme to him as he was assembling this. I might also add that he did a pretty good job assembling this object he created, allowing for the fact that he really needed to be connected to one other person to assemble it. With the connection to the one other person, though, he would have had not only the motivating power, but the navigating power. When he was building this, the idea was, This is it—but where? The "where" was the problem. I think he knew fairly early on that it was meant for something else.

The "meant for something else" factor has to do with a safety mechanism, because as a benevolent civilization somewhere (which is future-oriented), if you're going to influence people in the past, you want to give certain people parts of the puzzle who have acknowledged that this is all right for them to do, but you want to induce a safety mechanism so it will not be misused. The safety mechanism is the underlying feeling not only of morals and values and principles associated with their up-bringing, but also the idea that it isn't okay to utilize completely their creation (that they've reassembled, you might say, from future reference) until all of them (the other members of the team) are present.

I might add that David is one of the few members who was actually known to people in a position of influence. Most of the other members were in very innocuous backgrounds—as you like to say, just folks. It is intended that perhaps within the next twelve to fifteen years these people all get together. Now, I might say to Mr. Adair that it is safe to discuss this thing, because as this information gets out, the other members will hear about it and over the next twelve to fifteen years (maybe less— we'll see) get together and then be able to quickly and easily assemble the vehicle, which is not meant so much to take Earth people somewhere [chuckles] but really to receive others from other dimensions.

What appears to be a vehicle (one flying from point to point) is really a one-way machine that others can travel from where they are to where you are in your machine. So they'll just basically show up in the machine.

That's another safety factor built in. I'm putting it like that because I want to reassure the potential reader here that it is safer than it appears. Although the original participants Mr. Adair had to deal with when he was a youngster wanted to make it a delivery vehicle, it really isn't that.*

Some Day the Machine Might Be Reprogrammed

Someday when the vehicle (or object, let's call it) is built and others arrive, they would be able to reprogram the device so that it could go to other places and take Earth people there. But the nice little safety mechanism is that they won't do that unless these beings feel that the Earth people are trained, heart-centered, spiritual, benevolent beings. There is no way to fool them, so don't worry.

The F-22 and Pilot Modification

He gives a man's name from Princeton who had a contract to build a reverse symbiotic system for the F-22 pilots because they might come in angry. This was to screen their negative or unbenevolent emotions. Can you say something about that? Is the work at Princeton based on information given to one of these future friends of Adair?

For starters, the F-22 is beyond top secret, so I'm going to be discreet about that. In any military capability, when using technology whose point of origin is associated with beings who are basically benevolent or can be benevolent, if you attempt to adapt that to human fighter pilots, it's without changing the pilots. But at some point you have to change the people.

Here are military people who are encouraged to be aggressive and trained in military tactics and so on. Can you actually create something by which these people can be sufficiently drained of their discomforting energy or so-called negative energy so that they can participate in any technology that requires them to be benevolent? For starters (fair warning, all right?), if you do that, two things are going to happen: One, the pilots are probably not going to have as much aggression when you want them to have it; and two [chuckles], as individuals they're probably going to want to feel like that again.

It's like the ultimate destressing device. I might add that a lot of these exercises to let go of stress really came out of this whole business of needing to work with technology that's sufficiently organic that it has feelings. It's all in the feeling base. That's why I said the whole future is about feelings, not about thoughts at all. The technology basically forces individuals to be more benevolent, or it doesn't work. If you try to

---

* Adair's comment: "I'm an engineer. I don't know anything about channeling, but I need to say that the symbiotic ascension engine was designed to push through space in a linear fashion. It is totally unique in that it can project its own gravitron field around the ship, making the ship an artificial black hole that can travel millions of times faster than the speed of light—in distance —without violating the speed of light. It warps the space around it, yet still travels in a linear fashion."

combine technology that functions only by benevolence and fool the technology into thinking you're benevolent when you're not, it's not going to work. The technology itself is organic, like a person. It's like trying to fool a child. It's like being benevolent, being Santa Claus, and then switching and becoming the monster person. The child knows instantaneously, perhaps even before the moment of switching. You can't fool it.

Are they working on that? Sure they are, because the whole idea ultimately is to try and eliminate . . . you know, for the longest time advanced military aviation was working on eliminating the pilot until they realized that ultimately the pilot, as a feeling instrument (something they haven't been able to build into computers), is essential. Almost in spite of themselves (which is kind of amusing) they're now having to work toward achieving benevolence. The irony, the humor of it all, is that in the process of having to achieve benevolence in order to make the equipment work, they're going to cancel out aggression! You can't do that with human beings and expect them to be able to switch aggression on and off.

You've been able to switch aggression on and off in your day-to-day life. But when you have a situation in which you have absolutely no aggression, are totally benevolent, with heart-centered, benevolent feelings—everything I've been talking about for years—if you switch that on in a pilot, do you really think you're going to be able to switch that pilot off and on with aggression even with external stimuli? It just won't work. You think it will work, but it won't.

Area 51 Artifact Can't Work without Its Creators

Was the creation of this sentient technology that he called symbiotic one of the pieces given to one of the young men who will join with Adair in twelve years?

No. Think about it. Remember what I said. If the machine or the device or artifact (such a nice word) was created by beings, that means that any beings who attempt to use that particular artifact won't get it to work because they didn't create it. The whole key is to bring people together *to create their own vehicle.* They might create the internal mechanism, the parts—the navigation and so-called motivating factor—but they will also have to create the skin of the vehicle, the form. They won't be able to use the vehicle that's there because that vehicle is specifically connected or benevolently associated with the beings who were in it.

Let's say they sat around in a circle (although they don't). Then they would ask for anyone or anything available to form around them and become part of the vehicle. That's why I'm calling it organic. The vehicle is organic; it has the same feelings (and I'm not using some vague word like "emotions," but *feelings*) that any human being has. I'm telling you that the reason it responds to the feelings of individuals is because it also is a feeling network, just like a human being. So it's a great safety mechanism.

The principles of his rocket motor were the same as the big one. If he had not blown his rocket up, would they have reverse-engineered his machine and used the big one as a rocket motor?

Let's just remember that he was financed all the way. They know a lot about it. But to answer your question—yes and no, because they want the whole package. After all, they can build rockets. Their goal is not so much to build rockets—they've got them.

Not like his.

"First Strike": Taking War into Space

Well, you have to understand . . . let's go beyond what he heard. On one hand, he heard, "We've got to have first strike." He heard something that sounded like that. His natural assumption, from knowing the people he knew then and knowing the times, was that this would have to do with Earth war.

"First strike"—where did this stuff come from? First strike isn't about Earth war. It's about going out into space, capturing other people's stuff and essentially taking war beyond Earth. Certainly if he were to hear "first strike," he would naturally assume that it referred to this planet. They've got rockets; they can do a first strike here. What first strike would mean elsewhere is the ability to sneak up on somebody with something they can't see, deliver some weapon and then bring back the object you've used for your delivery vehicle so you can use it again— meaning an advanced extraterrestrial military weapon, to be used beyond this Earth.

That was the original plan even then. You've got to remember that toward the end of World War II that's the thing the Nazis were working on. They were well past thinking about anything to dominate the Earth. They were already working on, "What can we do to go beyond the Earth?"

But still it needs to be said that what that seventeen-year-old did was selfless and heroic and pretty awesome.

Oh, certainly. Also not surprising. Any of the other members would have done exactly the same thing. That's why it's an interesting thing that they're all basically living. He's kind of the point man. In that sense, he is known; the others are not (I'm sure not going to say who they are), but they will make themselves known.

Well, he's got a book coming out, so . . .

It will help, and at some point he'll probably begin more public speaking, and that will help. But ultimately people will find out about it because of an appearance he will have on television. (No, I won't say when or where.)

Congress Nervous about Black Projects

Adair said that at that joint session of Congress he felt that the senators and representatives had great pressure on them and that there was something more than he understood. What was really going on? Why did they call that session?

Well, let's remember: think of the billions and trillions of dollars that the U.S. has poured into various advanced projects, all right?

Black projects?

Yes, as the spy people like to call them. "Hidden" projects I like better. And that the senators and congressmen had basically said okay. Granted, in the beginning they were duped, and monies that went for these projects were essentially committed for what the Congress felt was something else. But eventually it came out. Even after all the apologies to the Congress, Congress was still convinced that there was purpose in this and reason for it.

Apologies by the military? By whom?

Yes, by the military and those in positions to say, "These projects will change everything," people who don't or can't really give them details but would basically say, "If you invest in this we'll be able ('we' meaning the United States) to have whatever we want whenever we want for as long as we want." Basically a blank check.

Supposedly Reagan gave them a trillion dollars for SDI?

Genetics, the Coming Transfer Technology

Well, think about SDI and these kinds of things. SDI is one of the very few things (with the possible exception of the new military technology, so-called Stealth) that people know about that's being done. As Mr. Adair pointed out, the rest of it is being trickled out to people. A lot of it is going to come pouring out in the form of what they can do with genetics. In the next dozen years the body chemistry—what is going to be not only possible but largely accepted by medical science—will go through a revolution, not just in research but in application. Most of the diseases you've known will be, not exactly eliminated, but totally controllable. This is not to say they *can't* be eliminated, but they will be totally controllable and people will not have crushing impacts from these illnesses.

But they could do that now; it's available now, you're saying.

This is your motivation: think about it. If you've put trillions of dollars into something and your ultimate motivation (I don't want to make people sound greedy) is to at least get your money back—and ideally, make a profit—then you might be disinclined to give people a pill that would make disease go away permanently. You might be more inclined (I'm not trying to make these people out to be monsters) to find something you can give to people that will control the *symptoms* of disease permanently. So you need to sort of dilute your cure pill into a *control* pill.

And still make money.

And get back your investment and a reasonable profit, as business would say. Granted, that's not the best system, but it's not the worst system, either. That's just an example.

New Wireless Technology Based on Organics

Other forms of technology, things that are just barely obvious, like wireless technology—cell phones are perhaps the most rudimentary example—are really coming on. In the next few years you're going to be able to sit down in front of your television set (and when I say next few years I mean in the next three to five years)—and it won't cost a bundle! We're not talking about $50,000 TVs, but about $700 to $800 devices—and talk to relatives. They'll see you and you'll see them, and it won't be a photograph. This stuff is all coming in. This is not new; I'm not telling you something you don't know.

They have video conferencing now. It will just be more . . .

Yes, it will be more easily done. A lot of stuff is coming.

He says computers running at 30 and 40 gigahertz. We now have 300 megahertz.

Yes. That's all coming down the line, as they say. Understand that what they're using is organics. The whole wave of all technological change in the future is entirely based on organics.

The Resolution of Atlantis Technology That Feels

Now, in the larger sense, what does this suggest to you? Atlantis, here we come! So here we are again right back in Atlantis where organics are being used without their permission. That is why, of course, there will be such resistance to doing anything else. If someone showed you that you could use organics not only for genetics within the physical body, but to create a computer that would not only have so many gigabytes on the hard drive but unlimited storage capacity, no matter what your moral qualms might be, it would be very hard to stem the tide of enthusiasm. This is like a tide. We've been talking for years now about the resolution of Atlantis. It's coming, because the whole idea of corporations owning life forms is here. And it's going to be a crisis.

Where did all this come from? Full circle, okay? We're right back to our organic vehicle. How do we know it's organic? Because it has feelings. When Mr. Adair touched it, it felt benevolent because he was curious and interested. The second time he was angry and upset when he touched it, and he felt more upset. He might as well have been touching a human being, because it wasn't just reflecting back his own feelings, it was reacting to his feelings as another human being. The vehicle itself felt; it was having a felt reaction to his feelings. That's the most important factor.

I'm telling you that organics are made up of the same feeling energies that you have in your own body. You will ultimately have to face the fact that you must ask organics to volunteer for what you would like them to do—essentially stand on the land and say, "Who would like to volunteer? Form up energetically around me and create a ship by which we can travel wherever we want to go; enjoy it as much as you want, and as soon as you want to go back, I'll ask for other organics to fill in for you." In other words, there are no prisoners, no slaves. There are only willing participants.

Freedom for Organics, a Future Controversy in the U.S.

The interesting thing is, that decision is coming down the pike very fast, and it's going to create a tremendous controversy. The nice thing here is that a lot of this controversy is going to come up in the U.S., and the U.S., regardless of how carefully public opinion is being structured, no matter what propaganda is used to manipulate people, it will be difficult if not impossible to talk people into giving up their desire for freedom. If individuals want freedom, they know that other individuals want freedom, too. It's a very small step to make, to say that if I and my friends want freedom, I know this object with feelings like mine wants freedom, too. It's a real tiny step there. There are a lot of other countries, but in terms of the energy, the money, the willingness to produce things and the overwhelming feeling of freedom . . . everybody in the world wants freedom, but in the U.S. they *expect* freedom.

Demand it.

Demand, yes, and expect it. And they are taught that they have it even though you don't have as much as you used to (that's another story). The main thing is that no matter how much propaganda people manage to put out about how it would be a good idea to give up freedom (if only you gave up this freedom or that, then you could have this and so on), it's not going to work. It will work up to a point, but that's it.

It's kind of nice that this decision is going to happen in the U.S. because a lot of other countries don't have the time, the effort and the resources to pour into the technology that will demand that this decision be made. You have people all over the world who want freedom, but the government is too poor to invest in these resources. But here in the U.S. the resources have already been invested and Congress and others are basically committed—businesses, corporations, everyone, are committed to it. It's a juggernaut. Ultimately, however, people will say, "This is wonderful," but once the honeymoon is over, they're going to say, "These devices, as you're calling them, these machines—they have feelings. I can tell because I can feel."

The object that Mr. Adair touched, he felt its reaction to him. What happens when a human being, even an insensitive human being, walks up to one of these things and the human being feels the so-called vehicle's or object's feelings? Just as when you walk into a room and somebody's mad, upset or disappointed—a child is disappointed or your wife or your husband is upset or mad—you can feel that something's going on before anything is said, before they even turn around and look at you. These so-called machines are going to be just like that; you're going to feel something from them. What happens then? This is all very important.

Atlanteans: 92% near the U.S. Coasts

You stressed that this is mostly going to happen in the United States. That's where most of the Atlantean lessons are to be relearned, right?

Ninety-two percent of the former Atlanteans are in the continental United States, meaning that one might expect some to be out on the islands, but almost all are in the forty-eight states.

On the East Coast more than the West?

They're pretty evenly distributed on the coasts, the exception being the Gulf Coast, not so much in Texas. Predominantly they're in the northeast corridor, in the Southwest and a little bit in the West. Northern California's got a lot and the northeast corridor has a lot. They're sprinkled across . . . they're in the Southeast, but not as much.

Congress to Restructure Priorities

I didn't feel that I got closure on this thing. He said he was talking to these congressmen and that it felt like the walls were closing in on them.

Yes, think about it: all this money they've committed, and the U.S. is, economically speaking, at a catastrophic point. Picture the U.S. being a corporation for a moment. If you've dumped all of your economic reserves into something and you are desperate to start showing some kind of profit, or at least getting your investment back, and it's not happening, you're going to begin to get the impression that if something doesn't happen real soon, things could fall apart economically.

There's one thing Congress people understand very well, and that is that it is their job to appropriate the money. It's not the executive branch's job to do that. They might have some ideas, but it's up to Congress to appropriate money. So Congress is like the banker. You could have the greatest investments in the world, but if those investments don't start to pay off, you're going to start getting nervous.

What you're saying is, there's going to be leakage soon about how much of that money went for what. Will that get out to the public?

I think that's less important. I'll tell you why. The only advantage in that would be that then you could figure out who to blame. Blaming is just energy, just anger turned within. Even if you're blaming somebody else, it's just an anger dance. There's no advantage in it. You know, some anger is useful, but this isn't an example of it.

So it's much less important who spent what when than to restructure priorities. At some point the U.S. would have to basically say okay. Here's a typical example: We outbluffed the Soviet Union in the war-toys game and we won, but at some point you've got to pay the piper. You can't keep that game up. At some point the money has to come back in. If it doesn't, you're going to float your currency or ask for debt forgiveness. In other words, you're going to have to change your perception of yourself from a First World country to a Third World country, and there's a lot of reluctance to do that. Can you imagine the U.S. standing up at the World Bank and quietly asking for debt forgiveness? I'm telling you now, there have been a lot of requests for delay. The U.S. is not quite ready to float the dollar yet, but it might come to that.

Ultimately what brings this country into much better alignment with other countries is coming in through the back door. If other countries have loaned you money through banks . . . and it's basically banks that consolidate resources and disseminate them. It's about disseminating resources. If other countries—or people in other countries—are the lenders and the U.S. is the debtor, at some point the U.S. has to say, "Please wait," or . . .

When it is time to pay off the treasury bonds or something like that.

That's right.

Ah. Now I understand.

It's one thing to give people money, but what's behind that money? Money is valuable on the basis of what it represents. Printing money and saying, "Oh, here's your money"—that's meaningless. If you don't own your resources, if you put your resources up as collateral and then print money to give to the person who's loaned you something, that's no good. You need to have real value. The U.S. is going to have face the music on that at some point. Congress usually gets nervous about money because that's their job. Money and Congress—that's what they do.

I thought it was something involving ETs that was about to come out.

No, it's not a matter of life and death like that. Besides, most people in Congress do not concern themselves with that professionally. If they're interested individually, that's different.

Tonight's Interferers: Come Clean, Write a Book and Be Forgiven

Well, since someone or ones have been bothering us tonight, what's the dynamics of that? How does it work that someone attempts to stop you from channeling?

Well, the nice thing is knowledge. There are no secrets. Anybody can know anything they want at any time. The more that people realize that, the more likely they are to listen in. For a while everybody will be nosy. At other times other people want only certain things discussed. If you have an exclusive on something and then suddenly everybody knows about it, your exclusive is suddenly worth nothing. So there's the money thing.

Then there's the control thing. The power and influence you had is suddenly nothing, because everybody else can do it or everybody knows about it. Then there's also self-preservation—people afraid to be exposed, afraid they're going to be hurt. That's another big one.

Basically I'm talking about people who would prefer that I don't talk about these things now. But really it's okay (speaking to beyond this room), it's okay. Recriminations now are not going to be what they once were. I might add (speaking again beyond this room) that the power of public confession is amazing. If you've noticed lately, there has been a lot of interest in scandal. The upshot of this is that just about anything you come out and confess these days, if you share the blame so no one person comes out looking like the monster, it will create only scandal, that's all. You'll get over it. You'll write a book and you'll get on with your lives, so don't worry about it.

So who specifically were you talking to? They have sensitives, they have beings who can operate on these dimensions and be here?

Scandal, a Way to Let Go of Revenge

Sure they can. And sometimes they get upset and they want to . . . "Oh, don't talk about that." But it's not the big secret that it once was. One of the ways you can tell that a society is getting ready to let go of revenge is the way it salaciously loves scandal. If you can enjoy your revenge through such scandal and such appetites, then the chances of your needing revenge beyond that are greatly limited. What's so bad about getting a mud pie in the face? You'll wash your face off and go on with your life.

So what is the concern now with the sinister secret government and the alternate negative future?

It's still there, but I'd say it's less of a threat.

You were very concerned about it for a while.

Realizing That Feelings Affect Everyone, That Suffering Must Cease

Yes, and I might be concerned about it again. But it's less of a threat at the moment largely because of the changes in people. People are, as I say, gradually beginning to realize that you can't go on with your life if other people are really suffering. The main thing is, what's going on now in the largest sense is in all ways a striving toward increased communication. If you look at technology as well as psychology, sociology and even other sciences, almost everything that's been going on for the past fifty years is an attempt to increase communication and the capacity for communication. You can't keep doing that until you realize on the feeling level that other people's feelings do affect everyone.

Believe me, this is not just something esoteric that you and I talk about; this is really beginning to come down the pike. People are beginning to understand this, and it's going to make all the difference. After all, even if people have committed terrible crimes and you execute them, you're going to feel them being executed just as you feel the pain of the victims they inflicted themselves on. And if you go back in their lives you might find that something warped and twisted them when they suffered as children, or maybe they were just anomalies.

The main thing is that most people experience circumstances that twist them and cause them to harm others. All these things that you've been studying for years is gradually becoming more and more well-known, sometimes in ways that offend large segments of the population, such as horror movies or movies showing aliens as monsters. But when the posters go out and amongst all their questions they ask, "Do you believe that extraterrestrials are benign?" the vast public believes that, yes, they're benign. Even in the face of all of this, the public understands the difference between fiction and reality.

Especially when it's comical, like the Men in Black *movie.*

That's right. And things that are just amusing and slapstick—everybody understands slapstick. It is based on the human condition.

Well, we're running out of enemies now on Earth, so they're trying to make up some someplace else.

Remember always that the desire for control is inevitably based on the fear of being controlled, and if and when there is no fear or experience of being controlled, the need to control simply disappears.

Is there anything else you'd like to tell Mr. Adair? We sort of got away from him.

Oh, I think that even this stuff we're talking about is probably in his field of interest. But no, not really, unless he wants to ask directly at some point in time. I'd be happy to talk to him.

40

No Catastrophes!

Zoosh through Robert Shapiro
January 8, 1998

Many doom-and-gloom questions have come in to the Sedona Journal of Emergence about plagues and anthrax and asteroids and solar flares, so we went over some of the questions with Zoosh through Robert Shapiro. Zoosh had this to say:

If people are talking about catastrophic occurrences taking place—something that tremendously impacts the entire world population—my response is that there will be

ABSOLUTELY, POSITIVELY, UNQUESTIONABLY NO CATASTROPHES!

Homeopathic Kits

I do recommend homeopathics for the general public, but I do not expect catastrophic plagues, period. Homeopathics in general can boost and support the immune system, and an emergency kit that has very clear instructions written in English that anybody can understand is a very good idea. It would be good to have such kits available through homeopathic physicians or any physician or medical professional who believes in it. It would be easy to make up such a kit the size of a lunch pail or a standard first-aid kit that people could carry around, with perhaps 8 to 10 or 12 bottles, maybe more, of important remedies that say, "If this happens, take this" and so on. It would be fairly easy to contact a good homeopathic manufacturer to suggest that such a kit be made available to the general public, to be disseminated either through the suggested health practitioners or even through health food stores or any store that has qualified people who can explain the products sufficiently to the customer. If marketed in a little container with a red cross on it and perhaps a handle, it could be carried around in a backpack or in a car or in the medicine chest at home and would likely be a big seller.

However, I stand on my opinion about worldwide plagues, though I am not ruling out outbursts of disease in certain places—which is why I feel such kits are valuable.

Would you include an antidote for anthrax?

In localized areas it might be useful, such as in the Middle East or anyplace where chemical and biological warfare agents have been tested. It is extremely unlikely that it would be needed where these agents have been stored in the U.S. It could be an optional item in a basic kit; you could have a grade 1 kit, a grade 2 kit—something like that.

Storing Food

If people are talking about an earthquake, a volcano or something like that, I support the Latter Day Saints Church here. I believe they say to have three months' supplies or thereabouts). The reason for that is if there is ever any inconvenience—an earthquake, fire or flood—you will have enough food for yourself and the neighborhood. There are always people in the neighborhood who haven't thought ahead or could not afford to buy ahead.

I salute the LDS Church for its desire to care for the community. If you wish to have food stored for yourself and your neighbors for those reasons, that is excellent, if you can do so. But to have food stores for only you and your family—what would you do when your neighbor comes over and says his family is hungry or thirsty? Are you going to say no? I do not think so.

That will answer categorically all these questions coming in. ABSOLUTELY, POSITIVELY, UNQUESTIONABLY NO CATASTROPHES! You can put that out on the Internet.

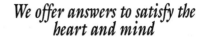

Mother Earth is a spiritual master, maternal master & teaching master. She's a dimensional master & she's working on quantum mastery (master of consequences)
P133 & 279

BOOKS PUBLISHED BY LIGHT TECHNOLOGY PUBLISHING

	No. Copies	Price	Total
ACUPRESSURE FOR THE SOUL		$11.95	$
ARCTURUS PROBE		$14.95	$
BEHOLD A PALE HORSE		$25.00	$
CACTUS EDDIE		$11.95	$
CHANNELLING: EVOLUTIONARY . . .		$ 9.95	$
COLOR MEDICINE		$11.95	$
FOREVER YOUNG		$ 9.95	$
GUARDIANS OF THE FLAME		$14.95	$
GREAT KACHINA		$11.95	$
I'M OK, I'M JUST MUTATING		$ 6.00	$
KEYS TO THE KINGDOM		$14.95	$
LEGEND OF THE EAGLE CLAN		$12.95	$
LIVING RAINBOWS		$14.95	$
MAHATMA I & II		$19.95	$
MILLENNIUM TABLETS		$14.95	$
NEW AGE PRIMER		$11.95	$
PATH OF THE MYSTIC		$11.95	$
POISONS THAT HEAL		$14.95	$
PRISONERS OF EARTH		$11.95	$
SEDONA VORTEX GUIDE BOOK		$14.95	$
SHADOW OF SAN FRANCISCO PEAKS		$ 9.95	$
THE SOUL REMEMBERS		$14.95	$
STORY OF THE PEOPLE		$11.95	$
THIS WORLD AND THE NEXT ONE		$ 9.95	$
ROBERT SHAPIRO/ARTHUR FANNING			
SHINING THE LIGHT		$12.95	$
SHINING THE LIGHT — BOOK II		$14.95	$
SHINING THE LIGHT — BOOK III		$14.95	$
SHINING THE LIGHT — BOOK IV		$14.95	$

	No. Copies	Price	Total
ROBERT SHAPIRO			
THE EXPLORER RACE		$25.00	$
ETs AND THE EXPLORER RACE		$14.95	$
EXPLORER RACE: ORIGINS . . .		$14.95	$
EXPLORER RACE: PARTICLE . . .		$14.95	$
EXPLORER RACE: CREATOR . . .		$19.95	$
ARTHUR FANNING			
SOUL, EVOLUTION, FATHER		$12.95	$
SIMON		$ 9.95	$
WESLEY H. BATEMAN			
DRAGONS & CHARIOTS		$ 9.95	$
KNOWLEDGE FROM THE STARS		$11.95	$
LYNN BUESS			
CHILDREN OF LIGHT, CHILDREN . . .		$ 8.95	$
NUMEROLOGY: NUANCES . . .		$13.75	$
NUMEROLOGY FOR THE NEW AGE		$11.00	$
RUTH RYDEN			
THE GOLDEN PATH		$11.95	$
LIVING THE GOLDEN PATH		$11.95	$
DOROTHY ROEDER			
CRYSTAL CO-CREATORS		$14.95	$
NEXT DIMENSION IS LOVE		$11.95	$
REACH FOR US		$14.95	$
HALLIE DEERING			
LIGHT FROM THE ANGELS		$15.00	$
DO-IT-YOURSELF POWER TOOLS		$25.00	$
JOSHUA DAVID STONE, PH.D.			
COMPLETE ASCENSION MANUAL		$14.95	$
SOUL PSYCHOLOGY		$14.95	$

	No. Copies	Price	Total
BEYOND ASCENSION		$14.95	$
HIDDEN MYSTERIES		$14.95	$
ASCENDED MASTERS		$14.95	$
VYWAMUS/JANET MCCLURE			
AHA! THE REALIZATION BOOK		$11.95	$
LIGHT TECHNIQUES		$11.95	$
SANAT KUMARA		$11.95	$
SCOPES OF DIMENSIONS		$11.95	$
THE SOURCE ADVENTURE		$11.95	$
PRELUDE TO ASCENSION		$29.95	$
LEIA STINNETT			
A CIRCLE OF ANGELS		$18.95	$
THE TWELVE UNIVERSAL LAWS		$18.95	$
ALL MY ANGEL FRIENDS		$10.95	$
ANIMAL TALES		$ 7.95	$
WHERE IS GOD?		$ 6.95	$
JUST LIGHTEN UP!		$ 9.95	$
HAPPY FEET		$ 6.95	$
WHEN THE EARTH WAS NEW		$ 6.95	$
THE ANGEL TOLD ME . . .		$ 6.95	$
COLOR ME ONE		$ 6.95	$
ONE RED ROSE		$ 6.95	$
EXPLORING THE CHAKRAS		$ 6.95	$
CRYSTALS R FOR KIDS		$ 6.95	$
WHO'S AFRAID OF THE DARK		$ 6.95	$
BRIDGE BETWEEN TWO WORLDS		$ 6.95	$

BOOKS PRINTED OR MARKETED BY LIGHT TECHNOLOGY PUBLISHING

Title		Price	
ACCESS YOUR BRAIN'S JOY CENTER		$14.95	___ $ ___
AWAKEN TO THE HEALER WITHIN		$16.50	___ $ ___
EARTH IN ASCENSION		$14.95	___ $ ___
GALAXY SEVEN		$15.95	___ $ ___
INNANA RETURNS		$14.00	___ $ ___
IT'S TIME TO REMEMBER		$19.95	___ $ ___
I WANT TO KNOW		$7.00	___ $ ___
LIFE IS THE FATHER WITHIN		$19.75	___ $ ___
LIFE ON THE CUTTING EDGE		$14.95	___ $ ___
LOOK WITHIN		$9.95	___ $ ___
MAYAN CALENDAR BIRTHDAY BOOK		$12.95	___ $ ___
MEDICAL ASTROLOGY		$29.95	___ $ ___
OUR COSMIC ANCESTORS		$9.95	___ $ ___
OUT-OF-BODY EXPLORATION		$8.95	___ $ ___
PRINCIPLES TO REMEMBER AND APPLY		$11.95	___ $ ___
SONG OF SIRIUS		$8.00	___ $ ___
SOUL RECOVERY AND EXTRACTION		$9.95	___ $ ___
SPIRIT OF THE NINJA		$7.95	___ $ ___
TEMPLE OF THE LIVING EARTH		$16.00	___ $ ___
THE ONLY PLANET OF CHOICE		$14.95	___ $ ___
THE PLEIADIAN AGENDA		$15.00	___ $ ___

JOSHUA DAVID STONE, PH.D.

ASCENSION ACTIVATION MEDITATION	S101	$12.00	___ $ ___
TREE OF LIFE ASCENSION MEDITATION	S102	$12.00	___ $ ___
MT. SHASTA ASCENSION ACTIVATION MEDITATION	S103	$12.00	___ $ ___
KABBALISTIC ASCENSION ACTIVATION	S104	$12.00	___ $ ___
COMPLETE ASCENSION MANUAL MEDITATION	S105	$12.00	___ $ ___
SET OF ALL 5 TAPES		$49.95	___ $ ___

VYWAMUS/BARBARA BURNS

THE QUANTUM MECHANICAL YOU (6 TAPES)	B101-6	$40.00	___ $ ___

TAKA

MAGICAL SEDONA THROUGH THE DIDGERIDOO	T101	$12.00	___ $ ___

BRIAN GRATTAN

SEATTLE SEMINAR RESURRECTION 1994 (12 TAPES)	M102	$79.95	___ $ ___

MSI

Title	Price	
THE TRANSFORMATIVE VISION	$14.95	___ $ ___
VOICES OF SPIRIT	$13.00	___ $ ___
WE ARE ONE	$14.95	___ $ ___

LEE CARROLL

Title	Price	
KRYON-BOOK I, THE END TIMES	$12.00	___ $ ___
KRYON-BOOK II, DON'T THINK LIKE...	$12.00	___ $ ___
KRYON-BOOK III, ALCHEMY OF...	$14.00	___ $ ___
KRYON-THE PARABLES OF KRYON	$17.00	___ $ ___
KRYON-THE JOURNEY HOME	$15.00	___ $ ___

RICHARD DANNELLEY

Title	Price	
SEDONA POWER SPOT/GUIDE	$11.00	___ $ ___
SEDONA: BEYOND THE VORTEX	$12.00	___ $ ___

TOM DONGO: MYSTERIES OF SEDONA

Title	Price	
MYSTERIES OF SEDONA — BOOK I	$6.95	___ $ ___
ALIEN TIDE — BOOK II	$7.95	___ $ ___
QUEST — BOOK III	$9.95	___ $ ___
UNSEEN BEINGS, UNSEEN WORLDS	$9.95	___ $ ___
MERGING DIMENSIONS	$14.95	___ $ ___

BARBARA MARCINIAK

Title	Price	
BRINGERS OF THE DAWN	$12.95	___ $ ___
EARTH	$12.95	___ $ ___

MSI

Title	Price	
ASCENSION!	$11.95	___ $ ___
FIRST THUNDER	$12.95	___ $ ___
SECOND THUNDER	$17.95	___ $ ___
ENLIGHTENMENT	$15.95	___ $ ___

PRESTON B. NICHOLS WITH PETER MOON

Title	Price	
MONTAUK PROJECT	$15.95	___ $ ___
MONTAUK REVISITED	$19.95	___ $ ___
PYRAMIDS OF MONTAUK	$19.95	___ $ ___
ENCOUNTER IN THE PLEIADES....	$19.95	___ $ ___
THE BLACK SUN	$19.95	___ $ ___

LYSSA ROYAL AND KEITH PRIEST

Title	Price	
PREPARING FOR CONTACT	$12.95	___ $ ___
PRISM OF LYRA	$11.95	___ $ ___
VISITORS FROM WITHIN	$12.95	___ $ ___

AMORAH QUAN YIN

Title	Price	
THE PLEIADIAN WORKBOOK	$16.00	___ $ ___
PLEIADIAN PERSPECTIVES ON	$15.00	___ $ ___

ASCENSION MEDITATION TAPES

YHWH/ARTHUR FANNING

ON BECOMING	F101	$10.00	___ $ ___
HEALING MEDITATIONS/KNOWING SELF	F102	$10.00	___ $ ___
MANIFESTATION & ALIGNMENT W/ POLES	F103	$10.00	___ $ ___
THE ART OF SHUTTING UP	F104	$10.00	___ $ ___
CONTINUITY OF CONSCIOUSNESS	F105	$25.00	___ $ ___
MERGING THE GOLDEN LIGHT REPLICAS OF YOU	F107	$10.00	___ $ ___

KRYON/LEE CARROLL

SEVEN RESPONSIBILITIES OF THE NEW AGE	K101	$10.00	___ $ ___
CO-CREATION IN THE NEW AGE	K102	$10.00	___ $ ___
ASCENSION AND THE NEW AGE	K103	$10.00	___ $ ___
NINE WAYS TO RAISE THE PLANET'S VIBRATION	K104	$10.00	___ $ ___
GIFTS AND TOOLS OF THE NEW AGE	K105	$10.00	___ $ ___

JAN TOBER

CRYSTAL SINGER	J101	$12.00	___ $ ___